JUMPING THE
S-CURVE

JUMPING THE
S-CURVE

HOW TO BEAT THE GROWTH CYCLE,
GET ON TOP, AND STAY THERE

PAUL NUNES

TIM BREENE

LEADERS OF ACCENTURE'S HIGH
PERFORMANCE BUSINESS RESEARCH

HARVARD BUSINESS REVIEW PRESS

Boston, Massachusetts

Library of Congress Cataloging-in-Publication Data

Nunes, Paul, 1963–
Jumping the S-curve : how to beat the growth cycle, get on top, and stay there / Paul Nunes and Tim Breene.
    p. cm.
  Includes bibliographical references.
  ISBN 978-1-4221-7558-3 (hbk. : alk. paper)
  1. Organizational effectiveness. 2. Performance. 3. Strategic planning.
4. Success in business. I. Breene, Tim. II. Title.
  HD58.9.N86 2011
  658.4'012—dc22   2010031416

CONTENTS

HIGH PERFORMANCE: THE BUSINESS OF JUMPING S-CURVES

FOR MANY DECADES, Zenith truly was—as its name suggests—at the top. Founded in 1918 and incorporated in 1923 as the Zenith Radio Corporation, the company introduced the world's first portable radio in 1924. Two decades later, with the advent of television, the company successfully shifted its focus. It introduced its first black-and-white sets in 1948 and later developed the first hand-held remote control in 1956 and a new standard for color television, the Chromacolor tube, in 1969.[1] By 1975, the company led the industry with a 24 percent share of the market for color televisions in the United States, 5 percent more than its nearest and only strong competitor at the time.[2] Throughout this period, Zenith was known by the slogan it coined for itself back in 1927: "The quality goes in before the name goes on."

But in the 1970s, the tide began to turn. Japanese manufacturers took an ever larger portion of U.S. television set sales, grabbing market share of 45 percent by 1976, triple its level at the beginning of the decade.

Zenith wasn't beaten yet, however. In the 1980s, it moved into the computer business with Zenith Data Systems (eventually selling out to the French company Groupe Bull for more than $600 million), even as its attempts to maintain a profitable television operation were likened to "rearranging deck chairs on the *Titanic*" by one publication.[3] Yet again, Zenith turned to its heritage as an innovator, this time focusing on promising—but costly—research into high-definition television (HDTV).[4]

It was at once too early and too late: well ahead with HDTV as a true consumer option, but too late to save its television business. The ship ultimately did go down, as longtime partner LG Electronics of South Korea acquired a 5 percent stake in 1991, which grew to 55 percent by 1995 when LG kicked in $350 million to gain control of the company—principally for its HDTV technology.[5] Finally, in 1999, Zenith filed for bankruptcy and LG took over the remains.

Zenith exemplifies both the success of the high-performance business and the limits that many companies reach. It scaled the heights of success first with its radio business and then did what few companies are able to do: it made the leap to a second successful business when it moved into television. Ultimately, however, it couldn't replicate that success yet a third time, either with computers or with HDTV.

Zenith had become a great company, twice (and may become one yet again, as LG has recently resurrected the brand with some early success). But high performance isn't about achieving "greatness," which is far too static a concept. It is about outperforming the competition again and again, even as the basis of competition in an industry or market changes. High-performance companies (or organizations) are those that continually repeat their success. They show the world that their first trip to the top was not an accident. These companies accomplish the difficult feat that gives rise to the title of this book: they jump the S-curve.

What exactly do we mean by *S-curve*? The term is widely used for a variety of reasons (for more, see "The Explanatory Power of the S-Curve"). But when we use the term, we simply mean the common pattern in which a successful business starts small with a few eager customers, grows rapidly as the masses seek out the new offering, and eventually peaks and levels off as the market matures. And when we speak of high-performance companies (or organizations), we mean those that somehow manage to climb that S-curve and then jump to a new one again and again (figure 1-1).

The Explanatory Power of the S-Curve

The use of the term *S-curve* in business circles goes back at least to the late 1800s, but it gained broader currency in the early 1960s, when Stanford University professor Everett Rogers published *Diffusion of Innovations*. In this book, Rogers shows how the cumulative sum of adopters of an innovation takes on the shape of the letter *S*. He then characterizes segments of adopters in terms that are still commonly used today. During the dot-com era, the meaning of the phenomenon was adapted to describe the rollout of the new Internet-related technologies. Best-selling books like Geoffrey Moore's *Crossing the Chasm* explained how new-technology companies could break out of the bottom of the curve and reach the top.

We have found that the term *S-curve* can be adapted yet again to explain business performance over time. Companies thrive, after all, by successfully delivering some form of innovation to customers. Performance starts slowly as the business is launched and the company experiments to find the right business formula. Then performance accelerates rapidly as word of the attractiveness of the offering spreads, and finally it fades as the market approaches saturation, imitators appear, and obsolescence leads to better substitutes. (See figure 1-2.)

FIGURE 1-1

High performance: the climbing and jumping of S-curves

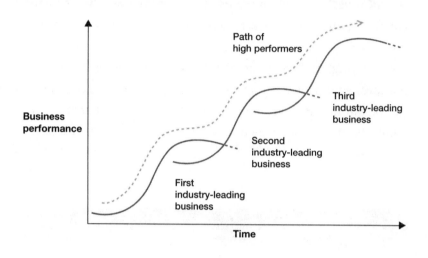

Path of high performers

Business performance

Third industry-leading business

Second industry-leading business

First industry-leading business

Time

FIGURE 1-2

Diffusion of successful business offerings

After a successful new business offering is taken up by the early adopters, its rate of adoption grows rapidly before leveling off as it approaches the market saturation point.

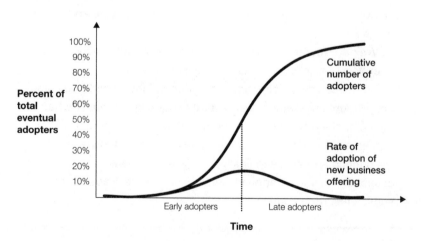

Percent of total eventual adopters

100%
90%
80%
70%
60%
50%
40%
30%
20%
10%

Cumulative number of adopters

Rate of adoption of new business offering

Early adopters   Late adopters

Time

Recognizing high performance as a series of climbs and jumps may sound intuitive, but it was not immediately obvious to us when we began our journey. A good deal of the literature on business performance at the time focused on providing a recipe for greatness—*In Search of Excellence, Good to Great,* and *Peak Performance* are a just a few of the classics in that category. Other works—books like *Built to Last, Creative Destruction,* and *What Really Works*—sought to unlock the secrets of company endurance. But a detailed, research-based analysis of the intersection of the two—how companies can achieve repeated peaks of high performance—was missing.

This was the gap that we sought to close as we took on responsibility for creating and leading the still ongoing program at Accenture to understand high performance in business—a program begun in 2003. In the near decade since, we have a learned a great deal about how companies achieve recurring greatness—which is our definition of high performance in a nutshell. For companies that want to achieve high performance, our lessons learned may sound counterintuitive: what matters most to long-term performance is not so much what you do to reach the top—though that is certainly important—but what you do to cross over to the bottom of the next S-curve and begin the climb again. Similarly, the secret to successfully jumping the S-curve is not about what you do at or near the top of the curve, but what you do to prepare for the jump on the way up. The ability of some companies to move to the bottom of the next curve, even as they climb the original one, is the focus of this book.

FINDING A PATTERN

Before we give an overview of our findings and the structure of the book, let's cover some of the why and how of our research.

What prompted our study in the first place were the questions frequently asked by Accenture's clients: How do we create lasting value? How do we make the transition from an existing business, which is destined to stall, to a new one? The context in which companies struggle to do this of course is familiar by now: successful companies with ever-shorter life spans on the Standard & Poor's 500, rapid industry reinvention, near borderless competition, and shorter periods of profitability from competitive advantages that were hard-won.

Of the more than eight hundred companies that we began our study with, roughly eighty were initially judged to be high performers through a peer-based quantitative analysis that relied on 13 different financial metrics to assess each organization's growth, profitability, consistency, longevity, and positioning for the future. (See "Separating Wheat from Chaff.") These were companies that had both truly outperformed their peers and withstood the test of time. They had succeeded in ringing up exemplary profits, revenue growth and gains in stock performance year after year, regardless of economic or industry circumstances.

Interestingly, although we found relatively few high performers, we found considerably more than the eleven companies featured in *Good to Great* and the eighteen highlighted in *Built to Last*— high performance is within the reach of many organizations, not just the extraordinary few. If some of our high performers like Intel; PepsiCo, Inc.; and UPS were obvious, others surprised us. At the time of our initial study, companies like Danaher, Illinois Tool Works, and Reckitt Benckiser were well regarded, but their real achievements in creating the essentials of high performance were not yet well publicized.

And what did this group have in common? At that point, we weren't sure. To find out, we conducted months of additional research, using techniques that included everything from in-depth executive surveys to multivariate regression analyses. In Accenture's industry practice areas, special teams were created; they were staffed with experienced consultants, internal and external industry experts, practitioners and professional researchers, including

Separating Wheat from Chaff

We set out with a very practical goal in mind. We wanted to study high performance in such a way that the findings would be helpful to practitioners, those who wake up every day to the challenges of running a business—managing existing operations while finding new markets to exploit.

Because we wanted only practical insights, we were less concerned about whether the companies we studied had always been, or would always be, high performers. It was enough that they had weathered the storms of their industry long enough and well enough to have successfully competed in multiple eras of competition. Some of the companies we highlight in this book have endured severe challenges in the past couple of years, and their status as high performers may seem in question as a result. But the label of *high performer* is not a promise of future performance; it is a recognition of past success so unusual (by statistical measures) that it warranted our careful study.

Likewise, relatively new entrants to the pantheon of business performance may seem conspicuous by their absence. New high performers are continually emerging, with many coming from rapidly maturing emerging markets, which is why we point you to a Web site that will give you a continuously refreshed set of industry insights into today's high performers (http://www.accenture.com/Global/High_Performance_Business/default.htm). But our focus remained fixed on companies that had already demonstrated an ability to jump the S-curve, and by definition, the newer superstars have not yet had to face that challenge. Nor were we interested in companies whose performance might indeed have been enviable, but whose success was not particularly noteworthy in the context of their industry because competitors had also attained similarly impressive results in the same period. Also conspicuously absent may be some top competitors from emerging markets. We were not able to judge the performance of many companies that are based in developing countries because they lacked a sufficient history of results that could be reasonably assessed and directly evaluated. That said, many if not most of the companies we studied are global entities that have been active in developing countries for decades.

Having determined what we hoped to find, our next challenge was how to conduct our study. Our basic philosophy, and the key differentiator in our approach, was that all performance is relative. While starting our research, we were shocked by the number of prominent studies of business performance that had selected their high performers after comparing them head-to-head across industries—ignoring the differences in the average profitability, maturity, and risk across those markets. Their victors had won what hardly seemed a fair fight. This led us to believe that our analysis could only be properly conducted on valid sets of peer companies. "Change the peer set, change the performance," became our mantra as we struggled to create suitable sets for comparison.

In the end, we settled on thirty-one peer sets encompassing more than eight hundred companies for our initial study. As these groups represented more than 80 percent of the market capitalization of the Russell 3000 Index at the time, we felt they were an excellent proxy for the broader market. Since then, we have identified and studied nearly one hundred peer sets. Interestingly, after our approach garnered wider public attention, thanks to an article in *Harvard Business Review* in 2005, we learned that some researchers outside Accenture were adjusting their methodology as a result.[a] While this is gratifying to us, we fully recognize that there are no enduring, permanent classifications of peer sets or even industry segments. Such categorizations can be made only on a case-by-case basis for a particular context at a specific period of time, given how company strategies continually evolve, technologies change, and industries converge (and at times diverge).

After determining the relevant peer groupings and companies to study, we still needed to crystallize our definition of high performance. After studying nearly a score of alternative methods, including the methods popularized by leading business authors of the past thirty years, we developed a definition that sets an exacting standard:

High performance is the consistent and enduring surpassing of peers in revenue growth, profitability, and total returns to shareholders, across business and economic cycles, often across generations of leadership, measured by widely accepted financial metrics.

How could we turn that definition into a useful tool for analysis? Using thirteen simple and common financial metrics, we measured performance in terms of growth, profitability, consistency, longevity, and positioning for the future—the last in order to avoid rewarding those companies that create high profits by cutting investment. In general, we applied the metrics over a ten-year span to ensure coverage across the average industry life cycle of seven years. (We allowed some variation in that time frame to account for different industries' business and investment cycles.) Our goal was to ensure the window of analysis was sufficiently long that it encompassed multiple eras of competition in the industry, during which the basis of competition shifts. Outperforming the competition for so long demands success on multiple S-curves, as companies in the peer group must both develop and respond to new technologies and ways of competing.

Most of the business studies we reviewed used simple cutoffs to pick the peak players—arbitrary cutoffs like the top quartile or the top five companies. But with that approach, the results can be skewed. In an industry where very little separates the top performers, the last one to make the cut will be heralded, while the nearly identical company just below will be unfairly overlooked. To avoid that, we scored companies on a curve in their industry peer set, assigning grades for each measure according to its relative deviation from the peer-set average. We then averaged each company's grades. Only companies that significantly out-performed the average score of their peer set were classified as high performers.

a. Julia Kirby, "Toward a Theory of High Performance," *Harvard Business Review*, July–August 2005, 30–39.

a number of academics. These teams then conducted studies to identify the drivers of sustained outperformance in the peer set of their expertise. And we had our own team integrate those peer-set insights into a cohesive set of findings, which are summarized in this book.

That's the very short version of how we came to our findings, and the method and program are an ongoing effort at Accenture. (For the long version, see the appendix, "How We Determined High Performance.") By our best estimate, more than a thousand individuals around the globe have participated in our research to date, with many hundreds continuing to participate every year. We have expanded to include regional- and emerging-market studies where possible and have extensively studied the role of expertise in seven core business functions, including supply chain and customer relationship management, for example. And we have regularly conducted a modified version of this research approach in public service sectors, where the shared insights have generated mutually enriching lessons. Though no large-scale, longitudinal research project is ever perfect—nor could it be—the level of consensus we have achieved with such an extensive group of expert participants during the long gestation of this book gives us great confidence in the ideas we have captured here.

TRUTHS, MYTHS, AND CYNICS

Perhaps it should go without saying that *we* are confident in our own ideas. But it's actually a more critical point than it might at first seem, because we knew we had to wrestle strenuously against the idea that our whole effort would come to naught—that it was doomed to fail by its very nature. For some critics, the mere attempt to find a pattern behind high performance is only so much tilting at windmills. According to such thinking, companies that seem to achieve it are more lucky than good, and the ultimate winners in an industry are crowned with a halo and go on to receive undeserved credit for having had superior insights about the market or greater capabilities than their competitors. But we firmly believe that our detailed peer-set research does indeed reveal the existence of real high performers, and the substance of this book will show that luck has very little to do with their long-term success or ability to jump the S-curve.

Another form of criticism comes under the banner of "nothing new under the sun." The rules of performance, according to this line of thinking, are immutable: giant scale is critical. Some industries are moribund—high performance isn't even an option—while others naturally give rise to high performers. Over the long haul, companies have to choose between growth in profits and growth in scale—even the best companies can't have both. Investments in high performance take a long time to mature, well beyond the time frame of most management life cycles. And—perhaps the most pernicious idea of all—near-great companies don't have as much to gain by striving for high performance as average or low-performing companies do. All of this in the end proved to be untrue. A closer look at those various myths, or what we think of as the urban legends of business, reveals how each simply doesn't stand up to scrutiny in light of Accenture's empirical research.

Legend: Some industries or market sectors are so mature or so competitive that it is impossible to substantially and continuously outperform competitors in them.

Reality: High performance is not dependent on industry factors or the general health of an industry.

We found that high-performance businesses exist in all but a tiny percentage of industries, even in those where growth and shareholder returns are, as a whole, anemic. In all but three of the thirty-one industries in our initial study, we found at least one company that dramatically outperformed its peer set. Nor were these high-performance companies simply outperforming a set of poor performers—the best of the worst, so to speak. Most high performers, no matter the industry, were also beating the Standard & Poor's 500 as well.

Legend: The bigger the better.

Reality: Industry-leading scale is not a requirement for high performance.

We found no correlation between a company's relative size in an industry and business performance. What can explain this? For one, massive size brings its own diseconomies in the form of intractable complexity. For another, giant scale increases a company's vulnerability to disruption from new competitors, especially if the incumbent's assets are largely fixed.

This is not to say that industry-leading scale and high performance don't sometimes coexist; a number of our high performers were also the largest players in their industry. But we found that high performers were broadly distributed in terms of revenue size. The lesson is that companies should not be obsessed with becoming the biggest in their industry when seeking high performance. Instead, they should always strive to determine and maintain efficient scale—a size that might (or might not) lead the industry, but one that enables the organization to compete effectively. Beyond that, scale should be carefully evaluated for its contribution in helping to deliver products that offer some differentiation of value (with respect to price, functionality, quality, or other attribute).

Legend: Companies can't pursue high growth and high profitability at the same time; they have to choose.

Reality: Consistently outperforming competitors in both growth and profitability is a competitive reality today and a hallmark of high performance.

In the past, a traditional responsibility of senior leadership, particularly for chief strategists, was determining when a business should go for continued growth and when it should instead just capture profits. The notion in business strategy that there is a time for milking the cash cow—taking the profits from one business to fund growth in other areas, until the cow eventually runs dry—illustrates how business thinking has, for decades, held that optimal profit making and expansion are strategic opposites. While this viewpoint is not entirely unfounded, it can produce self-limiting results. After all, investors shun high-growth companies with disappointing profits as surely as they turn away from highly profitable but shrinking ones.

The good news is that companies need not accept this trade-off. Accenture research has found that high-performance businesses consistently outperform their peers in both growth and *spread* (a standard measure of profit, defined as the difference between the company's return on capital and its cost of borrowing that capital). Our evidence suggests that this ability to do both is a predominant feature of high performers.

> **Legend:** The rewards of seeking high performance come only after years of hard work.
>
> **Reality:** The benefits of pursuing high performance can accrue well before actual operating measures improve.

Given how the market tends to punish companies for missing their earnings projections, it is easy to think that share price cannot improve until financial results do. Yet, our research confirms the fallacy of such thinking. Wall Street amply rewards businesses that demonstrate not only day-to-day operational excellence but also the development of strong capabilities and the creation of a powerful long-term strategic vision. To such companies, the markets grant substantial amounts of what Accenture calls "future value." For a basic understanding of that concept, think of the value of a company's existing business operations, measured over time—in perpetuity—as the *current-value* portion of its share price.

The part of the share price that remains after subtracting current value is the *future value*. The size of a company's future-value portion, particularly relative to the size of its current value, reflects the market's opinion of the future prospects of the company.

Over the seven-year period we studied, high-performance businesses far exceeded their peers in demonstrating to Wall Street that they deserve a high proportion of future value in their overall market values. High-performance businesses have, on average, nearly twice the median amount of future value in their industries. That is, while the market value of their current operations may be similar to those of lower-performing companies, high performers enjoy a 20 percent to 50 percent premium on their overall enterprise values—a premium that can be used to fund expansion, reward employees, and generally support the quest for even higher performance.

> **Legend:** Being consistently above average in an industry is probably good enough.
>
> **Reality:** Even above-average performers have a lot to gain from becoming high performers.

Our analysis shows that the gaps in revenue growth and profitability between high performers and above-average performers are every bit as large as the gaps in those measures between above-average and average performers—and as large as the same gaps between average and underperforming companies. Specifically, high performers as a group typically surpass the above-average performers in their industries by over 5 percent in cumulative growth and 1 percent in additional spread (profit) each year.

This continuous, near-linear improvement in business results even as companies reach into the high-performance category underscores how important it is that companies never quit in their efforts to improve their performance. This is especially true for longtime players that might be beginning to doubt their ability to remain great or to become great again. While our research found many high performers to be relative newcomers to their industries, other high performers were among their industries most well-established incumbents. Neither has an edge when it comes to achieving high performance, and both have everything to gain from not quitting until they achieve it.

Companies can achieve high performance even in slumbering, mature industries. They can do so even when the markets demand both growth and profits, when a dominant player seems to enjoy unfair advantages, and when long-term bets are years away from paying off. For true high performers, then, "wait til next year" is never an option. In fact, to them, challenging circumstances are just another opportunity for achieving something great.

In the first phase of our research, then, we accomplished two important tasks. We established that high performance was real and well beyond the realm of luck. We also showed that the conventional wisdom, again, had gotten it wrong.

THE PATTERN EMERGES

Of course, debunking business legends is one thing; truly understanding the makings of high performance is another. As we continued analyzing the data, a pattern emerged—just as it does when one stands back from a pointillist painting and the many thousands of dots reveal a picture full of recognizable images. In our case, the image that emerged describes why some companies scale and jump S-curves again and again. It also reveals why others never make it to the top or, if they do, quickly fade into the background.

Continuing with the painting metaphor, we saw essentially a diptych—a work of art on two panels. In the first, companies successfully scale the S-curve by following through on a winning business idea. The keys to that accomplishment are the focus of chapters 2 through 4, where we describe the essential elements required for climbing an S-curve, ones we call the building blocks of high performance. The next, and even harder, task is replicating that success. We take up the way high performers accomplish that in chapters 5 through 8. In chapter 5, we explain what derails most companies: the hidden S-curves that should be visible to executives but for many good reasons remain obscured until it is too late to act effectively. In chapters 6 through 8 we detail the steps high performers take to successfully manage their companies to the accelerated timetable imposed on them by the shorter hidden S-curves. We describe how high performers repeatedly jump S-curves and scale new heights by managing their organizations according to the three hidden S-curves, using a different approach to strategy, the evolution of their top teams, and talent formation. Figure 1-3 shows how these tasks break out into the overall categories of building high performance and sustaining it (with the challenge of addressing hidden S-curves falling in between). Although we discuss these tasks in a particular order, organizations need to act on them concurrently, and the responsibility for that is one of the primary duties of the top management team, either at the corporate or business-unit level.

Chapter 9 exposes some of the current global economic and technology trends that are shortening both the financial S-curve of companies and the hidden S-curves, explaining why, if the time to jump isn't now, it is certainly soon.

Each of the chapters will, we hope, provide insights into how companies can attain and sustain superior results over an extended period. As a prelude to those ideas, the following preview provides a high-level summary of what we learned throughout our research study on high performance.

Chapter 2, "A Big-Enough Market Insight," reveals a fundamental truth about high performance. It is not enough simply to win. To be a high performer, a company must win big—big enough to be noticed as playing in a different league from peers. That requires recognizing and following through on what we call

FIGURE 1-3

What it takes to climb and jump S-curves

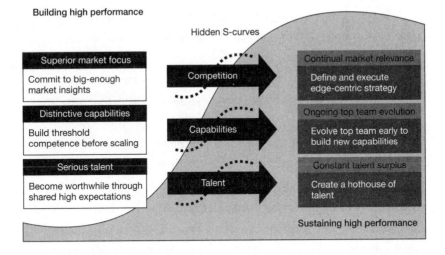

Building high performance

Hidden S-curves

Superior market focus	Competition	Continual market relevance
Commit to big-enough market insights		Define and execute edge-centric strategy
Distinctive capabilities	Capabilities	Ongoing top team evolution
Build threshold competence before scaling		Evolve top team early to build new capabilities
Serious talent	Talent	Constant talent surplus
Become worthwhile through shared high expectations		Create a hothouse of talent

Sustaining high performance

a big-enough market insight, or BEMI—an insight of so much potential that when it is turned into a successful business, the resulting financial rewards completely overshadow those of other competitors. In other words, merely managing a portfolio of existing businesses or brands and making incremental innovations to them is not enough over the long haul. Consistent among high performers is market prescience combined with aggressive moves into major new areas of opportunity. This is true whether the company is Novo Nordisk seeing the opportunity to meet the needs of the growing numbers of diabetics globally, Nokia discerning the potential of cell phones to take off in mass markets, or Lexus observing the market's readiness for a new kind of luxury car amid North America's growing affluence.

Companies may sometimes think in terms of "a big, hairy audacious goal," or BHAG, a term coined by Jim Collins, the noted management guru. In fact, if you'll forgive our multiple use of abbreviations here, a BEMI will often require the setting of a BHAG in order to realize the opportunity. But here's an important caveat:

17

not every BHAG is based on a BEMI. An audacious goal that is not aligned with a major market insight is likely to produce an unfortunate waste of time, talent, and energy.

Chapter 2 covers the core approaches to finding a BEMI and the importance of faith in the power of science and technology to provide solutions for the challenges in serving customer needs in a BEMI. It also describes how to break the future into manageable chunks so as not to be overwhelmed by the magnitude of the task.

Chapter 3, "Threshold Competence Before Scaling," examines a major failing of companies that begin to climb an S-curve—mismanagement of the pace and timing of the climb. We explain how high performers first develop what we call threshold competence. This pursuit is not to be confused with creating a core competency, which refers to the development of a group of abilities that lead to excellence in a specific activity. Threshold competence occurs when a company's newly developed offering surpasses the minimum level of improvement the market requires to get customers to purchase the new product or service. Because it is the threshold that breaks inertia in customer behavior, it is often a very high bar. Yet, it is the standard that high performers consider nonnegotiable. Threshold competence is achieved when the company can meet this standard consistently and repeatedly.

To create threshold competence, high performers like Apple, Procter & Gamble, and Nokia make a commitment to experimentation and discovery; in turn, this allows them to conceive and produce distinctive offerings that have tremendous customer value. In the process, the companies also produce distinctive capabilities in the organization by combining old capabilities with new ones. Distinctive capabilities are therefore not the drivers of new offerings but rather the result of successfully following through on a big-enough market insight.

When threshold competence has been attained, and only then, high performers take the next critical step: rapidly expanding their operations to bring an offering to market at a substantial level of scale, before competition can blunt its impact. High performers recognize the value in scaling quickly, but they also appreciate what has to be in place *before* they begin that process. They resist putting the cart of scale before the horse of competence, and do so in spite of investor pressures for early profits, the relentless need to meet or surpass aggressive quarterly projections, and other daunting pressures to scale early. Through cautionary tales like People Express, we see clearly how the rush to scale can consistently doom companies to weak performance and failure. By contrast, the example of Southwest Airlines shows how the commitment to market differentiation and planning for scale first, and then to the balanced and aggressive creation of scale, leads to ultimate success. How do high performers manage the fundamental task of rapid scaling? We identify and describe the three keys: the steadfast refusal to scale too fast, the ability to replicate the business in a repeatable way, and the early focus on mastering access to customer and market channels.

Chapter 4, "Worthy of Serious Talent," recognizes that vision and execution cannot be had without the right people. But it is not enough simply to get employees on the bus or under it, in Jim Collins's terminology—either committed to greatness or out of the company. High performers must in fact *keep* talent on the bus throughout the journey, which is long. As we have said, true greatness comes from success across eras of competition, which can entail decades of competition. Keeping the right people in the company requires understanding what serious talent demands of the companies it works for. Serious talent refers to employees that are both highly capable and highly committed—to both individual and team excellence. Those who exemplify such traits have high expectations. They seek to give their all to companies that share three traits that fulfill those expectations: the capability to achieve great success; predictability in the way that co-workers behave (and thus in the way the company operates); and reliability in times of great challenge. Talented people also seek to prove themselves worthy of their own investment of time and abilities.

High performers like global consumer goods company Reckitt Benckiser prove themselves capable of great success by creating, and rigorously ensuring, pervasive competence at all levels of the company—roles are filled with people who can, and do, get the job done and get it done right. These companies create high levels of predictability—the emboldening feeling that the business operates like a well-oiled machine—through transparency and mutual accountability in all relationships. And they create reliability by establishing a culture of honor that complements a culture of law. Such a commitment to enforcing particular honorable behaviors through the faithful actions of its members—like the U.S. Marine Corps commitment never to leave a fallen comrade behind—assures serious talent that they can depend on their colleagues to do the right thing when the time comes. Beyond this trio of traits, they also create not just stretch goals but shared *stretch mind-sets,* the organizational drive to be the best. In return, serious talent agrees to abide by the equally high expectations of colleagues and company.

Chapter 5, "Hidden S-Curves," sets the stage for the second half of the book: how high performers consistently jump from one S-curve to the next. We start by exploring how and why the building blocks of high performance described in chapter 2 through chapter 4 erode. We then describe the inevitable business stall that companies face when they fail to renew these building blocks and how that halt in momentum, while not always fatal, nevertheless signifies the death of high performance.

Next, we more carefully explore how and why companies fail to recognize the decline of the key elements that produced their initial success. One critical reason is that the average size and complexity of the world's largest companies is increasing. Consequently, our insights about how companies jump the S-curve are heavily focused on the need to overcome the disadvantages of scale—the seemingly paradoxical problem of having to man-age the downsides of overwhelming success. We also review why companies are poorly organized and ill prepared to re-create the building blocks and how success and unwieldy scale contribute to the inability to renew the organization.

We then begin outlining the three hidden S-curves. For each building block of high performance—the BEMI, the threshold competence, the serious talent—a shorter curve parallels the financial one. In effect, companies hit maturity with each one, even as they are still enjoying financial success. That's what makes those S-curves so hard to see—it's not easy to take your eye off the bouncing ball of financial performance in the apparent absence of need. Understanding hidden S-curves, then, is not a matter of obtaining esoteric management wisdom. You don't need special training or a sixth sense. But failure to detect and act on them spells long-term trouble for any business.

Chapter 6, "Edge-Centric Strategy," reveals how strategy making in high performers goes beyond traditional strategic planning. It instead operates along the hidden S-curve of market relevance, ensuring that strategy is evolving close to the speed of market evolution. Almost as soon as a market develops, the basis of competition within that market begins to shift. For example, in the cell-phone market, the basis of competition has evolved in multiple stages: first, price; then, network coverage and quality of service; next, value-added services; and now, design and branding. In general, however, the basis of competition after the introduction of an innovation moves from performance to reliability to convenience to price.

High performers recognize this inexorable pattern and develop strategic approaches that create real strategic change in the company early—on the edge of discovery. Low performers fail to recognize that the basis of competition will shift well before the sell-by date of a BEMI has expired.

We characterize high performers' new strategy formulation

and execution processes as "edge centric" because they get their strength from the edge in three ways. First, they operate on the *edge of the market*. High performers like Best Buy use unique tools and approaches to get to the periphery of market evolution and customer demand, setting up the necessary recognition and embrace of the next BEMI. Second, these processes in high performers occur on the *edge of the organization*. That is, they are directed from the center by top management, but not dominated by the center of the business. Instead, they rely on the contributions from the parameter. And third, these processes operate on the *edge of control*. To be effective enough to lead to an S-curve jump, strategy making cannot be so predictable that the forces of the status quo can game the system. It cannot be about routine five-year planning (though that remains necessary). It must instead be, paradoxically, episodic but continual, driven by a permanent commitment to strategy development and execution, but not a permanent strategic process.

Chapter 7, "Top Teams That Change Ahead of the Curve," describes how high performers divorce the evolution of their top teams from the financial evolution of the business. Rather than follow the natural maturity of the still-successful business, high performers drive their top teams to change before they have to—ahead of the financial performance curve. In effect, these businesses connect the evolution of their top management teams to the much shorter, hidden S-curve of distinctive capabilities.

High performers make this connection because they recognize that the real need for new management occurs when distinctiveness wanes, not when business performance starts to plateau. Low performers regularly allow their top team to mature with their business. As a result, they end up with a collection of very capable business runners, but not a team that can easily commit to and execute the level of change required to jump S-curves. High performers, in contrast, concentrate on succession planning not as a way of ensuring that the CEO or other high-level executives can be replaced in an emergency, but as a way of ensuring the steady and reliable evolution of the top team. Chapter 7 explains the particular ways in which high performers like P&G foster the early evolution of their top management teams and how those teams are balanced, organized, managed, and refreshed to create transformational change while the horses are still well inside the barn.

Chapter 8, "Hothouses of Talent," highlights our recognition that jumping the S-curve requires not just enough talent: it demands an excess. It first requires an abundance of talent to adequately supply the rapid scaling of the existing business—sufficient to ward off imitators and other competitors. Rapid scaling is enormously demanding of talent, as additional managers and directors are in need in new offices, regions, stores, and factories. But jumping the S-curve also requires spare talent in sufficient numbers to start and grow new businesses and initiatives.

Engaging in both scaling and startup activities simultaneously requires massive and uncommon quantities of talent, which is why so many low-performing companies choose instead to emphasize one need over the other. Alternatively, they lamely divide available talent across both activities, understaffing each. Complicating matters, many companies turn down the spigot of talent development to reduce costs and sustain earnings just when the flow should be greatest.

To be sure, the need for surpluses of talent comes amid a host of challenges: rapidly growing demand from emerging markets, the aging and retirement of many experts in the developed world, and schools that do not adequately prepare students for the "real world." That's why the best companies recognize the need to become *hothouses of talent*. Such organizations are able to grow enough talent internally not only to meet their needs to scale, but also to have the surplus required to concurrently search for new BEMIs, launch new businesses, and successfully jump S-curves.

Chapter 9, "Sharp Curves Ahead," serves as a call to immediate action for managers and top executives. The chapter explains why S-curves are getting shorter today, and indicates where readers can turn for additional insight into the forces that are driving change at an ever-faster pace.

At the highest level, our findings about what companies do to create and sustain high performance are deceptively simple once recognized. Still, they are difficult to execute. That is why so few companies in each of our industry peer sets passed our test of high performance. It is also why, over time, the vast majority of businesses disappear in the process of creative destruction—a process that typifies free-market capitalism.

Certainly, there are other ingredients to high performance—hard work, inspiration, and, yes, even luck, and these ingredients are hard to measure. And certainly, like a pointillist painting, our insights—and even our statistical data—are not perfectly shaped. They are colored by their context. But even though an artist's work might be an imperfect representation of reality, it can nonetheless capture certain fundamental truths of the world we inhabit. We believe that this book, similarly, will provide you with examples and insights you need to help you improve the performance of your company. For it to do so, you must see the painting not just from a distance but up close as well. Let's begin to do just that.

PART ONE

CLIMBING A CURVE

2 A BIG-ENOUGH MARKET INSIGHT

Y EARS AGO, Novo Nordisk had a shrewd insight. The global health-care company rightly recognized that the growing affluence of emerging countries like China would lead to changes in diet that would eventually result in a dramatic increase in diabetes. "As people become more and more affluent, and get less and less exercise, more and more are prone to develop diabetes," declared Lars Rebien Sorensen, executive vice president of Novo Nordisk's health-care business, in 1999. Back then, Sorensen made this bold prediction: "There will be 300 million diabetics 20 years from now, as opposed to 100 million today."[1] Novo Nordisk's history certainly made its executives more attuned to having that insight—the company was formed from the merger of two businesses that had been involved in diabetes treatment since their founding in the 1920s. Still, when Novo Nordisk decided to make a global push for dominating the market, it was just a midsize player in the pharmaceutical industry. Even in its core business of diabetes treatment, it was an also-ran in some major markets. In the United States, for example, the company lagged far behind Eli Lilly, which controlled

80 percent of the insulin business.[2] Today, thanks to that insight into emerging economies, Novo Nordisk is the global leader, with 52 percent of the total insulin market.[3]

High-performing companies like Novo Nordisk tend to be in the right place at the right time. When a market opportunity knocks, they're at the door with the right product or service. But that's not because high performers are somehow luckier than their competitors. Indeed, our research has found that serendipity has little to do with the uncanny market timing of high-performing businesses. We observed that high performers don't just happen to be in the right place to take advantage of a large market opportunity; their skill is in arriving at that position by constantly being on the lookout for the big-enough market insight, or BEMI. By *big enough*, we mean that the market insight must be far larger than just an idea for creating incremental products. We're talking about a substantial insight that would enable a company to build a major business with the potential of considerable growth over a number of years. It might even lead to a game-changing product that totally rewrites the rules of a given market. BEMIs, in other words, provide companies with a growth path to launch themselves to new, higher planes of success. (See "Identifying BEMIs.")

BEMIs will rarely lead to a growth surge over the short term. That's because today's winners have already anticipated the current business environment. The real opportunities lie in seeing where a market is likely to head over a longer time horizon. In our experience, attacking incumbents head-on under stable business conditions is hardly a smart strategy. Rather, the more effective approach is to look for major trends that could potentially upset those conditions in some significant way. The ability to see those trends and how they might intersect is what having a BEMI is all about.

Novo Nordisk's insight about diabetes certainly had huge, long-term implications for the company, but BEMIs do not necessarily have to be as momentous or as far-reaching. Often they are much

Identifying BEMIs

Alan Greenspan, the former head of the Federal Reserve, has said that the only way to definitively identify a market bubble is after the fact. The same could be said of big-enough market insights, or BEMIs. In essence, a BEMI is a considerable insight into a market that would enable a company to launch a major new line of business with the potential for years of solid growth. An example we'll explore in detail later is Nintendo's popular Wii game console, which was the result of the company's insight that videogames could be appealing not just to teenagers and young adults but also to older consumers *if* the products were easy to use and fun to play. And therein lies the rub: even though BEMIs might be identified with certainty only in hindsight, companies need to act in the present to prepare for what might eventually become a huge, lucrative market. At the same time, though, they can't be chasing every insight that comes their way. As a result, executives should use the following three criteria to identify a BEMI.

First, Is the Insight Big Enough?

Obviously, *big enough* is a relative term. For a large global conglomerate, annual sales of a new business might need to be $1 billion to justify a major investment. For a small startup, just a tiny fraction of that volume might suffice. Consider how two companies—Samsung and Ovideon Inc.—acted on the BEMI that advancements in plasma and liquid crystal display (LCD) technologies would enable the development of flat-panel TVs with such clear pictures that viewers would replace their conventional sets and pay a premium for watching programs in high definition. Samsung, the Korean consumer electronics giant, had to win big, so it bet big. It does its own TV manufacturing in order to control both quality and costs for its high-volume operations, and so far, the huge investment has paid off. In 2009, the company controlled about 17 percent of the total market, shipping more than 27 million LCD models and more than 3 million plasma sets.[a] In comparison, Ovideon's share of the market is minuscule, but that's just fine with the start-up from Aurora, Illinois. Ovideon doesn't need to move huge volumes, because it outsources its manufacturing and concentrates on small market niches, such as applications in offices and public spaces like airports. So, for both Samsung and Ovideon, flat-panel TVs were a BEMI, but in very different ways.

Second, Is the Insight Valuable Enough?

Specifically, what will customers be willing to pay for the new product or service, and how many such customers will there be? Admittedly, those are very difficult questions to answer. Few executives might have predicted the prices that millions of consumers would be willing to pay for bottled water or for a cup of coffee that's been freshly brewed by a barista, but those who could accurately anticipate this were able to build huge, profitable businesses. Companies need to test their assumptions, regularly and over time, about the prices that potential customers might be willing to pay. Otherwise, they could be setting themselves up for a disaster. Iridium, the satellite telephone service, is a case in point. When the system was envisioned in 1985, the insight was valuable enough. There was a lack of good cell phone service in many of the destinations visited by traveling business executives, Iridium's targeted customers.[b] But by 1998, the idea ceased to be valuable enough to justify the required investment in the face of advancing cellular technology. One telecom analyst accurately assessed the new market: "If all the revenue from international business travelers calling internationally from developing countries went to Iridium, Iridium would still not be able to cover its capital costs, let alone its operating costs."[c] Indeed, Iridium could not build a large enough customer base, and less than a year after starting service, it was forced to file for bankruptcy protection.

Third, Is the Insight Certain Enough?

Some fads seem to come out of nowhere. The hula hoop is the classic example. But other BEMI products have served a need that was all but inevitable, given certain technological, geopolitical, or demographic trends. Years ago, Novo Nordisk accurately predicted that the growing affluence and more sedentary lifestyle of people in China and other emerging countries would lead to a rise in the incidence of diabetes. In the United States, an aging population of healthy baby boomers with high disposable incomes has opened various market opportunities, such as vacation packages and retirement communities that emphasize an active senior lifestyle, including not just golf but tennis, yoga, bicycling, and daily physical exercise. Of course, timing is a huge factor. Apple was prescient in realizing that consumers would want personal digital assistant (PDA) devices, but the technology wasn't quite ready when the company introduced the Newton. A few years later, Palm, Inc., would bring to market a similar device to much success. Whatever the case, executives should be extremely wary of any insight that relies on a speculative potential trend. Remember the Segway Personal Transporter? Segway bet heavily (a reported $100 million in R&D) that consumers would adopt a revolutionary new form of transportation: a personal two-wheel electric vehicle that they could ride upright at speeds up to around 12 miles per hour.[d] When it was introduced to a fanfare of media hype in late 2001, the annual sales target of forty thousand units seemed almost cautious.[e] Six years later, though, a *total* of fewer than thirty thousand had been sold, mainly to niche applications, such as for law-enforcement agencies and theme parks.[f]

Finally, BEMIs don't necessarily require a huge technological innovation. Sometimes the insight is purely about an emerging market, such as Novo Nordisk's realization that diabetes would become an increasing health problem in emerging economies. On the other hand, technological innovations don't necessarily lead to BEMI opportunities. The Segway, which deploys a sophisticated self-balancing mechanism based on gyroscopes, is perhaps one of the most inventive devices in recent memory, but it is essentially a product that is still looking for its BEMI.

a. Evan Ramstad, "Samsung Edges Out TV Rivals," *Wall Street Journal*, February 17, 2010.

b. Sydney Finkelstein and Shade H. Sanford, "Learning from Corporate Mistakes: The Rise and Fall of Iridium," *Organizational Dynamics* 29, no. 2 (2000): 138–148.

c. Andrew Zajac, "Iridium: Pie in the Sky? Motorola's Bet on Global Wireless Communications Could Go Far to Reshape Its Image—And Send a Signal About the Future of Other Satellite Systems," *Chicago Tribune,* June 14, 1998, Business Section, 1.

d. Michael P. Regan, "Segway Sets Course for Stock Market," *USA Today,* May 30, 2006.

e. Nina Sovich, "Segway Slump," *Fortune Small Business,* April 1, 2004.

f. Wil Schroter, "When to Dump That Great Idea," *Forbes,* July 9, 2007.

more immediate but equally hidden from view to all but the most careful observers. Consider Porsche's decision to sell sport-utility vehicles (SUVs). When the company announced its entry into the already-crowded market a decade ago, purists shuddered and skepticism prevailed. Why was Porsche risking the reputation of its mighty brand to go after the soccer-mom market? But the Porsche Cayenne wasn't simply going to be a me-too product. From the inside out, it was going to be a true Porsche, worthy of the company's long heritage in building top sports cars with superior performance and handling. In fact, when the 2.2-ton Cayenne Turbo was pitted against a sleek Mercedes ML 63 AMG sedan in a sprint to reach a speed of 100 kilometers per hour, the difference was just a tenth of a second (5.1 seconds for the Cayenne versus 5.0 for the Mercedes)—and the Cayenne had better handling. Porsche's BEMI—that the seemingly overcrowded SUV market still had room for a high-performance, sportster-bred entry to satisfy high-end consumers—might not have been earth shattering, but it was big enough to launch a major new business. By 2008, the Cayenne was Porsche's most popular model, outselling even the 911 and accounting for about one-third of the company's total sales.

In other cases, BEMIs enable companies to totally redefine a mature market. Take, for example, Nintendo. In developing Wii, the popular videogame console, Nintendo rightly recognized that the potential market was far larger than just adolescent boys and young men who were buying Microsoft's Xbox and Sony's PlayStation for their sophisticated state-of-the-art technologies. Instead, Nintendo re-imagined the market for videogames to include everyone from teenagers to senior citizens. After all, the original games were products like Pong, which was played across generations. So, instead of concentrating on flashy graphics and snazzy features, Nintendo focused on ease of use and good, old-fashioned fun. One of the company's hits is a tennis simulator in which the user hits a virtual ball on the screen by swinging the Wii controller (which contains a motion sensor) as the racket. Thanks to those types of products, the videogame market has exploded across demographic lines. According to the Entertainment Software Association, 40 percent of users are now adult women, and a quarter of U.S. consumers over the age of fifty also play.[4]

As we conducted deeper investigations into our high-performance businesses, a distinct pattern emerged. The high performers were the companies that had identified BEMI opportunities from various trends and had prepared to exploit these trends well before they occurred. In other words, their skill wasn't necessarily in envisioning a world that could be but one that *would* be. What seemed obvious and doable in hindsight was based on insight and early commitment to an important shift in market conditions. The high performers looked to win big, and they looked long term.

In contrast, low and average performers failed to see a trend that would inevitably transform their industry or they tended to have market insights that weren't big enough. These companies were far more likely to churn out one incremental product after another than to develop innovative blockbusters. (But that's not to say that high performers forwent incremental advancements altogether. In fact, many of them continued developing incremental products in their core businesses while simultaneously working on more radical innovations to take advantage of a BEMI.)

Indeed a common fallacy of low and average performers was the mistaken belief that they could achieve superior results by managing a large portfolio of existing businesses, an approach that often resulted in a regression to the mean: a few of the businesses might have excelled, but the overall performance of the portfolio (and of the organization as a whole) was, at best, average. In contrast, companies like Novo Nordisk were able to achieve high performance by betting big and focusing their resources on BEMIs—sometimes a single BEMI spanned the entire corporation; other times separate business units pursued their individuals BEMIs. But high performers never allowed underperforming businesses to dilute their success.

Another tendency of low and average performers is that they often overreached—they tackled BEMI opportunities that were beyond their capabilities, in essence, biting off more than they could chew. And that's why we stress the words *big enough*. The insight has to be big, maybe even huge, to propel a company to a higher level of success, but it must still be manageable, given that organization's capabilities.

But how exactly do high-performance companies repeatedly find BEMIs and take advantage of them? Our research uncovered three crucial attributes. First, they are committed to understanding the subtle but important shifts in customers, markets, and industries, and invest heavily to create that intelligence. Next, they maintain an unshakeable faith in the power of science and technology to solve a problem, no matter how difficult and seemingly impossible it might first appear. Last, they handle the complexity of an uncertain future by breaking it into manageable pieces so that resources can be deployed accordingly.

IDENTIFYING A BEMI

High performers don't wait for divine inspiration for their BEMIs. Instead, they make substantial investments to understand a market and the numerous trends that could influence it. Those trends could come from a variety of sources—demographic, geopolitical, technological, societal, and so on. Consequently, high performers are continually on the lookout everywhere, trying to spot subtle changes and shifts in their business landscape. They leave no stone unturned, because they realize that BEMIs can sometimes arise from the most unlikely places.

Listen More

Obviously, customers are a good place to start when companies are looking for a BEMI, but high performers go well beyond just listening to customers; they take extra measures to ensure that the customer's voice is truly heard. Tesco, for instance, holds an annual Customer Question Time, which is attended by twelve thousand customers every year, to hear customers' views on everything, from products and prices to Tesco's role in the community.[5] Furthermore, through the company's TWIST (Tesco Week In Store Together) program, thousands of Tesco's head office managers are sent out every year to work in store for one week so that they can experience the products and processes that the consumers face and so that they can listen to employee suggestions.[6] Thanks to those and other efforts, Tesco has long been able to understand changing consumer attitudes, such as increasing concern for health and a preference for local produce, and to improve its own practices and offerings.

One way in which listening to customers led Tesco to exploit a new market opportunity was with Tesco's Fresh & Easy Neighborhood Markets, the chain of small food stores in western United States. Tesco executives came to the United States with the observation that smaller-size food stores were growing in many markets around the world but not in the United States. After speaking directly to American consumers, the executives indeed found a market niche for specialty fresh-food markets that would be located right in people's neighborhoods. This BEMI led to the creation of a new type of store that was based on insights drawn from listening to customers, and it proved to be a hit.[7]

Of course, customers aren't always able to articulate what they want, and that's why high performers go the extra distance to figure that out. Procter & Gamble, for example, invests more than $200 million each year on consumer research, and part of that effort consists of anthropological studies conducted in the field. Through a program called Living It, employees literally live with consumers in their homes, eating and shopping with them for several days at a time. Another program, called Working It, allows employees to work behind a retail counter to gain firsthand insights into what customers are—and are not—buying. And these immersion programs aren't just for staff employees and middle managers. In fact, roughly 70 percent of all P&G executives have participated.[8]

Moreover, high performers are well aware that the biggest market insights can often come from unlikely sources. Consider GE Healthcare's experience in emerging markets. In China, for example, doctors typically work in rural clinics, which can't afford pricey medical equipment like conventional ultrasounds that sell for more than $100,000 in the United States. So, to serve the Chinese market, GE developed a cheaper, portable machine that uses a laptop computer. Of course, the compact device isn't nearly as good as the bulkier, sophisticated equipment sold in the United States, but the performance is good enough for simple applications like detecting enlarged livers, and moreover, GE has managed to bring the price down to as low as $15,000. And that was just the beginning of the story. GE recognized that its compact ultrasound could be adapted for the U.S. market in applications where portability is crucial (for instance, for an ambulance crew at an accident site) or where space is an issue (such as in a cramped emergency or operating room). Thanks to that valuable insight, GE quickly grew the global sales of its portable ultrasound business from $4 million in 2002 to $278 million just six years later.[9]

In today's world, with the Internet and other information technologies, companies simply have no excuse for being out of touch with their customers. Crucial information about the market is out there, available to any business that expends the effort to look. Consider Dell, which actively monitors various blogs, Internet forums, and other communities to learn what customers are saying about the company. Not only does the information help identify common problems with products, but it also provides insight into the kinds of features and functionality that consumers might like in the future—data that could be crucial in helping Dell to identify its next BEMI. For example, after learning about the growing popularity of Linux from such sources, Dell launched a major initiative for the rapid development of a line of PCs to support this open-source operating system.[10] Is Linux going to be the company's next BEMI? Perhaps not, but at the very least, Dell has been aggressively searching for any such opportunities that could rejuvenate its business, which has been struggling for the past several years to recapture its earlier magic.

Listen Better

Of course, although information technologies might be well suited for collecting copious data, the resulting information will be of little use to companies that can't separate the proverbial wheat from the chaff. Dell has reported that through its various online initiatives, the company has 100 million interactions with customers every year.[11] Sifting through that mountain of data requires a powerful filter to detect signals (sometimes just faint ones) from the surrounding noise. Simply put, quantity is indeed important, because you need to listen to more numerous, varied sources of information, but quality is also crucial if you want to avoid chasing pseudo trends that lead nowhere.

One approach is to rely on the collective wisdom of a group of employees or customers, thus tapping into the so-called wisdom of crowds. Take, for example, Wells Fargo. Several years ago, the company was awash in a sea of data. Through an electronic suggestion box, the company was logging an annual average of eight thousand ideas. But how to make sense of that large, diverse dataset? The solution was to use wikis (open-source, participative Web sites) and other crowd-sourcing technologies. Wells Fargo implemented an application through which participants could develop seeds of ideas—anything from a suggestion for improving the customer experience at bank branches to a recommendation for making back-office operations more efficient. Participants continually develop and rate the different ideas, with the cream eventually rising to the top. The system is extremely scalable—anywhere from fifty to fifty thousand individuals can participate.[12]

Such technologies can be remarkable tools, but high-performance companies never discount the wisdom of a seasoned executive. Toyota's entry in the luxury-car market is a case in point. The origin of that BEMI came from Yukiyasu Togo, a Toyota executive with an intellectual and cultural curiosity that has become the stuff of corporate legend. In his first overseas assignment for Toyota, Togo learned about the Thai people and culture by shaving his head, dressing as a Buddhist monk, and begging on the streets of Bangkok. Later, when he was stationed in Canada as an executive vice president, he sold cars going door-to-door, visiting 150 homes, in order to understand why Toyota sales had been slow there.[13]

Back in the early 1980s, Togo was the head of Toyota Motor Sales USA. Living in Southern California, he noticed something that annoyed him—his friends who were also high-level execs tended to buy BMW and Mercedes-Benz cars but not Toyota. Why, Togo wondered, didn't his company have a luxury car that could compete?[14] And the problem extended far beyond Togo's circle of friends. The lack of a high-end vehicle left Toyota vulnerable to customer defections. As baby boomers were reaching their peak earning years and had more disposable income, many were stepping up from their Corollas, Cressidas, and Camrys and purchasing European luxury cars. In essence, those consumers were growing out of Toyota's reach.[15]

Togo brought his case back to the company's headquarters in Tokyo, appealing to then-chairman Eiji Toyoda. It was hardly a slam-dunk decision. In fact, many executives at Toyota felt that launching the Lexus brand would dilute resources such that the result would be two weak brands (Lexus and Toyota) instead of one strong one. The resistance was particularly vehement, with critics using the acronym NFL (for "no f—cking Lexus") to express their vigorous objections. But Togo persisted, at one point asserting that he would resign if Lexus flopped.[16] Fortunately, chairman Toyoda listened to Togo's BEMI, and Lexus has since grown into one of the world's strongest luxury brands.

Of course, Toyota didn't rely solely on the insights of a single executive. The company conducted focus groups and found that each of the major luxury brands had a perceived weakness: one was judged to have poor quality and service, while another's cars were thought too plentiful on the road, thus diminishing their exclusivity. Still other brands were considered either too boxy, having too small an interior, or having styling that was weak compared with another top competitor.[17] Thus Toyota confirmed that there was indeed room in the market for another entrant. But the point is this: the top brass at Toyota listened to Togo because of his proven track record. Under Togo's leadership, Toyota sales of new vehicles in the United States surged from around 720,000 in 1983 to more than 1 million just three years later.[18] And Togo was known for going above and beyond in his efforts to understand local markets, as evidenced by his experiences in Thailand and Canada. In other words, if any executive was primed to have a BEMI about the U.S. market, it was Togo. Fortunately for Toyota, the company pursued his insight about the luxury-car market instead of discounting it.

HAVING FAITH IN THE POWER OF
SCIENCE AND TECHNOLOGY

Having a BEMI is all well and good, but taking advantage of that insight is an entirely different matter. From our research, we found that average and low performers often underfund BEMI projects and frequently quit too early when the going gets rough. High performers, on the other hand, tend to stick with a BEMI project through its ups and downs, with unwavering commitment and faith in the power of R&D to address the identified market need.

Consider P&G's development of Pampers. When P&G introduced the product in 1961, disposable diapers had already been on the market for decades. The Chux brand had appeared in 1935 and was a leader at the time. What P&G had managed to do, however, was to see how major societal changes in the United States could exponentially grow the market. Specifically, the company recognized two crucial trends. First, the growing affluence of consumers was driving their desire for greater convenience, and second, women were increasingly joining the workforce.

But P&G faced a huge challenge: in those days, disposable diapers had to be made by hand because the paper used in them rendered mass production impossible. Thus, although families might purchase a small supply for travel purposes, the product was too pricey for everyday use. To tap into the mass market's growing desire and ability to pay for convenient diapering, P&G had to concentrate on dramatically lowering the costs, and after five years of intense research, it managed to bring the price down to 10 cents a diaper. But that wasn't good enough, because diaper services were then about 3.5 cents per diaper and home washing was about 1.5 cents. Finally, the breakthrough came when P&G developed a machine that could mass-produce diapers at 5.5 cents apiece. More expensive than diaper services, but affordable to increasingly affluent consumers. Thanks to that innovation, the market ballooned from $10 million in 1966 to

$370 million in just seven years.[19] Today, disposable diapers are a $10 billion industry that is still growing rapidly, as consumers in emerging markets increase their use of the product, thanks to their growing affluence and changing lifestyles.

Did P&G absolutely know that it could bring down the cost of disposable diapers to the right price point? No, but the company persisted in the face of that uncertainty because it had faith in the power of R&D. It worked tirelessly to act on its BEMI, persevering for years even through repeated setbacks. Of course, that kind of commitment doesn't come cheap. According to one source, P&G reportedly spent more to develop and test market Pampers than Henry Ford did to bring his first automobile to market.[20] But that's why high performers focus on BEMIs, because the potential pay-off has to be well worth the investment required.

Commit Fully

Often, a number of companies will have the same BEMI, but the winner will be the organization that is most willing to commit itself fully. Years ago, auto manufacturers were all aware that oil was becoming an increasingly precious commodity. But it was Toyota that wholeheartedly threw itself into seizing that market opportunity with Prius—a new type of vehicle that would reshape the industry. Back in the mid-1990s, the company launched a project called G21 (Global 21st Century) with a simple if daunting goal: build a car with a fuel efficiency of 47.5 miles per gallon, 50 percent more than that of a basic Corolla.[21] (In contrast, Honda, also a forerunner in developing hybrid technology, took a more restrained approach with Insight—a small, two-seat car that was never intended for high-volume sales.)[22]

The obvious solution was to work on improving the transmission and engine of existing cars. With that approach, Toyota engineers felt they could potentially improve fuel efficiency by as much as 50 percent. But Risuke Kubochi, general manager of General Engineering (and the former chief engineer of the Celica model), rejected the idea of leveraging conventional technology. So the Toyota engineers began looking at hybrid technology, which the company had been toying with for about twenty years. But the problem was that although a hybrid model could deliver dramatic fuel-cost savings, the technology was then prohibitively expensive. But Kubochi was undeterred. He ordered the engineers to create a concept hybrid car that would boost fuel efficiency by at least 100 percent *and* be cost effective. Moreover, he wanted the car in time for the 1995 Tokyo Motor Show, just twelve months later.

The project had Toyota's full commitment. The company assigned a thousand engineers to work on the initiative, and they investigated eighty alternative hybrid power trains, eventually narrowing the list to four. The engineers had barely gotten that far in the project when they received a new directive. In addition to having to develop a concept car within twelve months, Hiroshi Okuda, the new president, also needed a full-production vehicle within twenty-four months, roughly two-thirds the time it usually takes.

The obstacles were daunting. The battery that would drive the motor component of the vehicle, for instance, was a major headache. It had to be small but also have enough power. To complicate matters, the technology was very sensitive to temperature: the battery wouldn't work if it was either too hot or too cold, which was completely unacceptable for use in an automobile that might be driven in California or Alaska. (The solution? Put the battery in the trunk, away from the heat generated by the engine, in a location where its temperature could be more easily controlled.)[23] And that was just one of myriad major design issues that had to be addressed in bringing a novel technology to market.

But the development team literally worked around the clock, enabling Toyota to officially unveil the Prius in October 1997, two months ahead of schedule. And in the following December, just two months later, the car was already on the market. From the start, the Prius was a hit. It was the right car at the right time, appealing to the growing number of consumers who were becoming environmentally conscious and were beginning to identify themselves that way. (In a 2007 survey, the top reason that customers cited for buying a Prius was that the car "makes a statement about me." Interestingly, fuel economy was a distant third on that list.)[24] Thus, the hybrid automobile, which GM vice chairman Bob Lutz had once dismissed as "an interesting curiosity," had arrived.

The price of that success was not cheap. The total cost of bringing Prius to market was more than $1 billion.[25] The figure is all the more impressive given that, when Toyota was developing the revolutionary Prius, the company was not nearly as large as its main U.S. competitors. In fact, when Prius made its debut in 1997, Toyota was merely a fraction of their size, with annual sales of about $90 billion, versus $170 billion for GM and $150 billion for Ford.[26]

Perform Directed Research

Of course, companies should never just conduct R&D for the sake of conducting R&D. Otherwise, they could end up developing a technologically brilliant product for which no market exists. To avoid this, high performers always focus on performing *directed* research. They identify a BEMI and then figure out how best to serve that market. For P&G and disposable diapers, the company's research targeted one major issue: bringing costs down. And P&G had an unshakeable belief in the power of science and technology to do just that.

But that's not to say that high performers will stick with a technology through hell and high water. In fact, quite the opposite is true. High performers are focused on solving a BEMI market need through any means that work. That is, they don't wed themselves to any technology. Their primary concern is addressing an emerging market need; the technology is merely the means to accomplish it. So, for example, to satisfy the growing demand for "green" vehicles, Toyota is developing a number of alternatives, including hybrid, electric, and fuel-cell technologies. And even though the company has scored a huge hit with Prius, a hybrid car, Toyota is still making considerable investments in electric and fuel-cell technologies. "It's very important when you do R&D to widen the scope, to have several competing technologies or systems, and then to choose what is best," explains Masatami Takimoto, Toyota executive vice president. Even within hybrid technology, there are numerous types of systems, including several variations for the basic drivetrain. "We started our hybrid development work in 1969 and, since then, we've tried them all," says Takimoto.[27]

Not only are high performers flexible about the technologies they use, but they also avoid the not-invented-here syndrome. If a necessary technology or other industry know-how has already been developed on the outside, high performers might obtain it by licensing or by partnering with or acquiring the business that owns that intellectual property. Take, for instance, P&G, which was once considered a fortress of insularity. That closed approach to innovation used to be effective in an era when companies could control the flow of talent and knowledge. But around a decade ago, the company commenced a concerted effort to bring its walls down after realizing that greater employee mobility, the Internet, and other factors had led to a new age of open innovation.[28]

Now P&G freely reaches around the globe for new ideas and technologies to acquire. In fact, the company has some seventy-five innovation scouts located around the world, and its goal is that up to 50 percent of all new innovations should come from the outside. A huge success in that area was SpinBrush, a battery-operated toothbrush that sold for $5 and became the best-selling toothbrush in the United States. P&G got the idea for the product from four entrepreneurs in Cleveland.[29] Indeed, P&G will even partner with rivals: it competes with Clorox on cleaning products, but has partnered with the company to commercialize such innovations as Glad Press'n Seal (a plastic wrap that will seal to a variety of surfaces) and Glad ForceFlex (a plastic trash bag with a stretchable drawstring that keeps the bag in place), both of which have substantially grown their respective markets. Those products might not represent BEMIs, but they are evidence of P&G's commitment to the continual search for them.

BREAKING THE FUTURE INTO MANAGEABLE CHUNKS

Up to now, we've talked about how high performers identify and take advantage of singular BEMI opportunities. But high-performance companies are hardly one-hit wonders. Instead, they demonstrate a consistent ability to follow one BEMI success with another in a process that is not discretely sequential. That is, even while high performers are implementing one BEMI initiative, they are busy trying to identify the next BEMI to avoid any lags in business. Think of how Apple has moved smoothly from the iPod to iTunes to the iPhone. Ideally, as one BEMI market matures, high performers use its profits to fund their next BEMI initiative. But how exactly do they manage such orderly progression, given the myriad market, industry, and other uncertainties that can derail even the best of business plans? From our research, we found that the key is to break the future into manageable chunks.

Establish a Pipeline over Different Time Horizons

To understand how, consider Genentech, the San Francisco–based pharmaceutical company (which Roche Holdings fully acquired in 2009 after taking a majority stake in 1990). Founded in 1976, the company has successfully commercialized one major product after another, including Avastin (for colorectal cancer), Herceptin (for breast cancer), and Rituxan (for lymphoma and rheumatoid arthritis).[30] The impressive body of work is reflected in the company's financial performance: Genentech's sales revenue per employee was $1.11 million in 2009, a measure on which the company has consistently been an industry leader.[31]

To maintain a consistent flow of major innovations, the company has historically set ambitious long-term goals to ensure that its market insights are big enough. In 1999, for instance, Genentech conceived its "5 × 5" goals: five new products would be approved, and five significant products would be in late-stage clinical trials, all by 2005. After achieving both goals, the company announced its Horizon 2010 Vision and Goals, which set the bar even higher: Genentech planned to bring at least twenty new molecules into clinical development and at least fifteen major new products into the market by 2010.[32]

Indeed, Genentech has been the very embodiment of a product pipeline. As early as 2003, the company had already been recognized for its successful pipeline management and promising lineup.[33] In 2008 as it neared its Horizon 2010 target date, Genentech already had fifteen compounds ready to hit the market in two years and another thirty within five years.[34] Today the company's Research and Early Development center has thirteen new molecular entities in Phase I and four in Phase II.[35] (Phases refer to stages of clinical trials, with each phase involving progressively more extensive tests for safety and efficacy. Results must be approved by the FDA in order to continue to the next phase. Successful completion of Phase III is required by the FDA for the drug to be marketed). With parent company Roche, the combined counts are now thirty-seven in Phase I, fifteen in Phase II, and eight in Phase III.[36]

Meanwhile, the company also continually refines and reformulates its former winners. Its chief drug, Avastin, which was originally used to treat colorectal cancer, was approved in 2008 for treatment of breast cancer and in 2009 for a type of brain cancer, and further applications could include other types of cancers as well. In such ways, Genentech manages its development of both incremental and blockbuster innovations.[37]

But having fixed goals like those in its 5 × 5 initiative hasn't prevented the company from changing course quickly to move in promising directions. In 2000, after realizing that its Rituxan cancer drug might help rheumatoid arthritis sufferers, Genentech assigned a third of its one thousand researchers to the clinical trials and studies.[38] Six years later, the drug received FDA approval for use in treating rheumatoid arthritis. More recently, Genentech has been investigating the effectiveness of Rituxan for autoimmune diseases, including various types of lupus.[39] Because such diseases are not well understood by doctors, the research could be of great scientific (and commercial) importance.

Beware of All-or-Nothing Solutions

In addition to ensuring that their pipelines of innovation keep flowing, high-performance companies are also adept at breaking each individual project into manageable chunks. Like expert mountaineers, they create base camps at different elevations, never attempting to reach the summit in one trip. That way, they can remain flexible, doing heavy climbing when the conditions are favorable and resting at camp to wait out storms. All this might sound obvious, but far too many businesses have suffered, sometimes disastrously, from trying to do too much all at once.

Some companies will, for example, implement all-or-nothing technologies. The classic example here is Iridium, the multibillion-dollar satellite system that provides global telephony service. The original design for the system boasted impressive technology: when completed, sixty-six satellites would circle the earth in low orbit, providing complete telecommunications coverage anywhere in the world, even at the north and south poles. But the problem was that the handsets wouldn't work until the entire constellation of satellites was in place, thus requiring a massive upfront investment. The total price tag? No less than $5 billion.[40] Though the business plan may have been sound when it was conceived, it took eleven years (from concept through development) to launch the service, and during that time, cell phones had become increasingly popular, with cellular networks spreading even to emerging markets like China. Not surprisingly, in August 1999, just nine months after its service was launched, Iridium filed for bankruptcy protection. Today, the system is still operating under new ownership (which bought the assets for a mere $25 million), but serves a limited targeted customer base, including the petroleum industry, the scientific community, and the military.[41]

Not only should managers be wary of all-or-nothing technologies like Iridium, but they should also think twice about any business model that requires an all-out investment before it can be tested. Case in point: Webvan, the online grocery service that was launched in 1999. Backed by savvy investors like Goldman Sachs and Sequoia Capital, Webvan wanted to transform the way that people bought their groceries. Webvan's BEMI was certainly ambitious, and so was its solution. The company built a vast infrastructure of massive, automated warehouses, each of which cost $25 million. The problem was that margins in the industry are treacherous—on average, companies eke out a net margin of little more than 1 percent. Because of that, Webvan needed tremendous volume to make its business model work. Each of the warehouses required about four thousand orders a day just to break even. Unfortunately, Webvan never could attain that scale, and after burning through $1 billion in cash, the company was forced to close its doors in July 2001. "We made the assumption that capital was endless and demand was endless," admitted CEO Robert Swan.[42]

In contrast, the British retailer Tesco (one of our high performers) took a much more measured approach. It launched an online service through which orders are fulfilled from existing Tesco stores instead of from a network of warehouses, thus dramatically lowering costs. Of course, Tesco possessed a huge natural advantage: its considerable brick-and-mortar presence in the market. But the point here is that Webvan's business model was fundamentally unsound. Peapod, another dot-com startup, entered the online market by teaming with existing supermarkets in the United States.

In this chapter, we explored how high-performance companies consistently position themselves to be in the right place at the right time. But we purposely omitted something crucial. Yes, Toyota shrewdly recognized that the aging generation of baby boomers would present a huge market opportunity for selling luxury cars, but exactly how was the company able to bring Lexus to market, given that Toyota's history was in manufacturing reliable, economical vehicles and not classy, high-end products? In other words, being in the right place at the right time is a necessary but not sufficient condition for sustained business success. Indeed, many companies have had brilliant market insights but have flopped miserably because of poor execution. In order to implement a BEMI initiative, organizations need to acquire a distinct set of capabilities. In the next chapter, we'll explore how businesses can accomplish that through a number of effective processes.

Before You Jump to Conclusions, Ask Yourself These Questions:

1. What processes are used in your company to identify BEMIs?

2. Is your company currently working on a BEMI initiative?

3. If your company does have a BEMI project in place, is it adequately funded to overcome potential obstacles?

4. Is your BEMI initiative broken into manageable chunks so that various components can be tested before you launch the full system?

THRESHOLD COMPETENCE BEFORE SCALING

PEOPLE EXPRESS was an innovative airline. Founded in 1981, in the wake of industry deregulation, the company did just about everything differently. Its employees performed a variety of functions—pilots helped with baggage, and flight attendants checked passengers at the departure gates. All seats on a flight were the same price, and passengers could pay their fares while sitting in the plane en route to their destinations. The airline also charged for each checked bag as well as for food and beverages served on the flight—unheard-of during that time. As a result, the no-frills airline was able to discount its fares to unbelievably low prices, often comparable to bus or car transportation—just $23 from Newark, New Jersey, to Buffalo, New York, for example. Those rock-bottom prices opened up air travel to many consumers who previously couldn't afford it, and from the start, the airline was a smashing success. In just a few years, People Express became the fifth-largest airline in the United States.

But then the cracks started to show. The company was hiring workers so quickly that it couldn't train them properly. Moreover, long-established carriers like American Airlines, United Airlines, and Continental Airlines had figured out how to cut costs and had slashed their fares for a certain number of seats on each flight, thus attracting many of People Express's budget-conscious customers. And the enormous debt that People Express had acquired in order to expand was beginning to crush the airline. By one analyst's estimate, interest payments and preferred dividends to service that debt was consuming nearly 8 percent of revenues.[1] As the company's finances headed south, worker morale took a huge hit because employees had become accustomed to healthy profit-sharing and a rising stock price. Not surprisingly, customer service began to suffer, and soon disgruntled consumers had tagged the airline with the derisive nickname "People Distress." The company, unable to overcome those various missteps, eventually had to sell itself to Texas Air Corp. (owner of Continental Airlines) just six years after its promising launch.

As People Express and countless other companies have discovered, ramping up a business is an inherently tricky endeavor. On the one hand, executives might have good reasons for wanting to scale up their operations quickly—to take advantage of a market opportunity for example. They might, for instance, need to establish their new technology as the de facto standard, and even if they haven't yet determined exactly what their business model should be, they assume they will figure that out along the way. On the other hand, they may want to scale for reasons less likely to lead to success: the desire to increase revenues quickly in advance of an initial public offering or company merger, for example. Or they could simply be the victims of their own egos and hubris in their quest to be bigger faster—a drive that is sometimes reinforced by executive compensation packages that reward rapid growth and short-term success. Regardless of the reasons for doing so, however, scaling too soon or too quickly can lead to a number of serious problems. In particular, the following three syndromes can easily derail any company's expansion into a new market.

First, scaling too hastily can obfuscate the reasons for a company's initial success. Executives might not replicate what works, because they haven't figured out the formula yet or they may not fully realize the importance of certain processes. The danger is that they could dilute the very characteristics and features that customers value most. From the start, People Express was focused on serving smaller cities like Newark and Buffalo by using smaller aircraft for short flights between those destinations. But later, it began flying longer hauls, even inaugurating a transatlantic flight from Newark to London, and it bought Boeing 747s to serve those routes, thus dramatically altering the company's fundamental business model. To make matters worse, as People Express began to hit the skids, it tried to woo business customers by offering premium seating and frequent-flyer programs. In other words, instead of leveraging its distinctiveness (namely, the reasons for its initial success), People Express diluted it by becoming more like the legacy airlines.

Second, scaling too soon or too quickly can introduce problems that distract management from perfecting the distinctive value of the offering. In 1985, People Express bought Frontier Airlines for $300 million. That acquisition not only added to the company's debt load, but also brought together two very different workforces. People Express's employees were not unionized; Frontier's were. The integration challenge was a huge management headache that also absorbed considerable time on the part of the company's leaders.

Third, scaling too soon or too quickly can invite unwanted attention from incumbent competitors. Had People Express remained focused on serving smaller cities, it might have been able to expand across the United States without posing a huge threat to the established airlines. But once it started flying into major cities like Chicago, Los Angeles, and San Francisco, the legacy airlines had no choice but to take notice. Moreover, People Express's acquisition of Frontier Airlines, which was based in Denver, was a direct assault on Continental Airlines and United Airlines, both of which use Denver as a major hub.[2] The result was a nasty fare war that People Express could not withstand because of the debt it had amassed in trying to scale up its operations.

This is not to say that rapid scaling should be avoided at all costs. Hardly. In fact, companies frequently need to expand their operations quickly in order to bring new products to market at sufficient scale before their window of opportunity closes and competitors overtake them. But the danger is when companies pursue industry-leading scale before they possess what we call *threshold competence:* the level of competence required to sustain the business as it progresses to become a major force in its industry. Even high performers that have proven themselves adept at jumping the S-curve are not immune to the siren song of scale for its own sake. Toyota's massive recall of millions of vehicles in 2010, after reports of sudden unintended acceleration in certain models, is a case in point. That crisis became a corporate nightmare not only because of the huge financial damage (by one estimate, Toyota was suffering more than $150 million a week from lost sales) but also because of the enormous hit taken by the company's esteemed brand.[3] How did it come to this for the company that had for decades been synonymous with quality throughout the world—a corporation that we have profiled as a high performer and exemplar of how to jump the S-curve?

The answer may have been provided by CEO Akio Toyoda in his testimony before the U.S. Congress in the winter of 2010: "I fear the pace at which we have grown may have been too quick."[4] Indeed, from 2000 to 2008, the company doubled its sales—a remarkable feat for a corporation of that size—and it eventually supplanted General Motors as the leading auto manufacturer in the world. Along the way, though, Toyota had begun to stray from some of the very practices that had made it so successful in the past. A 2006 internal review, for example, found that Toyota's product development was too rushed, with not enough quality checks and too much reliance on computer simulation rather than the construction of physical prototypes.[5] The company had also violated other tenets of its culture, such as the rule never to build a new product in a new factory with a new workforce. In 2006, for instance, it began building new Tundra pickup trucks in a new plant in San Antonio. Those vehicles, along with millions of others, have been recalled for a variety of problems, not the least of which is the possibility of a sticking gas pedal.[6]

But speed alone isn't the problem. Sometimes, companies can be very successful with a quickly scaled business. Consider, again, Toyota. When the Japanese automaker decided to develop Lexus in the mid-1980s, the company had virtually no experience in the luxury market. Yes, it had proven itself selling reliable, economical vehicles like the popular Corolla and Camry, but what did the company really know about high-end consumers? Skeptics argued that Toyota simply had no business trying to compete against companies like Audi, BMW, Jaguar, Mercedes-Benz, and Volvo. But the Japanese automaker ultimately triumphed, with Lexus becoming one of the world's strongest luxury brands. How did Toyota achieve such spectacular success, seemingly against all odds, and in such short order? And why did that same company lose its way in the 2000s, when it was on the road to becoming the world's largest automaker?

PUTTING THE HORSE BEFORE THE CART

To answer our questions about successful scaling and later challenges, we conducted in-depth studies of numerous corporations that exploited large market opportunities. We looked at historic examples, such as P&G's development of Pampers more than a half century ago, along with the many successes that have followed. And we investigated recent cases, including Porsche's successful entry into the SUV market. To identify what was separating the high performers from their peers, we also looked at the companies that failed to exploit a promising opportunity. And, of course, we studied the challenges and successes that mark the long history of Toyota.

Here's what we found: functional excellence, such as expertise in supply-chain management, is indeed important, but it's hardly enough. Our research confirmed that high performers do possess many world-class capabilities and core competencies, more so than low or average performers, but the mere presence of these qualities did not necessarily lead to superior results.

When the Cayenne, Porsche's new SUV, was first introduced, critics were highly skeptical. "Teaching a bear how to dance does not automatically qualify it for the lead role in *Swan Lake*," sniffed George Kacher, a well-known European auto journalist.[7] Kacher had a point about functional skills in that they do not automatically lead to superior products (whether they be SUVs or ballet performances). But as it turned out, he was dead wrong about Porsche. Cayenne would become a best seller, accounting for roughly one-third of the company's overall sales. So, then, how did Porsche not only learn to dance but also star in *Swan Lake*?

That question was at the crux of our research. Consider that Porsche was hardly the first auto manufacturer into the SUV market. In fact, it was among the last, but it more than compensated for that with a market entrance that was near flawless. In our efforts to decode that kind of superior ability to execute, we found that high performers follow a number of fundamental rules.

The first rule is, "Know the thresholds of value that customers will demand, and never settle for less." High performers understand, from the customer's perspective, precisely the level of distinctiveness and value that they need to produce, and they refuse to bring to market anything that falls short.

Interestingly, high performers are rarely first to market. Rather, they invest in learning the thresholds of performance that will make customers sit up and take notice, and then they commit themselves to meeting or even surpassing those specifications.

Porsche might have been among the last of the automakers to sell SUVs, but it shrewdly used that delay to its advantage. After most of the other car manufacturers had introduced their models, many of which were essentially me-too products, the market was primed for something different. Enter the Cayenne, an SUV that drew on the company's sports-car heritage to offer superior speed and handling as well as the space to carry a family of five.

The second rule is, "Don't scale what doesn't work (yet)." High performers always achieve competency by building or acquiring various essential capabilities *before* scaling their operations. The point might sound obvious, but in their haste to capture market share, many low and average performers, like People Express, have tried to scale before establishing the necessary competencies, in essence putting the cart before the horse.

High performers don't do that; they purposefully build time into their schedules to learn what they need before scaling up. Porsche certainly left itself with enough breathing room with the manufacturing of Cayennes at its Leipzig, Germany, plant. According to one analyst's estimate, the facility could break even just by running at 20 percent capacity.[8] Porsche also could afford to take the time to get things right because the company didn't wait until its existing businesses were waning before investing heavily in the development of its new offering. In fact, in the fiscal year leading up to the Cayenne's debut, Porsche's sales of its flagship 911 sports cars were up by more than 20 percent.

The third rule is, "Show you expect success by planning for it from the beginning." High performers don't merely anticipate success; they expect and fully plan for it. As a result, they work out all the necessary details from the start: How will customers learn about the product, and through what channels will they purchase it? At what pace should demand be fulfilled? Exactly how will production ramp up? Those and other issues are addressed far upstream so that, as high performers are defining the new product, they are also simultaneously determining the manufacturing and channel strategy. That kind of advance planning can be the difference between a blockbuster and an also-ran. Consider that about 150,000 Cayennes were sold in the first five years—a huge number for an automaker of Porsche's size.[9] Having planned ahead with plants that could break even at 20 percent capacity not only bought Porsche time to scale, as noted above, but also gave the company the surplus production capacity it needed to scale rapidly when the time came.

By following those three rules, companies can attain both competence and scale and will thereby naturally build a set of distinctive capabilities for a particular market. For instance, one distinctive capability that Toyota acquired with Lexus was the ability to sell luxury products to high-end consumers. It is crucial to remember that distinctive capabilities are the result of sustained efforts at finding solutions to challenges that a company faces in going after a market opportunity; they are not the end goal in and of themselves. Consequently, managers should focus on solving a unique customer problem, not on developing a set of distinctive capabilities.

Moreover, from our research we found that the two major steps of the journey—building threshold competence and scaling—must be executed in specific ways. High performers first define the exact requirements for success by relating various criteria to important customer needs. Next, they buy time, distancing themselves from competitors, by implementing solutions that are difficult (if not impossible) to copy. Then, after attaining the necessary competencies, high performers scale their operations quickly but resist the temptation to move so fast that the expansion becomes unmanageable. They also learn to replicate what works (and to avoid what doesn't). And they never forget the crucial importance of distribution, getting their products into the right channels in ways that make their business models all the more effective. A closer look at each of those two essential steps—creating competence and scaling—reveals how their effective execution separates the high performers from the also-rans.

CREATING THRESHOLD COMPETENCE

Low and average performers tend to concentrate too much on today. They might dwell on an existing core competence, but this only limits their vision of the future. The classic example is Polaroid, which couldn't see beyond its traditional business in instant film and cameras to appreciate how digital photography would revolutionize the industry. In contrast, high performers look at the future first. They identify a big-enough market insight, or BEMI, and then they figure out what they need to do in order to take advantage of that opportunity.

Define the Thresholds of Success

As an essential part of that process, companies have to know the exact attributes and levels of performance that a new product must possess or that a new service or approach to business must deliver. Companies need to understand the *real* problems—the "pain points" that customers want removed as well as the specific obstacles that have kept competitors from addressing those issues. They also need to know what level of pain relief customers will be willing to pay for—how high the bar is for success. Doing so is by definition a stretch. A BEMI alone is never enough; rather, it sets a company off on a journey of discovery and innovation. In short, businesses must know what they need to know (but don't currently know).

All this might sound overly simplistic, but we have observed countless companies make crucial mistakes. They enter a market without first truly uncovering, defining, and targeting the challenges that customers want the companies to overcome. What's more important, the companies fail to quantify the specific level of improvement that will make customers want—if not covet—a new product. As a result, a business ends up offering partial solutions that leave customers cold and then justifies that effort as working incrementally.

In contrast, high performers clearly define and articulate the critical attributes and the corresponding performance levels that will truly entice customers to open their pocketbooks. These companies then bring together the full range of innovation types and approaches—including product and service, process, and management innovation—to meet the needs. The following sections review some of the critical attributes and thresholds from past BEMIs.

Affordability. When P&G developed Pampers, remember, the company knew it had to get the per-diaper cost down to a certain level. At the time, diaper services charged roughly 3.5 cents per diaper, and washing them at home cost around 1.5 cents per diaper. P&G knew that to be competitive, it had to be able to mass-produce its disposable diapers at a cost to the consumer of 5.5 cents. Similarly, after seeing countless families stacked up on motorbikes, Tata Motors realized that to capture those customers, it had to bring the price of its cheapest car down to $2,500—a price competitive with purchasing a motorcycle. The lesson? Companies need to figure out their price points before they launch a major R&D initiative and not during the final stages of the project.

Recently, Reckitt Benckiser, the global manufacturer of household, health, and personal care brands like Lysol, Woolite, and Nurofen, was working on a hands-free soap dispenser for the home, similar in principle to the sensor-activated dispensers at airports, malls, and other public areas. But the battery-operated product had to be affordable for consumers, a tall order in a device with more than fifty parts. After intense efforts to optimize the product's design and overhaul its supply chain, Reckitt Benckiser was able to bring the price point below $10.[10] What might be the BEMI behind such a product? As consumers become increasingly concerned about preventing the spread of germs, a device at this price point is likely to become increasingly popular.

Luxury and reliability. Traditional measures of luxury have always come with a bit of imperfection—hand-tailored suits, and at one time stylish but unreliable luxury cars, spoke of a certain amount of inefficiency in production and expense in maintenance that only the rich could be presumed to afford. Until the Lexus. Toyota entered the luxury-car market with a simple directive from then-chairman Eiji Toyoda: "Make the best car in the world." So company engineers studied competitors like BMW and Mercedes-Benz and arrived at some detailed, quantifiable criteria that then became nonnegotiable targets. For instance, the Lexus had to be extremely quiet—no more than 60 decibels of noise for a speed around 60 miles per hour, and 75 decibels for 125 miles per hour.[11] But the engineers couldn't simply add sound insulation, because they also had to minimize the car's weight to achieve a fuel efficiency that would help avoid the U.S. "gas guzzler" tax. To meet those stringent requirements, Toyota had to design the Lexus with painstaking detail. As just one example, technicians cut the space between adjoining engine parts by a third, including placing the starter motor inside the "V" of the car engine instead of bolting it to the outside, in order to reduce friction and noise.[12] In the end, Toyota was able to redefine luxury in the auto market from stylish imperfection to perfection.

Usability. Making products usable means more than just providing basic functionality; it also requires companies to anticipate needs that customers themselves might not consciously be aware of. Nokia is a master of that. The company, which hires "user anthropologists," sends teams of these consumer behavior researchers around the world to observe how consumers interact with its products. From such research, it developed products like cell phones that have usability as a key attribute. In this way, the company was able to expand the customer base beyond early adopters (such as busy execs) to the mass market. After Nokia realized that people often use their cell phones to show photos to friends, for example, it designed some of its new models with screens that swivel, enabling consumers to share photos without having to pass over their handsets.[13]

Nokia has also deployed such global usability research to understand how customers often adapt products to perform functions other than those they were intended to perform. For example, when researchers observed Africans using phones communally to listen to conversations and music, Nokia provided more powerful speakers in some models—a feature that is now available in the United States, where young people use the phones to watch videos together.[14] Nokia continues to mine that kind of consumer research: a few years back, the company set up a temporary design studio in a rural town in Ghana. The company invited villagers to offer their ideas about what would be, to them, the perfect mobile phone. The sign over the door read, "Your Dream Phone. Share it with the world."[15]

Design, novelty, and impact. Many high performers succeed by exploiting the wow factor. They clearly understand which products would be sufficiently breakthrough and which would merely be incremental offerings. Apple has regularly excelled in this area, thrilling and delighting consumers with snazzy product features (think of the iPhone's "pinch" function) and stylish designs. Cisco is another company that has learned the power of novelty. Using state-of-the-art technologies, it developed TelePresence, a video-conferencing system that boasts a generational leap in audio and visual quality. "Most people are agape when they walk in," says Jim Kittridge, a senior vice president for Wachovia Corporation, an early customer of the product. "They literally gasp; they can't believe what they're seeing."[16] Cisco also recently acquired Pure Digital Technologies, which has been wowing consumers for years with the Flip, a tiny video camcorder remarkable for its elegantly simple design.

That's not to say, however, that businesses should always favor the new and give short shrift to incremental improvement. Indeed, profits from incremental products are often necessary to fund breakthrough projects. "Innovation is about getting many base hits and occasionally hitting the home run," explains Bart Becht, CEO of Reckitt Benckiser. "You very rarely win a baseball game just by hitting home runs."[17] Nevertheless, high-performance businesses like Reckitt Benckiser always distinguish between the two types of innovations: incremental and breakthrough. In contrast, low and average performers sometimes confuse the two, leading these businesses to underfund a breakthrough initiative while overfunding the R&D of incremental products. Moreover, because high-performance companies are so keenly aware of the thresholds of success, they don't waste their time on things that are unimportant. "Apple's iPod ... actually has fewer features than existing products on the market," notes Navi Radjou, a vice president at Forrester Research. "But because of Apple's longstanding investment in understanding how consumers use technology, they understood which features really mattered."[18]

Buy Time to Get Ahead

After clearly defining the parameters for success, companies need to begin building, acquiring, and assembling the organizational capabilities necessary to achieve that criteria. But here is where high performers separate themselves from other businesses. Low and average performers concentrate simply on attaining the required competence. High performers do that, too, but they also do so in specific ways that buy themselves crucial time—a process that is far easier said than done. Indeed, many companies could have been major contenders, but before they could establish their dominance, they were too easily imitated and they lacked the necessary defenses to prevent that incursion.

Consider TiVo, one of the best known brands in the world. It has reached that vaunted pantheon of famous brand names that have come to represent a particular class of products. *TiVo* has become a verb meaning to record a TV show for later viewing. But, sadly, TiVo's business has yet to attain anywhere near the success that many had predicted, and today it remains vulnerable to becoming just a niche company.[19] The basic problem has been that TiVo took too long to secure important deals with cable companies and other potential partners, and during that time, competitors made significant inroads. In 2000, for example, TiVo was in negotiations with Comcast, with the latter agreeing to offer TiVo digital video recorders (DVRs) to some of its subscribers on a trial basis. Unfortunately, that emerging partnership soured. Eventually, TiVo was able to resurrect the deal, but it would take five years to do so—ample time for the industry landscape to shift. Cable operators developed their own competing products, striking manufacturing deals with Motorola and Scientific-Atlanta. And to make matters worse, the technology had evolved, with cable companies exploring alternative approaches like a networked service that uses large servers (instead of set-top boxes) to store programs, which consumers can then access remotely.[20]

To avoid TiVo's woes, many companies have bought crucial time in their markets by relying on intellectual property laws. Pharmaceutical companies in the United States, for instance, routinely apply for patents to protect new drugs for a period before generic ones are allowed. But depending on the industry, that process by itself might not offer sufficient protection. After all, TiVo at one point held 85 patents, with another 117 pending.[21] That's why the technology in and of itself isn't often as crucial as how it's implemented. The implementation might require combinations of technologies that are difficult to acquire or assemble. Or perhaps the technology just simply requires tremendous expertise and substantial re-engineering. Consider how Walmart has deployed the practice of cross-docking to streamline the company's logistics and supply-chain management.

In cross-docking, materials are unloaded from an incoming

truck and then placed directly on outgoing vehicles. Say, for example, a huge semitrailer arrives with literally tons of P&G products like Duracell batteries, Cascade dishwashing detergent, Pampers disposable diapers, Scope mouthwash, and so on. Those products are then divided on a dock and placed on smaller trucks to be delivered to individual stores according to each location's specific demand. This practice not only enables products to be delivered more quickly, but also dramatically lowers inventory and handling costs because it virtually eliminates the need for warehousing. The concept of cross-docking is hardly new; the U.S. trucking industry invented it in the 1930s. But Walmart has taken the practice to new levels of efficiency through the use of information technologies. The company has, for instance, set up a satellite network through which the different stores, distribution centers, and suppliers can exchange up-to-date information about what products are needed at what locations. In addition, Walmart owns a fleet of more than three thousand trucks and twelve thousand trailers, whereas, traditionally, retailers have outsourced that function.[22] In other words, through the years, Walmart has established in cross-docking an expertise and functional capability that would take considerable time and resources for another competitor to copy.

Other companies have put time on their side by relying on large networks that are difficult to assemble. That was certainly the case for online social-networking companies like Facebook. The companies exploit the so-called network effect, in which the value of a product or service increases as more people become users. But brick-and-mortar companies have also relied on large networks as a competitive defense. For 120 years, Avon Products, Inc., one of the high-performance businesses in our study, has used its direct-sales model to build its brand, assembling a large network of independent sales representatives selling mostly door-to-door. However, face-to-face may not be the future, now that a growing number of people shop online. Recognizing this transformation, Avon in 2007 began to use a more advanced, online-friendly direct-to-consumer model, fully supporting and supported by its huge salesperson network. Each "Avon lady" is provided with a personalized online store through which to connect and sell to a wider customer base of online shoppers on top of her door-to-door customers. This capability allows reps to chat and blog about beauty tips and post pictures, sustaining Avon's appeal as a personal and relational vendor.[23] Innovative recruiting incentives, such as giving each rep a percentage of the sales of each rep she recruits, and of each rep that the recruits engage, down to the third generation, stimulate the continued growth of the extensive network, which now consists of over six million independent sales reps worldwide, a huge barrier of entry for any competitor.[24]

Building networks is not the only way to buy time in a market. Some businesses have found other creative ways. They might, for instance, tie up crucial suppliers or distributors to shut out competitors. Or they could lock in customers to a particular platform by making their products incompatible with the offerings of others. Software and high-tech companies are well known for that tactic, but many businesses have successfully deployed it in other markets. The single-serving coffee brewing systems of Keurig and Senseo, for example, require individual coffee packets (or "pods") of different shapes, so that they can't be interchanged.

But that's not to say that high performers are always first to enter a market, after which they establish a defensible beachhead. Remember that Porsche was among the last of the automakers to sell SUVs. But Porsche nevertheless made time an ally to its market entry strategy. The company didn't rush to market with a copycat product. Instead, it took its time and waited until the other automakers had made their entrances and then, like a celebrity arriving fashionably late to a crowded cocktail party, it made a big splash with a sporty SUV that only a company like Porsche could have built. The result: Since its introduction in 2003, the Cayenne has quickly become Porsche's top-selling vehicle.[25]

SCALING AS DISTINCTIVE CAPABILITY

After they've attained competency, using time as their ally, high performers then rapidly scale their operations. Think of how fast Dell, in its heyday, transformed the PC industry. Similarly, Ryanair, the low-cost airline based in Ireland, revolutionized European air travel seemingly overnight. But that's hardly to say that companies need to expand as fast as they can. Instead, they need to grow in ways that make the best sense for their particular businesses.

We saw, in fact, that high performers actually turn the way they approach scaling into a distinctive capability of its own. Three elements of that approach stood out.

Start with *speed*. Remember the exhortation to "get big fast"? That was the recipe for success in the dot-com era: while absorbing losses all the while, you'd build market share and a brand that would later allow you to charge your customers premium prices. Sprinters out of the box, most dot-commers had to drop out of the race early. High-performance businesses are more like world-class marathoners: they *find the right pace* that allows them to scale properly. It's fast, but it doesn't exhaust them.

Next up: high performers develop a unique formula that allows them to *replicate, not reinvent,* the way they scale. They understand that creating a great product or service is only the beginning—the ante that gets them into the game. What comes next? High performers figure out an end-to-end process that captures exactly what works for them, in every detail, at every stage of the value chain. And then they put that into practice, over and over again.

Finally, high performers *create a distribution strategy* that isn't an afterthought to scaling but a core component of that growth. Wait too long to factor in distribution at a strategic level, and the opportunity is likely to diminish. Companies have to be prepared at the outset to determine how they can either dominate a channel or seek new or alternative channels to effectively reach their markets.

Let's look at each component of this approach to scaling in more detail.

Proceed Allegro, Non Troppo (Fast but Not Too Fast)

In music, performing a piece too slowly or too quickly can easily ruin it. In business, tempo is likewise essential. In fact, the rate at which companies scale up their operations is one of the key determinants of success. Organizations need to move fast to avoid missing a market opportunity, but they also should be careful not to proceed so hastily that they get ahead of themselves. High performers strike the right balance, whereas low- and average-performance businesses tend to scale too slowly or too quickly. Krispy Kreme is a classic example of the latter.

Back in the early 2000s, Krispy Kreme was the darling of the business world. People just couldn't get enough of the tasty, sugary doughnuts, and *Fortune* magazine devoted a glowing cover story to the company, calling it the "hottest brand in America."[26] But the company was expanding at a breakneck pace, frenetically adding one franchise after another. Soon, even celebrities wanted in on the action, which only added to the buzz and frenzy. Hank Aaron opened a store in Atlanta; Jimmy Buffet started another in Palm Beach; and Dick Clark secured the rights for franchises in Great Britain.[27] Moreover, Krispy Kreme began selling its doughnuts in supermarkets and convenience stores, which cannibalized sales from the franchise stores.

Less than a year after the flattering cover story in *Fortune,* Krispy Kreme began to hit the skids. Profits plunged, and the company's stock plummeted from a high of $50 per share to less than $10. Analysts linked the decline to several problems connected to scaling too fast. The first was market saturation. With over four hundred "factory stores" and a walloping 20,000-plus grocery outlets, there were simply too many distribution points for the level of consumer demand. This problem might have been manageable had demand simply leveled off. But the near ubiquity of the product and the fad-like frenzy that accompanied the product's rapid rise hastened customer burnout. After the novelty wore off, customers couldn't keep eating Krispy Kreme's doughnuts at the same pace. At the same time, the public-health drive to raise awareness about obesity in the United States sensitized consumers to health risks associated with overindulging in doughnuts.

This brings us to the third problem with the company's overly rapid scaling: its reliance on a single product. At that time, 90 percent of totals sales came from doughnuts—compared with only 32 percent at Dunkin' Donuts. Krispy Kreme had not adequately developed its menu, in particular, its drinks menu. Almost all similar businesses required the sale of high-margin beverages like coffee, not only for the margins, but also to ensure repeat customers. At the time, one segment of Starbucks customers was averaging more than sixteen visits per month.[28]

Contrast that too-much-too-soon approach with the controlled pace at which competitor Dunkin' Donuts has grown. Even though Dunkin' Donuts has amassed a huge, loyal base of customers, particularly in the Northeastern and mid-Atlantic states, it has yet to expand significantly west of the Mississippi River.

But it's not that high performers have some sort of remarkable innate sense of timing through which they continually match their supply with customer demand. Instead, they have learned to control demand; they don't let demand control them. In our research, we found that high performers are masters at deploying scarcity at scale. They create the perception of scarcity while selling large (but not unlimited) volumes of product.

One effective tactic for accomplishing that is to stage demand. Think about how Apple balanced limited availability with rapid volume selling for the iPhone. At first, the company sold the product at $600, but then quickly dropped the price to $400. Many in the industry called the initial pricing a huge mistake, and Apple publicly admitted as much. But the move might have also been a shrewd maneuver to establish a high price point in the minds of consumers. That way, the subsequent price drop to $400 made the iPhone all the more attractive, stoking demand. And then, when Apple further slashed the price to $200, the product became a fantastic bargain, and demand surged.[29]

Of course, many businesses might want to start slowly and then ramp up in a controlled way, but they lack the financial resources to be patient. So they expand precipitously because they need to become profitable as quickly as possible. To avoid being forced into that position, high performers like Porsche plan their operations so that the ongoing profits from a core business (the 911 sports car) can help fund the development of a new one (the Cayenne). Other companies free up resources by divesting assets that will no longer be important. Before Nokia made its big push to become a mobile telecommunications giant, it sold its various ancillary businesses in personal computers, rubber footwear, chemicals, and television so that it could invest the proceeds of those sales in its new strategy.

In business as in music, tempo is crucial. Often, as many high performers have discovered, the most effective pace for entering a new market is the foxtrot: operations need to start slow-slow, but finish quick-quick. And to avoid ruining that delicate dance, companies like Porsche and Nokia provide the necessary financial resources so that the business never has to rush.

Rely on Replication

Successful franchise operations are experts at reproducing whatever works from one location to another. Similarly, other types of companies have learned not to tamper with success. At Intel Corporation, for instance, the company's motto is "Copy exactly," which the chip maker takes quite literally. To keep manufacturing defects to a minimum, for example, the company uses exactly the same paint to coat the walls of all its semiconductor fabrication plants. But high performers don't just copy their successes in some ad hoc, unstructured way; instead, they create a defined process for that replication.

Consider how Nike has used a simple formula to reproduce its success from one sport to another, including basketball, tennis, baseball, football, cycling, volleyball, hiking, soccer, and golf. The template goes something like this. At the start, Nike makes inroads into a sport by selling shoes. Then it signs up that sport's top athletes (like Michael Jordan for basketball or Tiger Woods for golf) and begins to offer a line of clothing. After having established credibility in the market, Nike then expands into other products while setting up new distribution channels and striking deals with suppliers to lock them in. With those pieces in place, the company starts selling higher-margin equipment. Finally, it moves to global distribution.[30] Thanks to that structured, proven process, Nike has expanded its operations quickly and profitably from one market to another.

That's exactly the approach of Illinois Tool Works (ITW), one of the high performers in our study. Nearly a century old, the global, diversified manufacturer of industrial products and equipment deploys a simple but powerful template based on a version of the 80/20 rule that states that 80 percent of a company's business often comes from just 20 percent of its customers. With that in mind, ITW always stays focused on that 20 percent. So, for instance, ITW will develop products with that key 20 percent in mind and service those customers in person with a field sales staff, leaving distributors to handle the remaining 80 percent. Moreover, if a particular business becomes too large, ITW quickly spins off that group into an independent unit that would then be better able to serve its top 20 percent accounts. "When a business hits $50 million, we have the view that it is going to lose its growth focus," explains Frank Ptak, ITW vice chairman. "So we will take the $50 million business, split it into three $15 million to $18 million businesses, narrowly niched and refocused on whatever their specific opportunity is."[31]

ITW also deploys a tried-and-true process whenever it acquires another company: it segments the business, applies 80/20 principles, simplifies the operations, and implements various techniques for increasing efficiencies, including just-in-time manufacturing systems. That template has enabled ITW to buy and retool businesses at a fast clip. In just 2007 alone, it acquired fifty-two firms with combined annual revenue of about $1 billion.[32] The result is that ITW has essentially become a large holding company that oversees hundreds of individual business units (more than eight hundred, at last count). That type of organizational structure might appear unwieldy to outsiders, but over the years, ITW has honed it to consistently outperform competitors. Interestingly, not only does the company's template enable the fast replication of individual ITW units, but it also helps avoid the problem of too-fast growth. Because independent businesses are capped at $50 million, the most successful, fast-growing units must split their operations every so often. Each resulting entity can then restructure itself to concentrate on the needs of its top 20 percent customers. This helps ITW to avoid some of the problems (such as a loss of customer focus) that can accompany the rapid expansion of any business.

Deploy Strategic Distribution

Low and average performers often underestimate the crucial importance of having an effective distribution strategy. Not so at high-performance companies. Executives there fully recognize that distribution is a distinctive capability that is crucial to the scaling process. Indeed, even mediocre and bad products can become profitable with the right channel strategy. Think of all the dreadful movies that have turned a profit even after flopping in the theaters, thanks to foreign distribution and DVD sales and rentals. On the other hand, good products can easily languish in the market without the right channels. Consider that while many great tasting craft beers fail to obtain enough retail shelf space to become known and loved by a mass market, one of the most popular "microbrewery" beers is Blue Moon, a brand that was launched by Coors in the mid-1990s (now MillerCoors). Anything Blue Moon might lack in terms of taste when compared with beers from true microbreweries, it more than makes up for with the formidable distribution strength of the Molson Coors Brewing Company.

Perhaps one of best masters at managing its distribution channels is Frito-Lay, which is owned by PepsiCo, another of the high-performance businesses in our study. Indeed, virtually everything that Frito-Lay does seems geared to one thing: securing as much retail shelf space as possible. One tactic that Frito-Lay has used to great success is to offer numerous variations of a product. In addition to the original Lay's potato chips, consumers can choose from an assortment of flavors and types (baked or wavy). Although too many choices can confuse shoppers, all those variations take up additional shelf space, which means less room for competitors' products. And Frito-Lay is always eager to work with stores in ways that could widen its edge. At one retailer, Frito-Lay helped to investigate the total return on investment for products that are delivered directly to stores (as is the case with Frito-Lay snacks), compared to that of brands that are shipped to warehouses first.[33]

Sometimes a company will need to create an entirely new distribution channel, particularly when pursuing a BEMI opportunity. When Toyota launched Lexus, the Japanese automaker expended tremendous effort to reinvent the showroom for selling high-end cars. At the time, Toyota dealers weren't particularly known for their customer care and service, so, after heated internal debate, the company decided that Lexus needed its own, separate network of dealerships. From the start, the Lexus dealerships were designed with premium service in mind. Large picture windows allowed customers to watch their cars being serviced, and the plush waiting areas were filled with a variety of amenities, including espresso machines and mini putting greens. One dealership even boasted an on-site manicurist.[34] And the Lexus dealers were benchmarked against the best—companies like Nordstrom and Ritz-Carlton, which were renowned for their customer care.[35] So, for example, every month each Lexus employee had to call four past customers to ask about their satisfaction with their cars.[36] To achieve and sustain that kind of service, Toyota strictly limited the number of Lexus dealerships (out of more than 1,500 applicants, just 100 were selected).[37] This restraint helped ensure that each location had healthy profits—money that could then be reinvested into even better customer-care programs and improved showrooms.

Like Toyota, Apple has also incorporated its distribution strategy into the company's basic business model. Unlike other manufacturers of cell phones, Apple services its iPhone through its own retail stores, thus freeing its wireless partner AT&T from having to provide this customer support. In return, Apple has gotten AT&T to substantially subsidize the iPhone's high cost. In fact, Apple's average selling price of the iPhone to AT&T in 2009 was more than twice what consumers were paying.[38]

Other companies have shrewdly taken advantage of customer trends to find alternative ways to distribute their products. In the United States, consumers have increasingly been buying some food products from vending machines, small stores at gas stations, and other convenient outlets. Recognizing this trend, Kellogg Company spent more than $4 billion to buy the Keebler Food Company in 2001. In addition to acquiring Keebler's cookies, crackers, and other snacks, Kellogg also obtained the company's competitive strength in direct distribution.[39] For one thing, Keebler's vast presence in vending machines provided a powerful new channel for Kellogg to sell its products. Thanks to Keebler,

Kellogg has transformed itself from being a mere manufacturer of breakfast cereals to becoming a supplier of various snacks to consumers on a 24/7 basis.[40]

Of course, achieving both competence and scale—and in that order—is infinitely easier said than done. But many low- and average-performance companies make the process all the more difficult by not working out crucial issues early on. Once a business has traveled along the S-curve and is grappling with the issues of scaling, it's much too late to be fixing fundamental competency problems, especially when stakeholders are already clamoring for an ever-increasing stream of revenues and profits. And this is why high performers make every effort to address those basic issues at the start, literally ahead of the curve. Once that's done, they can begin creating competence and then scale, embarking on a journey of learning and discovery through which they will acquire the distinctive capabilities necessary to serve a market. But in our discussion thus far, we haven't really talked about one essential element: who exactly are the people on that journey? Who are the individuals helping the organization to gain competence and scale? How are those employees managed, and how do they manage others? Moreover, what kind of culture do they operate in? In the next chapter, we will discuss those crucial issues.

Before You Jump to Conclusions, Ask Yourself These Questions:

1. What are the parameters and thresholds of success for your current BEMI project? Are they clearly defined and is each of those criteria directly tied to customer needs?

2. What are the specific ways in which your company buys time in the market or otherwise uses time as an ally against the competition?

3. Are there warning signs that your business might be moving too slowly or quickly in a particular market?

4. Has your company developed a template for success? What are the essential steps of that formula for replicating your business into new markets and geographic regions?

5. When entering a new market, is your distribution strategy a high priority? And is that strategy interwoven tightly with your business model?

WORTHY OF SERIOUS TALENT

EW PEOPLE remember Shockley Semiconductor Laboratory (SSL) in Mountain View, California. Truth be told, the lab is much more famous for what it could have been than for what it was. Founded in 1956 by William Shockley, a brilliant scientist from Bell Labs who coinvented the transistor, SSL was stocked with serious talent—some of the best minds in the electronics industry. But the lab was hardly the ideal workplace. Management was dysfunctional, and trust was in short supply. In one infamous incident, Shockley, who headed the lab, wanted employees to take lie-detector tests after one staffer suffered a minor injury on the job.[1] Eventually, a group of SSL's top scientists (later dubbed the "Traitorous Eight") would leave to form Fairchild Semiconductor. But Fairchild itself would suffer its own share of defections, losing supremely talented individuals who would become some of Silicon Valley's brightest luminaries: Bob Noyce and Gordon Moore, cofounders of Intel; Jerry Sanders, cofounder and former CEO of Advanced Micro Devices; Charlie Sporck, former head of National Semiconductor; and Eugene Kleiner, cofounder of the venture capital firm that would later become Kleiner Perkins Caufield & Byers.

Why did SSL and Fairchild Semiconductor lose so much world-class talent that they could no longer sustain their businesses? And perhaps more important, why are other high-performance companies able to retain such individuals, while they also supply top talent to the market (a topic we will return to in chapter 8)? Such questions were at the heart of our research. In particular, we investigated why serious talent like Bob Noyce, Gordon Moore, and Eugene Kleiner leave certain companies and why they tend to stay at other organizations. By *serious,* we are talking not only about people who are at the top of their professions (the best programmers in the software industry, for example), but also about those who are just very good at what they do (such as salespeople who consistently land big new accounts). We are not talking about stars, however—those charismatic A types who are captured in the war for talent and who populated the halls of Enron just before its fall.

We are also referring to the individuals who take their careers very seriously, those for whom work is not just a job but rather a source of personal pride. In short, employees who are serious talent have both superior capability as well as the right attitude.

Keeping such individuals from defecting is necessary to prevent the talent "death spiral." Whenever people have lost confidence in an organization, serious talent is typically the first out the door. Because those top employees invest so much of themselves in their work, they regularly evaluate the likely rewards and level of risk they are taking in devoting years of their careers at the same company. Rather than selling themselves to the highest bidder, they recognize that their ultimate ability to be successful depends on the support they receive from the company they work for, the synergies they can create working in the company's particular culture and environment, and the ability of the company itself to be successful. When opportunities at other companies become more attractive, they seek those greener pastures, and with their credentials and drive, serious talent is usually able to find other jobs quickly.

When those individuals leave, their work has to be done by their less-skilled colleagues, who aren't able to fully pick up the slack. As a result, the organization's competence declines and customers begin to notice a drop in quality. The company then becomes a less attractive place to work, making it all the more difficult to hire the serious talent needed to turn things around. That death spiral is one reason why top companies know the crucial importance of preemptively keeping their top talent from defecting. "We essentially treat attrition, especially if someone has a high potential, as a catastrophic incident," states S. Eric Bartz, a manager with Schlumberger, one of the high-performance businesses in our study.[2]

To prevent the loss of serious talent and fully benefit from its presence, companies need to provide the right environment for those individuals to flourish. But exactly what kind of environment is that? Certainly, organizational culture is a huge factor, but what attributes are crucial and which might be important but not necessarily vital? No single human-capital strategy works for all high performers. Yet, there is a common thread. From our research, we found that one characteristic that is absolutely essential is trust. We learned that even highly engaged employees—those who are deeply involved in their work and will go the extra mile in their jobs—say they are unlikely to remain with a company when they don't trust management and the organization as a whole.[3] To put it bluntly, the top performers in any business must trust that they're working for an organization that is worth the expenditure of their talents, skills, and effort. It must, for them, be a company *worthy of serious talent*. They need to have that confidence; otherwise, they'll leave.

And exactly what instills that feeling of confidence? We found that organizations must establish a virtuous cycle of talent (in which top-notch workers attract other highly capable people). They must place expectations of merit on themselves—expectations that are every bit as high as those they place on recruits. This turns the focus of the war for talent on its head; the focus moves away from enticing star performers, toward becoming the kind of company any employee serious about his or her work would want to be a part of.

High performers earn the right to serious talent by providing an environment that demonstrates to their employees the presence of three fundamental qualities: *capability*, which employees observe through pervasive competence; *predictability*, which they experience through mutual accountability; and *reliability*, which they come to believe in through a culture of honor. In addition, serious talent needs to be working with others who share a mind-set that won't settle for harmful compromises and is always striving for continual improvement.

CAPABILITY THROUGH PERVASIVE COMPETENCE

In order to keep serious talent on the team, companies must demonstrate a real ability to scale the heights. What they need is pervasive competence—employees with the right knowledge, skills, abilities, and other characteristics (known as KSAOs) at every level of the organization. The need for pervasive competence is twofold. First, it is important for instilling confidence in the organization as a whole, requiring more than just pockets of excellence. Consider the broken-window syndrome, which has been used as a basis for fighting crime in urban areas and seems to hold considerable truth for organizations. The theory asserts that vandalism—graffiti, broken windows, and the like—should be repaired because leaving the damage encourages more vandalism by sending a signal to others that no one cares. Incompetent employees who are allowed to keep their jobs are like broken windows—they send a signal to coworkers, customers, partners, and others that no one cares how they perform and that no one really is in control. High performers know that tolerating low performance, even out of a misguided sense of loyalty, destroys the trust and confidence of the companies' best employees.

Second, pervasive competence is particularly important for companies that are striving for excellence, because in top-performing businesses the *fault tolerance* before failure occurs is usually much smaller. That is, when an organization is operating at the limit of what can be done in a business or industry, seemingly minor lapses are more visible and can have large repercussions. So how, then, can companies achieve pervasive competence? First, they need to know what kind of skills and capabilities are required at each level of the organization. Then they need to enforce those standards across the board.

Defining Exactly What Competence Is

High-performance companies know exactly what constitutes valuable competence in their business. With that information in mind, they design their performance measurement systems. That is, they have their own definition of what competence is and rigorously adhere to it. This goes beyond general competence to specific elements that are known to drive business success. Requirements for roles are clear and consistent, and people throughout the organization are aware of what they need to do to perform their jobs well. At Danaher, the industrial conglomerate best known for its Craftsman brand of hand tools sold through Sears, Roebuck and Co. and one of the high-performance companies in our study, employees know exactly what is expected of them, and this goes for everyone, from the top executives to the building janitors.[4] At UPS, truck drivers need to know the "340 methods," which inform them precisely how to do their jobs, including the most efficient way to carry their keys (to avoid fumbling for them) and the number of steps per second that would be considered walking "briskly."[5]

Moreover, when corporate goals change, so must the employee requirements to ensure that the two stay closely linked. Consider what P&G did when, in the early 2000s, it realized that it needed to foster greater innovation. First, the company conducted a major study of two thousand former and current employees to identify the leadership behaviors that were necessary to achieve that objective. Using the results from that survey, it implemented a new performance evaluation system that emphasized various key attributes, including the ability to generate innovations by building collaborative relationships. Those criteria were then used to assess managers regularly, for example, by looking at whether a particular individual had built a sustainable pipeline of innovation that drove business results. Managers who had failed in that regard weren't allowed to become line-group presidents, even if they had demonstrated outstanding qualities in other areas.[6]

High-performance companies don't necessarily limit their competence criteria to just the attributes that are linked directly to their primary lines of business. Novo Nordisk, for instance, uses a triple-bottom-line system to assess its competence with respect to achieving both environmental and social goals in addition to financial performance. "We track and report business by all three methods," notes Jeff Frazier, vice president of human resources.[7]

Some high-performance companies are so sure they know exactly what competencies their employees need to possess that they take steps to ensure that individuals are properly trained *before* they enter the organization. Consider Schlumberger, which has assigned a number of "ambassadors" to dozens of top engineering schools around the world, including the Massachusetts Institute of Technology, Peking University, and the Kazakh National Technical University in Kazakhstan. These ambassadors include high-level Schlumberger executives who manage large budgets and can approve the donation of equipment and research funding at those universities.[8] Close ties with the schools help Schlumberger get the pick of the litter when it is recruiting, and the relationships also provide the company with an avenue to influence how students are prepared in terms of the technical skills required for their profession.

Enforcing Minimum High Standards Each Step of the Way

It would be wrong to assert that low performers fail to enforce standards of competence for their people. But those standards can be inconsistently applied, even when it comes to promotion. For example, seniority or connections may hold sway over clearly demonstrated competence. High-performance businesses, however, don't promote employees who lack key attributes, with the hope that they'll grow into their jobs. Instead, the companies ensure that individuals have the proper skills, training, and experience required for a position before they're promoted into it. That is, successful employees require demonstrated competence *before* promotion.

What do minimum high standards look like at a high performer? Consider the approach Best Buy took with its salespeople when it launched an initiative to shift from a product-centered strategy to a customer-centric one. All new hires had to first undergo online training and then take an exam after each segment of a particular course. After that initiation, they shadowed a more-experienced salesperson until they were ready to fly solo. Even then, they continued to receive monthly training to stay abreast of new technologies, and they were responsible for learning about products outside their department so that they would be better able to cross-sell them to customers. The salespeople who showed leadership promise weren't then promoted automatically into managerial roles. Instead, they had to first take a four-week training program with a coach, undergo more job shadowing, and work on small teams to solve real business problems. That type of employee development doesn't come cheap—Best Buy was spending about 5 percent of its payroll on training at the time, reportedly more than any other retailer.[9] In contrast, rival retailer Circuit City took the opposite approach. To cut costs, Circuit City laid off its best and most experienced salespeople, a move that seemed only to have hastened the company's demise into bankruptcy.[10]

Low- and average-performance businesses often suffer from the so-called Peter Principle, in which employees are promoted to their level of incompetence. Not so at high-performance companies, which don't fall into the trap of trying to keep people happy with inflated titles when the company can't pay them more. With that approach, you end up with too many vice presidents and associate directors in small niches, many of whom are in over their heads. High performers actually prefer to go in the other direction, paying an employee well into the next title range as the person develops but holding back on the promotion until there's no question that all the role requirements are fully met. If anything, employees at high-performance companies are typically *over*qualified for their positions, and people are given stretch projects in their current roles (rather than being prematurely promoted to stretch jobs with responsibilities that they might not be ready for). Phil Thomas, U.K. marketing director at Reckitt Benckiser, describes how employees at his company are routinely pushed to develop their skills: "The amount of responsibility people have . . . is incredible. It is definitely at the high end of what people feel comfortable with."[11] The approach is nothing less than managerial pragmatism, asserts Dave Barnes, CIO of UPS. "If we only challenge people for their current job and we don't look down the road at what the next job is," he explains, "we're probably going to fall short of getting the person ready."[12]

In fact, high performers demonstrate the reverse of the Peter Principle. They focus less on the hierarchy and are not constrained by career ladders. They recognize that the accumulation of diverse skills and experience is the key to building capabilities; indeed, Accenture research shows that such an approach is critical to retaining top talent.[13] A senior executive could, for example, take a "demotion" to head up the operations of a small business within the large organization to learn about a new, potentially important technology. At Nokia, that kind of movement is not uncommon, and the company even has a term for it. "A high vice president moves to another function to expand his knowledge and skills. We call this 'downing the ladder,'" explains Lea Myyrylainen, Nokia manager of mobile Internet interfaces.[14]

Furthermore, competence must be demonstrated across a variety of environments. That's one reason why companies like Marriott have an active job-rotation program. It's not just for high-potential employees to gain a broad range of experience; it's also for the organization to observe those individuals in different situations. Marriott might, for example, transfer a manager of a very successful property to one that is struggling. Interestingly, the company has found that such job rotations have an ancillary benefit: better employee retention. That is, managers who have been frequently transferred tend to stay with the company longer.[15] UPS is another company known to constantly rotate employees into different and demanding assignments. "We push them beyond their comfort zone and see how they react," says former CEO Mike Eskew.[16]

PREDICTABILITY THROUGH MUTUAL ACCOUNTABILITY

At high-performance businesses, management objectives are typically made more public than at most companies. Sometimes, the targets are financial, like sales or profitability goals. Or they could be specific to a certain function, such as a promise to manufacture all products locally. Other times, the goal pertains to the competition. Michael O'Leary, the CEO of Ryanair, for instance, has pledged to make his airline the largest in Europe through its business model based on low-cost fares.[17] But the important thing is that the goal becomes a public promise to accomplish something, and people are held accountable for achieving it. At high performers, accountability is a key component of the organizational culture; employees aren't governed as much by rules, regulations, and standards as they are by a system of mutual accountability.

Take, for example, Best Buy. At its corporate offices, the giant electronics retailer has implemented a system called Results Only Work Environment (ROWE), which goes way beyond traditional flex-time approaches. In ROWE, not only are employees free to set their own schedules, but they can also decide for themselves where and how to get their work done. Best Buy likens the system to college—students must study and write term papers, but they can decide when, how, and where (in the library, their dorm room, or a student lounge) to do the work. "ROWE . . . completely alters the way people work," notes Ellen Galinsky, president of the Families and Work Institute. "You're in control of everything—not just where and when you work but whether you go to meetings, for example. The only thing you're judged on is whether you get results. It's flexibility—and accountability—to the fullest."[18]

But that wasn't always the case. When Best Buy surveyed people at its corporate offices in 2001, management was taken aback by the results. "Basically, the employees said they didn't think their supervisors trusted them to do their work, that someone always was looking over their shoulders," recalls Cali Ressler, who, along with Jody Thompson, helped implement ROWE.[19] In essence, people were putting in face time, because they felt management assumed that the more physically present they were, the more work they were getting done. And that's why Best Buy implemented ROWE.

At one point, more than 60 percent of the four thousand employees at corporate headquarters had adopted ROWE, and the results were impressive. Productivity shot up by 35 percent, along with increases in employee loyalty, engagement, and satisfaction.[20] At one procurement division, the annual voluntary employee turnover plunged from 37 percent to less than 6 percent.[21] Such figures, however, don't capture the full story. Under ROWE, not only do employees perform their work with greater efficiency, but they also become more mutually accountable to one another because they enjoy the greater freedom. "Everyone wants the benefit, everyone is jazzed up about it, and no one wants to screw it up," says Thompson. "Managers find out pretty quickly they can trust people."[22]

And therein lies another huge benefit of a system like ROWE—when employees are mutually accountable to each other, the working environment becomes more predictable. If a project depends on task A's happening before task B, the employee responsible for B can safely assume that A will be done on schedule. And that's exactly the type of environment that appeals to serious talent. "We've had improved retention of strong performers and seen a greater increase in involuntary terminations of poor performers," notes John Moynihan, a vice president in Best Buy's HR department.[23] Interestingly, Moynihan adds that underperformers at Best Buy are typically pressured to step it up more by their coworkers than by their managers. And that's yet another benefit of mutual accountability—it helps free up management from having to exert a lot of top-down control (and intervention) to ensure that work gets done.

Frequent Measurements Against Promises

In any system of mutual accountability, all employees need to have clear requirements against which each individual's progress must be regularly measured. Otherwise, "broken windows" go unfixed, and serious talent begins to lose confidence in the organization. In other words, because the system is only as good as its weakest link, everyone needs to be held accountable. There are no sacred-cow employees, and nobody—not even a top executive with numerous past successes to his or her credit—is allowed to "retire in place." That kind of philosophy is a hallmark of high performers like UPS. "Accountability ... means making good on promises and meeting targets—or paying the price. This may sound hard-nosed, but when it's done objectively and by the numbers, it creates a sense of fairness," explains Cal Darden, UPS's vice president of operations.[24]

To ensure this quantitative objectivity, UPS relies on a variety of metrics, such as a customer satisfaction index that takes into account how the company is doing with respect to package handling, claims processing, billing, pricing, and so on. And customers are just one of four major areas of emphasis. The other three are financial, people, and internal processes. "We measure everything we do," explains Darden. "We don't apologize for our attention to detail if the details help us execute against our customer objectives. We measure to make us more accountable."[25]

That type of comprehensive tracking is also a crucial aspect of the corporate culture at Danaher. At the industrial conglomerate, senior managers set aggressive targets and all employees know what they must do to help achieve those objectives. A tool called the Danaher Business System follows the company's advancements toward those goals, and tracking boards display up-to-date details (often by worker shifts) of that progress. The overall system is based on the Japanese philosophy of *kaizen,* or continuous improvement, which pays attention to even seemingly insignificant details. At Danaher factories, for instance, managers are responsible for figuring out the best physical layout for everything—not only heavy machinery, but also each individual trash can—so that work is performed as efficiently as possible. While these approaches have been applied for years now, including at Danaher, the rigor with which they are applied at Danaher helps keep it a place worthy of serious talent.[26]

A Two-Way Street

At high performers like UPS and Danaher, mutual accountability is both lateral (between coworkers) and vertical (between supervisor and employee). In contrast, many low- and average-performance companies make the mistake of focusing only on upward obligations—what employees must do for their bosses.

But the accountability has to be a two-way street, as much downward as upward (if not more downward than upward). As a consequence, high-performance businesses make the development of people an obligation of company leaders—meaning they are measured on their skill at this task. This doesn't mean just 360-degree performance reviews for employees and their managers, which can easily become popularity contests if not done properly. It means serious requirements for the development of subordinates.

At high-performance companies, mentoring, counseling, and leadership development programs are not just paid lip service; they are taken seriously. Novo Nordisk, for example, assesses its managers partly by how well they develop and retain talented employees. Thanks to that system, the company boasts that it loses no more than 4 percent of its top talent every year.[27] At UPS, hiring outsiders for anything other than entry-level positions is generally frowned upon. Specifically, it raises questions about the managers involved—why couldn't they develop someone internally for that position? As a high-performance company, UPS expects its managers at the district, regional, and senior levels to have in place a succession plan that they must keep updated so that the company always has an accurate view of its leadership pipeline.[28]

RELIABILITY THROUGH A CULTURE OF HONOR

An organization that is filled with serious talent is difficult to manage. Remember that these are individuals who are extremely capable, smart, and ambitious. Consequently, disagreements over the allocation of resources, opportunities, profits, and so on, could easily become disruptive to the group as a whole. For one thing, companies need to protect people from having their contributions misappropriated by others, particularly by those who have more clout or authority.

To prevent such thievery and other misconduct in the wider world, societies typically rely on a *culture of law,* in which the group enacts and enforces a body of rules and regulations to keep people in line. But a culture of law by itself is not sufficient, either in society or in business. The primary reason is that even myriad rules can't cover every conceivable infraction, and enforcement can be costly and impractical. A second reason is that serious talent wants to know that the actions of colleagues are not governed by rules alone, so that when an urgent situation arises, colleagues will act out of duty, conviction, and courage, not mere compliance. In that sense, serious talent looks for companies that are both reliable followers of the rules, and reliable in a crisis. And that's why high-performance businesses also tend to rely on another system—a *culture of honor.*

In a culture of honor, a self-policing mechanism helps instill order. (See the box "Three Types of Justice.") When a person violates some generally accepted norm, others in the group ostracize or otherwise punish that individual swiftly to set an example. Because people are concerned with maintaining their reputations (and honor) within the culture, they are less prone to become transgressors and more likely to punish those who do. Perhaps the most famous example of a culture of honor is the legendary Knights of the Round Table of King Arthur folklore. In this group, all members had equal status and were expected to abide by a code of chivalry. People can find loopholes in laws or can otherwise discover ways to sidestep a rule or regulation, but they can never truly outsmart a code of honor, because it is self-policing. And that's why cultures of honor can be particularly effective for maintaining order in an organization stocked with serious talent, because those types of individuals tend to be especially concerned about their professional reputations (as well as the reputations of the groups they associate with).

Creating Camelot

One of the best ways to establish a culture of honor is to hire people with the right values in the first place and then reinforce those qualities regularly, a process that takes concerted corporate commitment. Novo Nordisk is a case in point. "Every ad, site, and selection tool has a strong component of individual value and alignment with our culture," says Jeff Frazier, vice president of human resources. "Culture and values are a significant component of management training."[29] Indeed, Jim Kelly, the former CEO of UPS, says that instilling a culture is a combination of hiring the right people and then reinforcing the desired values, so that the culture makes employees become more like who they already are. And that goes for even the top executives. "One of our chairmen, George Lamb . . . would tell you that the culture influenced what he did and what he was more than he influenced the culture," recalls Kelly. "And most of us who've been here for a while believe that."[30]

To continually reinforce a culture of honor, many high-performance companies rely on judicious storytelling, such that the information relayed becomes the stuff of corporate lore. At UPS, managers frequently tell anecdotes about employees who have gone above and beyond the call of duty, like the driver who was delivering a package on Christmas Eve to a military base in Aberdeen, Maryland. The address wasn't properly filled out, but instead of leaving the package at the base to be routed later, the driver made the extra effort to locate the soldier, who was delighted because it contained a surprise gift—airline tickets for him to be home for Christmas, and the flight was leaving later that day.[31] Those types of stories regularly make the rounds at UPS, reinforcing the core values of the company.

Instilling Rites of Passage

Typically, cultures of honor require some sort of rigorous initiation for new members. At Schlumberger, the process takes years of hard work for college graduates who are hired to become field engineers in North and South America. Those individuals first need to go through an intensive three-year program that includes

Three Types of Justice

A culture of honor typically provides three types of justice: distributive, procedural, and interactive. For this reason, they can be very effective in supplementing a culture of law by addressing issues that are not covered by an organization's rules and regulations, by handling any gray areas of dispute, and by helping to mete out swift punishment to offenders, thus discouraging any future infractions. Each of those three justices is essential for the smooth functioning of any organization.

Distributive Justice

Employees need to feel that their work will be rewarded appropriately and that the spoils of the organization will be shared and distributed equitably to people according to their individual contributions. This is especially true for serious talent. In fact, many highly talented people will work only at companies that are meritocracies, because these people recognize that if a particular business won't adequately reward them for their efforts, then another firm will. And this includes employees at all levels, not just those at the top. Consider P&G, the consumer-goods giant. More than a century ago, the company introduced both a profit-sharing plan and an employee stock ownership program, allowing workers to share the rewards during prosperous times.

Procedural Justice

In cultures of honor, people believe that their voices will truly be heard and that various processes (for hiring, performance evaluations, job assignments, project funding, and so on) are fair and that everyone will adhere to them. At Genentech, drug development is a major undertaking, with the average cost of a project about $800 million. Consequently, deciding which drugs to pursue is a crucial process, and to keep favoritism and backroom deals to a minimum, the company has implemented a transparent, well-defined procedure. At least once a year, scientists have to defend their research to a committee of about a dozen people—all with PhDs—who will ultimately make decisions about which projects to fund and which to scuttle. The open, vigorous debate focuses on the technical merits of the different initiatives, thus encouraging decisions to be based more on science and less on organizational politics.[a]

Interactional Justice

Another hallmark of honor cultures is that people are treated with politeness, dignity, and respect. Nevertheless, everyone is still encouraged to fight the good fight. At Novo Nordisk, for example, employees are urged to argue vigorously whenever they disagree with a proposed policy, but that dissension has to cease once the debate has run its course. "People can argue internally, but externally we show extreme loyalty to the company once decisions are made," says Lars Christian Lassen, manager of a Novo Nordisk clinical business unit. "Grumbling after the fact, or saying 'I was just following orders,' isn't tolerated here."[b] That type of environment is also a hallmark of the UPS culture. "I can think of a hundred times we've had knockdown fights about what we were going to do and how we were going to do it," recalls former CEO Jim Kelly. "But 99 percent of the time, when we came out of the room, we were all going in the same direction."[c]

a. Rob Goffee and Gareth Jones, "Leading Clever People," *Harvard Business Review,* March 2007, 116–123.

b. Lars Christian Lassen, quoted in Robert Levering and Milton Moskowitz, "Best Companies to Work For: 10 Great Companies in Europe," *Fortune Europe,* February 4, 2002, 30.

c. Jim Kelly, quoted in Julia Kirby, "Reinvention with Respect: An Interview with Jim Kelly of UPS," *Harvard Business Review,* November 2001, 72–79.

classroom work at training centers as well as on-the-job experi- ence at various sites. After that, they have to complete a proj- ect that addresses a real business need, and only those who pass that test are eligible for promotions. According to the company, 40 percent of the newly hired engineers don't make it through their third year.[32]

Moreover, leaders in cultures of honor are traditionally pro- moted from within, after additional screening processes. The Hells Angels Motorcycle Club, perhaps a curious high-performance or- ganization in its own right, displays many of the qualities of an honor culture. To test its potential future leaders, it requires them to organize and manage a motorcycle run—a difficult task because those events can be hundreds of miles long, often crossing into the territories of rival clubs and hostile law-enforcement agencies. "The run organizer's got to figure out the route and who we're go- ing to have to negotiate with to get it done," explains one Hells Angel chapter leader.[33] Those who are able to pull off a run suc- cessfully are deemed leadership material.

Staying True to the Code

But perhaps the best way to establish a culture of honor is to lead by example and to have a zero tolerance for violators, no matter how high up the corporate ladder they might be. This is one of the most important (if controversial) aspects of a culture of honor. People need to believe that punishment for violating an honor code will be swift and harsh, no matter the status of the of- fender. Otherwise, they will quickly lose faith in the system. Con- sider the case of Jon Corzine, the recent governor and U.S. senator of New Jersey who was previously chairman and co-CEO of Gold- man Sachs in the 1990s. Corzine was promptly ousted from the top spot at Goldman Sachs in a management coup after he report- edly made several key decisions—for example, approaching Chase Manhattan Bank about a potential merger—without adequately consulting the other members of the firm's executive committee.[34]

Furthermore, companies desiring to maintain a culture of honor need to ensure that important values are taken seriously in performance reviews. At Danaher, sales and other financial targets are just part of how managers are assessed. "If you achieve the numbers as a leader but without the core values, ... we will say, 'Hey, great numbers, but we're concerned that they are not sustainable,'" says H. Lawrence Culp Jr., CEO of Danaher. "By the same token, if someone is working very hard to live our core values ... but some of the results perhaps aren't as they should be, we have time for that person."[35]

If, after reading about cultures of honor, you begin to wonder about a downward trend in your organization's commitment to it, that's actually a good sign. "Honor cultures always tend to be nostalgic about the past ... since honor's tendency to venerate the authoritative and traditional naturally creates a built-in dissatisfaction with the present," writes James Bowman in his book on the history of honor.[36] In other words, people in honor cultures always worry about their best days being behind them. On the other hand, if you don't have any idea what an honor culture is or how it operates, that's a bad sign.

A SHARED MIND-SET OF RELENTLESS IMPROVEMENT

When companies provide a working environment with those three essential qualities—capability through pervasive competence, predictability through mutual accountability, and reliability through a culture of honor—they set the stage for serious talent to shine and for the organization as a whole to thrive. Yet we have found that although those three attributes might lead to a period of profitable growth, they aren't sufficient for attaining sustained excellence over the long term. To achieve that, the high-performance businesses in our study possess one other crucial cultural ingredient: the organizational drive to be the best. It's not just that everyone is personally ambitious; it's more that collectively, they are never content to rest on their laurels. "There are a lot of companies where if you win 10-9, nobody wants to talk about the nine runs [he or she] just gave up," says Danaher's Larry Culp. "We'll celebrate the win, but we'll talk about 'How did we give up nine runs? Why didn't we score 12?'"[37] That mind-set also pervades UPS, and in fact, the company has a name for it: *constructive dissatisfaction*. UPS's Jim Kelly explains: "Traditionally, we have focused on the good things maybe 5 percent of the time and spent the other 95 percent of the time focusing on what we had to do better."[38] And at UPS, the words *constructive* and *dissatisfaction* are equally important. "Around here, you can't just be a critic," explains Dave Barnes, CIO of UPS. "You have to be constructive and focused on finding better solutions."[39]

One of the ways in which the constant striving for improvement manifests itself on a daily basis is through the fundamental process of problem solving. In short, Danaher, UPS, and other high-performance companies rarely make compromises that will hurt their businesses. Instead of settling on an either-or approach, they look for a "both and" solution. In chapter 3, we discussed how Toyota developed Lexus. The luxury car had to be quiet *and* relatively light to avoid the U.S. gas-guzzler tax. This meant that engineers couldn't just add acoustic insulation to the vehicle, which would have been the easy either-or approach. So, instead, they pursued the much more difficult "both and" solution of cutting down on vibrations by aggressively designing and manufacturing the vehicle's engine to the tightest of tolerances.[40]

Another aspect of the shared mind-set of high-performance businesses is how they view human capital. High performers do more than just manage talent; they multiply it by investing a disproportionate amount of time in recruiting and developing employees. In such organizations, talent is viewed as a key element of strategy, and top management is actively involved. When A. G. Lafley was CEO of P&G, he estimated that he spent about a third to half of his time just on leadership development. Moreover, P&G board directors were expected to make on-site visits to become familiar with the high-potential managers who might be tapped in the future for senior positions.[41] The goal is to create a virtuous self-reinforcing cycle: the more serious talent that a company has, the more attractive it becomes as a place to work, thus enhancing the organization's ability to hire additional top-notch individuals.

Employees at high-performance businesses also think of change differently than workers at other companies do. Consider UPS's mind-set of "constructive dissatisfaction." In essence, UPS people are encouraged to think of change (and improvement) not as occasional, discrete events but as a continuous process. And indeed, over the company's history of more than a century, it has continually reinvented itself from its humble origins as a local bike messenger service in Seattle to a global logistics, package-delivery, and supply-chain company. Along the way, the company has built its own airline, implemented an extensive real-time system for tracking packages, and launched a financial-services business. That type of continuous change is part of the shared mind-set of employees at high-performance businesses.

Recently, we have been observing an additional component of the shared mind-set of the high-performance companies in our study—achieving corporate social responsibility and not just shareholder returns. Novo Nordisk, for example, does not judge itself solely by its balance sheet; it also looks at its performance with respect to the environment (for example, its emissions of carbon dioxide and use of energy and water) and social criteria (such as the number of on-the-job injuries). To encourage employees throughout the global corporation to adopt that mind-set, a full-time team studies each department for a week and then issues a report detailing how that group might improve its performance with respect to environmental and social goals.[42]

Much has been written about the generational differences of employees. Baby boomers are supposedly more loyal to their companies and willing to sacrifice their personal lives for their careers. Gen Xers, on the other hand, tend to insist on work-life balance and require more hand holding on the job. And Gen Yers are much more likely to change jobs frequently, constantly seeking new challenges. There is probably a bit of truth to those sweeping stereotypes, but we have found that seriously talented individuals tend to share the same thing across generations: namely, they want to work for a company that is worthy of their efforts and expertise.

Perhaps the best way to assess whether your business is such an organization is to ask yourself this: are your employees being recruited heavily by competitors? When they leave, is it because they are the most talented in the industry and have been persuaded by generous enticements? Schlumberger, for example, has seen many of its best engineers lured away by competitors that poached them with offers of substantially higher salaries. Other high-performance businesses like PepsiCo, P&G, and Danaher have become veritable breeding grounds for the future executives of other corporations. Former Danaher managers, for instance, are now the CEOs of several other industrial companies, including Belden, IDEX, and Polaris Industries.[43] And, here, we need to make a crucial distinction—the nature of your business is not nearly as important as the nature of your organization. By that, we mean that any company can become a magnet for serious talent, regardless of the products it sells. Yes, Apple attracts some of the best minds in its industry, but that's not necessarily because it makes snazzy, buzz-worthy products like the iPhone and iPad. Companies that sell more mundane items, such as laundry detergent and disposable diapers, can also become powerful magnets for serious talent. P&G is one example of such a company. And what do Apple, P&G, and other high performers have in common? A keen sense of purpose and constant striving to be the best at what they do, as well as an organizational environment with demonstrated capability, predictability, and reliability.

To be sure, though, high-performance companies are not the ideal working environments for everyone. Reckitt Benckiser, for instance, aims to be very transparent about its distinctive culture. "You either love Reckitt Benckiser and consider it exactly what you always wanted in corporate life but could never get, or you don't like it," says marketing director Phil Thomas.[44] And for all its success, Schlumberger has sometimes been criticized for being insular and cliquish.[45] But in that way, high-performance businesses like Reckitt Benckiser and Schlumberger exploit a powerful self-selecting mechanism that attracts and retains the serious talent that will flourish in those organizations. And, well, those who don't fit the bill need not apply.

Before You Jump to Conclusions, Ask Yourself These Questions:

1. How many departments and employees are "broken windows" in your organization?

2. How committed to staying are your most engaged employees, at all levels in the company?

3. How many of your employees have areas of weaknesses that are below what's acceptable but are tolerated because of other positive traits?

4. How openly and accurately do you measure employee objectives and contributions? How tight is the link between this and

your pay and promotion system? Is the entire process simple and transparent enough to be highly credible?

5. How do your employees treat one other when no one is looking? Does that make you proud or embarrassed?

6. Think of a recent problem in your department. Was it handled with an either-or approach, or did people search for a "both and" solution?

PART TWO

JUMPING TO
A NEW CURVE

5 HIDDEN S-CURVES

THUS FAR, we've traveled through the exhilarating part of the S-curve: the ride up. In doing so, we explored the core elements of high performance. We saw how high-performance businesses achieve superior market focus by committing to—and exploiting—big enough market insights, or BEMIs. We then revealed that high performers create and develop distinctive capabilities *before* they scale the business, although they plan their approach to scaling well in advance. Finally, we showed how they create a company that serious talent finds worthwhile as a place to invest its time, skills, and energy, often for decades.

But success with a BEMI can't last forever. Rapid, sustained growth eventually hits a ceiling. Capabilities lose their distinctive edge, and serious talent becomes disgruntled as opportunities dry up. Even at the best businesses, growth wanes. Consider just one example: Starbucks was built on the insight that European-style cafés could flourish in the United States and—when replicated with great discipline—could flourish at scale. With more than eleven thousand outlets in the United States alone, however, that formula has bumped up against natural limits to growth. A few years ago, in its fervor to meet a target of thirty thousand locations globally, Starbucks was opening seven stores a day. But its previously successful formula foundered when Starbucks was just a little over halfway to its goal, and the company has closed nearly nine hundred stores since 2008.[1]

Yet Starbucks' retrenchment pales in comparison with the hit taken by the once-mighty enclosed shopping mall. In the United States, such retail centers were spreading at a rate of some 140 per year in the mid-1990s, but since 2006, only one new mall has opened.[2] And retail outlets aren't the only BEMI to run up against natural limits: eBay's online-auction model has struggled to keep pace since 2005, when its market cap was three times that of rival Amazon.com.[3]

In these and countless other examples, the period of ascent came to an end: the S-curve flattened out. Most executives, however, have trouble recognizing that time starts running out well *before* results begin to taper off.

KNOWING WHEN THE END IS NEAR

We're not suggesting that such recognition is easy—if that were the case, companies would act to build new businesses much more quickly than they typically do. But if you want to jump the S-curve, you have to know where to look for signs of trouble before it's too late to change. The best way to gauge the time left on the clock is by looking at each of the three building blocks of the last three chapters; each one erodes in its own way and signals danger to the still-successful business.

An early harbinger of trouble can be seen in the shrinking power of a BEMI. What are some of the signs? For one thing, the trends that made your market insight once so powerful begin to wane: the rate of growth of diabetes slows; a period of relative austerity reduces spending on new cars; fewer babies mean fewer diapers. Another good indicator is the presence of new market entrants—or the absence of former competitors. An influx of strong, new competitors means they are onto you, and your market share may shrink even in the presence of strong sales growth. Oddly enough, the reverse can be a sign of trouble as well. If your market share is increasing while sales growth is modest, it may be a sign that competitors are abandoning the marketplace, and for good reason. For example, sitting atop the brick-and-mortar movie rental business empire in 2010 is small comfort when the entire industry appears to be on the brink of extinction.

Direct hits to the size of the market opportunity aren't the only way companies get stuck on the S-curve. At some point, the capabilities you developed to exploit your market insight lose their distinctiveness: patents expire; new technologies are copied; the components of your business model, once distinctive, become standard—if not obsolete. A quick look at the shelf your product sits on (virtual shelves, too, of course) is often enough to tell you whether your distinctiveness is fading. Trouble may be on the horizon if that shelf is filled with many new—and possibly better—products. And likewise, if you're having a hard time telling which is yours, then you're probably losing your unique edge.

Another sure sign of waning distinctiveness: when your pricing power trends downward over time. The ability to generate greater margins than those of direct competitors is a true measure of valuable distinctiveness and of the distinctive organizational capabilities that generate superior customer value. Commodity pricing almost always indicates a commodity offering.

Along the way, the culture that made your success possible also starts to decline. As employees find it tougher to move upward in the organization because of a paucity of opportunities, your ability to attract and retain serious talent becomes increasingly compromised. And the initial slide along a downward spiral begins to gain momentum. This can be a hard problem to detect, but a close watch on attrition can uncover telltale signs. An increase in unplanned or unintended attrition, especially of top performers, is a warning sign not only of the maturing of an S-curve, but also of employees' lack of confidence that the company can jump to a new S-curve and produce a new round of opportunities for high-potential employees.

So here's the bottom line: without a focus on rebuilding the foundations of high performance with new market insights, distinctive capabilities, and a culture attractive to serious talent, companies will first stall and then begin to decline.

STALLING YOUR WAY TO PERMANENT DECLINE

This isn't just hyperbole: once a company stalls, it usually falls into a slump from which it never fully recovers. As Matthew Olson and Derek Van Bever point out in their book *Stall Points,* once a company suffers a significant downturn in revenue growth, it has only a 7 percent chance of ever recovering to see moderate or high growth.[4] In *Unstoppable,* Chris Zook similarly discovered that fewer than one in five companies that stall for five years were able to return to their previous level of growth within the next five years.[5] And Jim Collins, in *How the Mighty Fall,* shows that by the time companies understand the trouble they are in and begin "grasping for salvation," few can claw their way out of the depths.[6] (Collins notes that some do, citing Xerox as a prominent case, but such companies are the exceptions to the rule.) These findings lead to an uncomfortable truth—once a company stalls, its life as a high performer is essentially over. In fact, Olson and Van Bever found that about two-thirds of stalled companies were acquired, declared bankruptcy, or were taken private.[7]

What causes a stall? Olson and Van Bever detail a list of more than forty reasons—from the impact of new regulations to dependence on particular customers, and even voluntary slowdown. A good many reasons are clearly derived from the challenges of scale and success, and the vast majority of causes of stalling are within a company's control, related to strategy or organization design.[8]

But the outcome is always the same: the near impossibility of ever again substantially outperforming the competition.

A few companies, however, manage to avoid stalling the engine of their business. That is, they keep managing the still-successful BEMI that is running through its natural course, but they also lay the groundwork for future success with a completely new business. How do they manage to act with foresight well before growth evaporates and the need for change is not only abundantly clear but dire?

The secret lies in managing the business according to the pace and duration of three hidden S-curves. These curves are more compressed than the traditional S-curve—the financial one—that drives the management of most companies, and it is the rare company that organizes itself to the timing and pace of these curves. High performers, however, see these curves clearly for what they are, and actively manage their businesses according to the accelerated pace of these curves.

We'll explore the nature of the hidden curves later in this chapter, and in the second part of this book, we'll show how high performers anticipate and successfully manage each one. But before we get to that, we need to spend time showing why companies have such a hard time seeing the hidden curves and why companies continue to manage their business according to the financial results of their original BEMI business.

The first problem—the inability to see the hidden curves—results largely from the blinding effects of scale. Consider that when a company's business begins to flourish, executives may be tempted to scale operations quickly to grab as much market share as possible. This approach can obscure a variety of pitfalls. For example, when management focuses on achieving scale for scale's sake, they may not be able to maintain the quality standards that helped the company climb to the top in the first place. In another scenario, the myopic drive for scale may net only a bigger slice of a shrinking pie.

The second problem also stems from the company's early success. As the business ascends the financial curve, management's natural instinct is to focus on the climb—an activity that is often rewarded by Wall Street as well as by executive compensation packages that encourage managers to generate increased profits from existing operations. Management is less inclined to identify and develop new business—activities that prepare the company to jump an S-curve, but which have low short-term returns and can be a distraction to effectively managing the core business. As a result, the company becomes organized for maximum efficiency, not for potentially disruptive change. Thus, the organizational structure itself ends up standing in the way of new-business invention. As the company stares through the lens of its current business, it becomes oblivious to how a future BEMI could completely transform the industry.

Both forms of nearsightedness—the obsession with scale and the instinct to drive organizational efficiency over exploration of the new—often lead to positive results in the short term, but they are not viable strategies over the long haul. These are the reasons we frequently see improvements in company results just before a stall, and then we see their collapse.

BLINDED BY A VISION OF SCALE

As companies become very successful (and very large), they will have an increasingly difficult time taking their foot off the gas of their current business long enough to create something new. Indeed, the sheer size of large companies often prohibits them from sensing or seeking new opportunities, evolving their capabilities quickly, or reinforcing their backbone with the right talent. And to make matters worse, rather than scale back, they will often seek to become even larger, in the mistaken view that size alone can save them from the inevitable shifting of market relevance, obsolescence of their commodities, and erosion of their culture.

But the bigger they get, the harder it usually is for them to jump S-curves. For one thing, large corporations typically have a built-in impatience with new ventures. What represents significant new innovation in a midsize company barely registers in a megacorporation. Given that it can take up to a decade to build a new business of even a few hundred million dollars from scratch—a period longer than the average tenure of a CEO today—the height of the hurdle facing even the most future-oriented leadership teams becomes even clearer.

Of course, the challenge of scaling a company is not new, but it is certainly different today. Being an industry leader and high-performance business generally requires operating globally, and at an unprecedented scale. Academics once contended that a few hundred thousand employees were the limit of what one company could ever effectively manage; today, Walmart has more than two million on its worldwide payroll, and many other corporations operate with hundreds of thousands.[9]

It's no wonder that recently, the average size of large companies has increased substantially. For example, Accenture research found that between 2000 and 2008, the average sales revenue for the *Fortune* Global 500 companies grew by over 52 percent in real dollar terms, from roughly $33 billion to over $50 billion (in 2000 dollars).[10] Further, during the past two decades, as sector after sector has moved through consolidation, some of the most admired public companies have been explicitly built on the promise of dominant scale. Executives observe that as industries mature, the companies that scale up are those that also survive the shakeout. What they miss, however, is that the scale of the winners may be an effect of their success rather than the cause.

Contrary to the belief that size can serve as a proxy for success, Accenture research shows that there are significant limitations to the advantages of scale. Indeed, we have found that high-performance businesses are rarely those that have sought success through scale alone. From automobile manufacturers to personal computer makers, the list of companies that dominated their industries for a time, only to fade away as shifts in demand, technology, or business models eroded their base, is a long one. No wonder that the average life span of an S&P 500 company is now only about fifteen years (and is expected to shrink to about ten years by 2020).[11]

The Scale-as-Endgame Approach

But that's not to say that big is always bad. In the right context, scale can deliver certain well-documented competitive advantages: increased production efficiencies and purchasing power, greater brand prominence, and more widespread amortization of general and administrative expenses, among them. However, the results of our investigation suggest that the scale-as-endgame approach is not sufficient to sustain high performance. In fact, only a few of the companies Accenture has identified as high performers are the absolute revenue leaders in their industries. Indeed, many high performers have competed successfully at a fraction of the size of the revenue leaders in their markets. In 2004, for example, high-performance businesses on average ranked roughly in the *middle* of their peer sets in revenue terms. In other words, although some high performers were the largest in the industry, most weren't. (All, however, had achieved what we would consider "efficient scale"—a size that allowed the organization to capture most if not all of the important economies of scale.)

Consider the individual standings of some high performers in 1997 and again in 2004. High-performance business Target, for example, was in the middle of the pack among its competitor set, seventh out of sixteen competitors in revenues, at both the beginning and the end of that period. In the food industry, high performer PepsiCo ranked just fourth in revenues among its peers in both those years. In the personal-care industry, Avon, another high-performance business, ranked only seventh in revenues at the end of 2004, up slightly from being the eighth-largest company in its industry in 1997. In the automotive sector, of the four companies that met our high-performance criteria, only Toyota was a tier-one global scale player at the time—and the Japanese giant has certainly had its own challenges as it has moved from number two to number one in the industry.

We found even less correlation between return to shareholders and scale-driven strategies. Accenture examined the performance of the U.S. companies that grew their capital bases the most—in actual dollars, not percentages—to see if these likely scale players were equally successful in growing market values in proportion to capital growth. Very few could keep up the pace, and most only diluted their market-value-to-capital ratio (see figures 5-1a and 5-1b).

Despite all these observations, note that the biggest businesses can achieve high performance, too. Walmart is a high performer; it is also the absolute leader in revenues in the industry. Indeed, the biggest players have sometimes defined high performance in a sector, and scale is absolutely essential at certain stages of a sector maturity cycle. But scale alone does not drive high performance. Our research has consistently found that high-performance businesses achieve their extraordinary success by balancing management's concentration on gaining scale with a proportional focus on the mastery of distinctive capabilities and the creation of a culture of serious talent. That is, the scale-driven perspective is not without merit; it is simply incomplete.

Even General Electric, for many years the paragon of a scale-driven business, didn't focus on size for its own sake. Its ruthless insistence on a number one or number two market position in every business in which it competed is often cited, perhaps simplistically, as the driver of its extraordinary revenue, profit, and stock-price growth. Published accounts by executives who led the company during this period suggest, however, that GE's real accomplishment was in building the organizational attributes that enabled it to tackle changes more effectively than any other company.[12] GE's current emphasis on innovation and organic growth, sometimes portrayed as a departure from the previous approach, actually builds on this less-appreciated achievement.

In summary, our cross-industry study of high-performance businesses found no correlation between size (which we measured as each company's percentage of the industry leader's revenue) and business performance. The lesson is that companies should not focus on becoming the biggest in their industry; instead, they should concentrate on being the best. (See "The False Promise of Mergers and Acquisitions: When All You Get Is Scale.")

Positively Letting Go

Being the best sometimes means thinking small—or at least smaller—when it makes strategic sense to do so. Indeed, high performers are adept at recognizing when a business no longer fits with their long-term ambitions, and they deliberately shrink themselves when they need to. To put it another way, high performers divest *intelligently:* they don't let the drive for scale get in the way of the connection between their unique capabilities and their market insights. They shed businesses that would distract them from strategic goals, freeing up resources for their big bets and BEMIs. Take, for example, P&G, which has refused to be held hostage to the past successes of famous brands, especially when it discerns a change in customer behavior. The consumer-products giant has sold Comet, Crisco, Jif, and other lines when they didn't square with the company's goals. And while P&G made a winner out of Olay skin creams, it closed down Olay Cosmetics.

To be sure, these can be very tough decisions, with jobs, company culture, and a hit to company finances at stake. In 2003, for example, Best Buy decided to put its 1,200-store Musicland Group on the auction block. Just two years before, the electronics retailer had paid close to $700 million for Musicland, but CD sales at the stores were already down in the face of online music downloading. Best Buy knew its best chances for recapturing some of its investment—and more importantly, for refocusing itself on its core business—were in making a quick sale. The eventual buyer, Sun Capital Partners, obtained Musicland simply by assuming its liabilities. Although Best Buy lost hundreds of millions in the short term, it was able to refocus on its core entertainment and computer business, which, in the following years, soared.

Sometimes, divestiture is necessary to open up entirely new paths to business success. Following the fall of the Soviet Union, at the time a major buyer for its commodity businesses, Nokia divested its operations in paper, rubber, and chemicals operations to concentrate on making mobile phones. By 2001, Nokia needed to carry out a second round of divestitures. When many of the thirty-eight ventures it had embarked upon in the late 1990s (in an attempt to diversify itself) were found to be failing, Nokia nipped them at the bud.[13] Today, Nokia continues to quickly divest ventures that are deemed unproductive. The company's automotive business, for instance, was started to sell wiring and devices for hands-free car phones. But competition was killing profits, and so by 2008, Nokia had spun the unit off to a former employee and a German venture-capital firm.[14]

Illinois Tool Works, or ITW, is another top performer that regularly divests businesses that are at odds with its strategic direction. A few years ago, for instance, it spun off a laminates business it had held for nearly a decade, but also an industrial software business it had acquired just eighteen months earlier. The two businesses had accounted for $1.3 billion of ITW's $16.2 billion revenues in 2007. But the company's leadership determined that the business model of those units was not a good fit with ITW's typical industrial-based operations. On that basis, ITW's leadership decided to act quickly to shed those concerns. Divestitures are nothing new for ITW, however. A spokesperson noted at the time that the company typically divests eight or nine companies a year.[15]

FIGURE 5-1a

The relationship between scale and value creation (Part 1): capital growth versus market-value growth (1995–2002)

A company's share-price growth frequently fails to keep pace with its capital growth, as measured by total equity.

Note: Capital = total equity. Graph based on top 50 companies (listed on U.S. stock exchanges on December 31, 2002) that grew their capital by the largest amount in nominal dollars during the period 1995–2002.

Source: Stern Stewart Russell 3000 data, Accenture analysis.

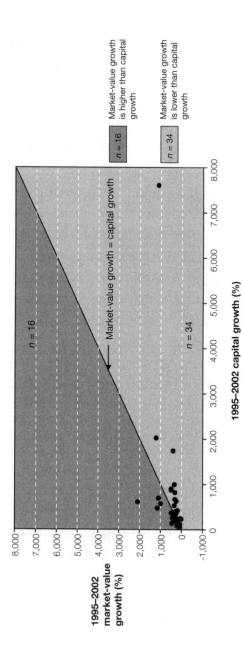

FIGURE 5-1b

The relationship between scale and value creation (part 2): capital growth versus market-value growth (2002–2009)

Note: Capital = total equity. Graph based on top 50 companies (listed on U.S. stock exchanges on December 31, 2009) that grew their capital by the largest amount in nominal dollars during the period 2002–2009.

Source: Stern Stewart Russell 3000 data, Accenture analysis.

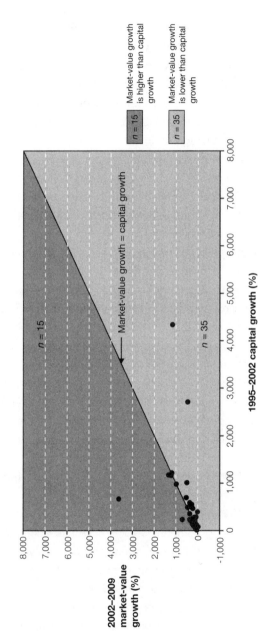

Companies often seek to go from large scale to megascale through the type of mergers and acquisitions (M&A) that gets front-page attention. This strategy is especially tempting for mature businesses, where leaders at the end of their S-curve may feel pressure to swing for the fences with a radical business-diversification strategy or with a scale play in the belief that bigger is better. And yet it's well documented that most large-scale M&A do not create lasting, above-average returns.

Accenture's own analysis of the share-price performance among acquirers in the fifty largest M&A transactions for 1996–1999 and 2003–2007 bears this out (see figures 5-2a and 5-2b). The correlation we found between the increased level of scale and the stock performance postmerger was slim. Only nineteen of the companies resulting from the fifty largest mergers between 1996 and 1999 performed better in the three years postmerger than their core acquiring company did in the three years prior to the merger. And roughly a third of those did only marginally better. Between 2003 and 2007, only eighteen of the fifty did better postmerger.

The work of other researchers has supported our conclusions. For example, one study of three hundred and two M&A deals worth at least $500 million announced between July 1995 and August 2001 found that 61 percent of acquiring companies actually eroded value for their shareholders.[a] By one estimate, more than $1 trillion in shareholder wealth was destroyed during the M&A boom of 1995 to 2000.[b]

Why do the big mergers so often disappoint? Our research pointed to two reasons.

First, companies underestimate the *diseconomies* of scale. The acquiring companies fail to take into account the subtle changes that result from the increased complexity of and that accompany most mergers. The economic benefits of scaled production can be outweighed by associated losses in flexibility, market responsiveness, and employee engagement. The real costs of these diseconomies can also be hidden by a failure to recognize that large acquired companies are often already well managed, particularly those in mature industries. This makes it easy to overestimate the likely savings from increased postmerger efficiencies. A 2006

Accenture/Economist Intelligence Unit survey revealed that only half of senior executives believed that they had realized the revenue synergies from M&A that they had anticipated, and less than half said that they had found the expected cost synergies.[c] Further, culture clash is likelier when management groups of different nationalities are involved.

Second, M&A transactions, especially major ones, consume precious management time and attention. Big deals thus shift C-level focus away from a company's core capabilities and business model, and the problem is exacerbated when there are clashes in the organizational cultures of the two companies.

Given the daunting odds, why do so many companies continue in the seemingly quixotic quest to acquire other businesses? Our research suggests that long-term trends in the capital markets play a large role. An increasing proportion of market value today is based not on traditional operating-performance criteria, but on investor expectations for future revenue growth. These expectations can create an imperative for growth at a level that companies cannot achieve organically, at least within the average tenure of a CEO. M&A can appear to be the only direct way to grow into an expectations-driven stock price.

In general, it takes courage and conviction at the C-level to opt for organic growth or to divest, particularly when others in the industry are announcing major deals or when organic growth has previously been elusive. But we're not suggesting an either-or solution. Indeed, high performers are adept at balancing M&A activity with organic growth. Cisco Systems, for example, is renowned for its deployment of the strategy of acquiring relatively small companies with the technologies it needs and then growing those businesses to fulfill certain market needs.[d]

a. David Henry and Frederick F. Jespersen. "Mergers: Why Most Big Deals Don't Pay Off," *BusinessWeek,* October 14, 2002.

b. Larry Selden and Geoffrey Colvin, "M&A Needn't Be a Loser's Game," *Harvard Business Review,* June 2003, 70–79.

c. Kristin Ficery, Tom Herd, and Bill Pursche, "The Synergy Enigma," Accenture, Strategy in Action (2007), http://www.accenture.com/NR/rdonlyres/AC9AF0B4-4E5D-4039-82E8-8DAC8A68CCCD/0/119685_SynergyEnigma_4.pdf.

d. David Mayer and Martin Kenney, "Economic Action Does Not Take Place in a Vacuum: Understanding Cisco's Acquisition and Development Strategy," *Industry and Innovation* 11, no. 4 (December 2004): 299–325.

FIGURE 5-2a

A matter of returns (part 1): premerger versus postmerger TRS (1996–1999)

The performance of large-scale mergers is at best uncertain. Since 1995, postmerger returns were lower than premerger perfor-mance in more than 60 percent of such deals.

Note: All companies performance has been analyzed against their respective Global MSCI world industry indices. Graph based on the 50 largest global merg-ers that occurred during the period January 1, 1996 to December 31, 1999. TRS is total returns to shareholder.

Source: Capital IQ, Accenture analysis.

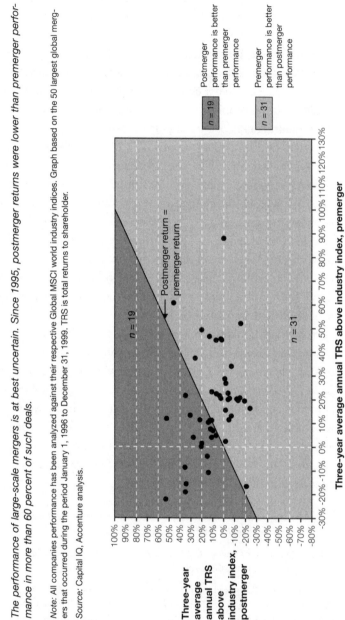

FIGURE 5-2b

A matter of returns (part 2): premerger versus postmerger TRS (2003–2007)

Note: All companies performance has been analyzed against their respective Global MSCI world industry indices. Graph based on the 50 largest global mergers that occurred during the period January 1, 2003, to June 30, 2007. TRS is total returns to shareholder.

Source: Capital IQ, Accenture analysis.

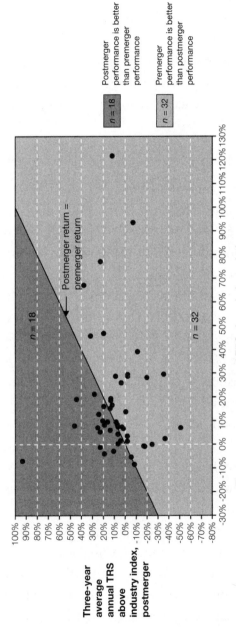

At most companies, though, divestitures are still typically viewed as indications of failure. High-performance businesses see them as a healthy part of the business cycle. Their business leaders realize that coddling an underperformer may delay the pain but will not eliminate the final reckoning. Cleaning out the dead wood is the only way to move forward to new opportunities. But moving forward is possible only if the company can conquer some of its instinctual drive to optimize its current business.

THE (DANGEROUS) INSTINCT FOR EFFICIENCY

When a company follows its natural instincts to seek the perfection of its current business, it can actually put itself in danger through well-intentioned but counterproductive management decisions. It might, for example, organize itself in ways that inadvertently discourage employees from thinking in terms of market insights, distinctive capabilities, and a culture of talent for the business as a whole. That is, the organizational structure (by geography, product line, function, or business unit, for example) might bias everyone's thinking toward improving the efficiency of existing operations at the expense of finding new market opportunities. This can occur even within the top team, and annual budgeting processes can easily compound the problem. In essence, when a company focuses too heavily on optimizing its current business—improving operations, squeezing out higher margins, and so on—what it's really doing is entrenching the old ways of doing things.

And there's another potential issue. Consider the challenge of decision making amid the "fog of war." As the lieutenants in the trenches on the Western Front of the Great War knew, in the midst of an enemy barrage, the smoke and din hampered judicious decision making. And although no lives are at stake, the same is true today in the competitive landscape. In fact, as the authors of *Stall Points* make clear, one key reason companies stall is because they stay with their core business too long—and another is that they abandon it too quickly. In the trenches of global competition, it's not easy to see which path to take.

Nevertheless, a business built on the solid foundation of high performance (as described in chapters 2, 3, and 4) rarely sinks quickly out of sight—the recent implosion in the financial industry being the exception that proves the rule. What happens instead is a slow erosion of each block of that foundation, as the market insight loses force, the unique set of capabilities deteriorates, and the culture fails to sustain serious talent. But rather than rebuild for the future, many companies err in focusing on what still may seem to be driving high performance. And that can lead to the following crucial mistakes that can easily cost companies their chance to jump the S-curve.

Waiting Too Long to Seek the Next BEMI

Companies typically find it extremely difficult to get people focused on seeking out major new ventures when the current business is thriving and absorbing tremendous managerial energy on its own. Sure, executives will oversee experiments in some areas, the company will continue to invest in R&D, and strategic plans will nod in the direction of emerging technological or consumer trends. But when push comes to shove, the urgency to find a true BEMI will be lacking.

The failure to even start searching for new market insights often comes from an inability to foresee or interpret transformational events. For example, erstwhile industry leaders were caught off guard as Apple reinvented first the music business and then the mobile-device business. As iTunes gained a near monopoly on digital music, Apple wrestled pricing control away from record labels.[16] Both products companies and the owners of content have scrambled to catch up ever since. Not every organization can be a market catalyst like Apple, but every company needs to understand what can and will reinvent its business.

These weaknesses reveal themselves in investment strategies that deliver only incremental—or what Clay Christensen in *The Innovator's Dilemma* calls "sustaining"—innovation. From big steel companies and computer manufacturers to newspapers and advertising agencies, examples abound of major companies that acted too late to respond to trends that others capitalized on.

Not Committing Fully to the Next BEMI

Sometimes, companies do recognize a major change on the horizon—they may even be developing the technology to make it happen—but for a variety of reasons, they can't make the hard choices necessary to make the jump. Maybe the new insight is at odds with the core business. Or perhaps management incentives make staying the course safer and more remunerative. Or management is just too exhausted to muster the wherewithal to start up a new curve again.

Perhaps unfairly, companies like Kodak, Polaroid, Digital Equipment Corporation, and Xerox (via Xerox's Palo Alto Research Center, or PARC) have become poster children of sorts for businesses that failed to exploit technology opportunities that were seemingly within their grasp. No doubt those organizations made big blunders along the way, but they are far from unique. In Kodak's case, the company identified digital possibilities relatively early, but continued to push the film and cameras that sustained its growth along the financial S-curve. Meanwhile, competitors went full bore into digital photography. (Note that Kodak eventually became a major player in digital camera sales, ranking number one in the United States in 2005, for example.)[17]

Misjudging How Quickly Capabilities Can Be Copied

Capabilities, like market insights, are not static. After all, smart people all over the world are taking note of successes with a particular business model or technology, and they will work overtime to copy what's effective. For instance, one technique that has been effective in U.S. professional baseball is the use of analytics to uncover new ways of judging talent. Famously, the Oakland A's team was an early pioneer in the use of analytics under general manager Billy Beane.[18] For a small-market team (that is, one with a relatively low payroll because of its limited television and other revenue streams), the A's enjoyed a good deal of success early in the 2000s. However, as other teams have developed their own analytical capabilities *and* outspent the A's for players, Oakland has since fallen on harder times.

The digital video recorder (DVR) phenomenon is also illuminating. With that new technology, TiVo had an early lead, as we chronicled in chapter 3. But as other companies caught up on the capabilities curve, TiVo had less leverage in the marketplace and never took off in the mass market. Now it faces competitors like Comcast, which can offer DVR services in a bundle with its cable television offerings.

Whether a company is selling mocha lattes, consulting services, cruise vacations, or passenger jets, its capabilities can and will be reverse-engineered. In other words, unless the organization is constantly developing new hard-to-copy sets of capabilities, its competitive position is bound to weaken over time.

Failing to Recognize How Quickly Capabilities Can Become Obsolete

Several factors can lead to a slow response to rapidly changing markets: a lack of real market understanding, an insular R&D group, an inbred culture, and poor choices about allocating resources. Together, these weaknesses degrade and destroy the company's existing capabilities. Failure is also courted when a company underestimates just how quickly it can lose its edge in a particular distinctive capability.

Consider Motorola's experience with the RAZR cell phone. Launched in November 2004, the snazzy snap-shut, ultrathin device sent the company's revenues soaring and helped make

Motorola the world's number two cell phone supplier after Nokia in 2006, with a 22 percent market share.[19] However, the glory was to be short-lived. Competitors quickly overtook Motorola in 2007, offering phones with more advanced, 3G network technology and emerging smartphone capabilities. By 2007, Motorola's global market share had fallen to 14 percent, and in 2008 to just 8 percent.[20] Motorola had begun to create a 3G phone as early as when the RAZR launched, but the delivery was half a year too late in the fast-changing market for mobile devices.[21]

IDENTIFYING THE HIDDEN S-CURVES

We've talked at length about the common mistakes that low- and average-performance companies make that prevent them from jumping S-curves. So the question remains: how do high performers avoid those pitfalls? The answer lies in the realization that there is more than just one type of S-curve. As we noted in chapter 1, an S-curve represents an area just over the first half of a bell curve, in which growth turns to maturity and then declines. In business, the term *S-curve* has been popularized as a way of describing the evolution of technologies. In applying the term to organizations, the most visible manifestation of an S-curve is the slope and trend of a company's financial performance. So to this point, we've been discussing the S-curve as a business reader would usually understand it: as a way of describing the rapid growth of a business and the eventual slowing of its rate of growth.

In the course of our research, however, we came to recognize that the financial-performance S-curve is only the most visible one and, as a result, the one that gets the lion's share of management attention. We've already started to discuss some of the damaging effects of that myopia. Company leaders should discern—and at high-performance businesses, they do discern—the three hidden S-curves that correspond to the maturing of each of the building

FIGURE 5-3

Hidden S-curves of high performance

Three key aspects of a company's business mature and start to decline much faster than its financial performance.

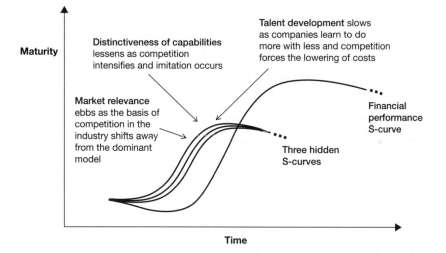

blocks of high performance (see figure 5-3). The most important point is this: these hidden curves mature much faster than the financial curve. They all hit their apex and start to dwindle just as the business itself is beginning to enjoy its greatest success. It's no wonder that management fails to notice them until it's too late.

The first hidden S-curve tracks how the basis of competition in an industry changes. It depicts how a once-dominant business model or product is superseded by inevitable changes in consumer needs and radically new innovations. In shorthand, we call this the *market relevance S-curve.* It clearly corresponds to the eventual death of your BEMI: over time, what your customers want will change, and your current offerings and how you deliver them will no longer suffice. New entrants, smaller and more nimble, may jump ahead of you. Sometimes, government takes a hand, with new regulations or changes in laws aimed at loosening or restricting trade; these actions, too, can change what is relevant in the market.

The solution, as high performers understand, lies in your approach to strategy. Most companies rely on strategic and long-range planning activities that smooth their path to a plateau on the financial S-curve. As we'll show in chapter 6, high performers do the opposite, keeping their strategy-development activities grounded on the competition S-curve.

The second veiled curve, which we call the *capabilities S-curve,* represents the uniqueness of your business abilities in the marketplace. Your capabilities are usually at their peak of differentiation just as the business starts to break away. At that particular moment, no competitor can touch you—but only for some brief period. By the time your business really takes off, imitators have usually had time to plan and begin their attack, and others, attracted by your success, are sure to follow. Of course, you can't just order up a new set of distinctive capabilities, which is why changes in leadership are critical to jumping to the next capabilities S-curve. High performers take action, reinventing their top teams. Low performers leave their teams in place, letting them continue to manage the still-rising financial S-curve. Or worse, their chief executive becomes a "celebrity CEO": someone who basks in the full run of financial dominance of a BEMI and then moves on just as the company is on the brink of suffering from a lack of new distinctive capabilities. In chapter 7, we'll discuss the specific ways high performers renew their top management teams to avoid such pitfalls.

The third buried curve is especially hard to detect, the one we call the *talent development S-curve.* Consider why: intuition suggests that talent growth in companies must be nearly linear; that is, it will grow roughly in proportion to revenue growth. What usually happens is very different. As your business hits its stride, your management and other ranks of serious talent—as a proportion of both total employees and revenues—are likely to shrink. As the company moves up the learning curve, it needs fewer expensive managers and experts per capita. Seeking further cost reductions, it may then tighten the spigot on talent development.

In the end, companies can sometimes double their revenues over a few years while barely growing their management or expert ranks. That is all well and good if you only hope to exploit one S-curve. But if you desire to successfully develop and jump to a new S-curve, you'll need a surplus of talent, and waiting until the initial BEMI-led business is near the end of its natural life to begin to gather the necessary talent means failure. High performers know this and keep a constant, even flow in their talent pipeline. How they do it is the topic of chapter 8.

We've touched on the nature of the hidden S-curves, and we've briefly explained why most companies can't see them just at the moment they need to focus beyond their current financial success. High performers, on the other hand, are able to successfully jump financial S-curves because they design and manage their organizations to those three hidden S-curves, using different approaches to strategy, top-team evolution, and talent formation. Let's now drill down into each of those hidden curves, starting with the way high performers respond to the changing basis of competition.

Before You Jump to Conclusions, Ask Yourself These Questions:

1. How robust are your company's building blocks of high performance? By what measures have they started to erode?

2. How close is your company to a stall point?

3. What challenges are preventing your company from renewing the three building blocks of high performance?

4. To what extent does your company rely on scale for success? To what extent is your company's strategy focused on growth at all costs?

5. How willing is your company to part with businesses that no longer drive its performance? And how quickly can it act to divest once the decision to do so is made?

6   EDGE-CENTRIC STRATEGY

I
N ITS HEYDAY, Blockbuster, Inc., certainly lived
up to its name. From a single storefront in Dallas
in the mid 1980s, the company quickly expanded
to thousands of retail locations worldwide, displacing countless
mom-and-pop operations to become the dominant force in video
rentals. At one point, Blockbuster boasted 7,700 stores in North
America, Europe, Asia, and Australia, and in 2002, its stock had
reached a high of $30 a share. But then the company hit a wall.
Sales stagnated and profits evaporated, and soon Blockbuster was
struggling for its very survival. The dramatic decline wasn't simply a case of too much, too fast. Yes, the company did expand at a
fast clip, but that growth might have been manageable had it not
been for something else: Netflix, Inc.

Founded in 1997, Netflix might first have seemed like any other
dot-com firm, indistinguishable from Pets.com; Kozmo.com, Inc.;
Webvan; and the countless other bright start-ups that eventually
flamed out. Netflix, however, had something those other companies didn't: a profitable business model. But Netflix did much
more than figure out how to make money renting movie videos;
it completely changed the rules of the game to do so. Instead

of establishing a bricks-and-mortar presence to compete against Blockbuster, it set up a mail-order operation that delivered DVDs to consumers directly at their homes. And it didn't charge late fees, which had become a bone of contention for many Blockbuster customers. People could keep the DVDs for however long they liked.

As Netflix gained ground in the market, Blockbuster scrambled to play catch-up. It, too, set up a mail-order operation and dropped its late fees—a move that reportedly cost the company $400 million.[1] That hefty chunk from the bottom line wreaked havoc with the company's financials. Soon Blockbuster was awash in red ink, and by early 2010, it had closed hundreds of stores and was struggling to service a debt of $1 billion. After the company issued a warning that it might have to file for bankruptcy protection, its stock plunged, trading at less than $1.

The short explanation for Blockbuster's downfall is the hoary tale of a complacent incumbent that gets blindsided by an entrepreneurial start-up with a new business model that disrupts the market. But that's far too easy a way to view what happened, and it's not particularly informative. A closer analysis reveals how companies like Blockbuster often have a fundamental ignorance of how competition changes in the business world.

COMPETITION'S HIDDEN S-CURVE

In any given market, the basis of competition evolves over time. Companies might, for example, initially compete against one another by designing products with ever-increasing functionality, but that bells-and-whistles strategy could then give way to standardization and price wars. (Think of how the PC market has evolved.) Of course, though they realize that markets are not static, executives don't fully understand how—and perhaps more importantly, *when*—major changes will occur. For example, when Netflix entered the market in 1997, Blockbuster was still flying

FIGURE 6-1

Hidden S-curve of market relevance

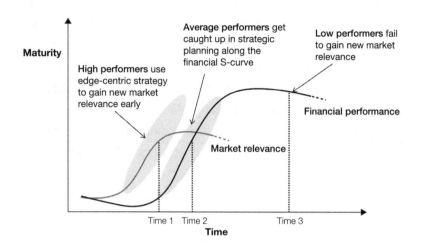

high—revenues were surging, and the company was on its way to posting healthy profits. In other words, Blockbuster was still riding up its financial S-curve while the industry was already shifting around it.

And that's where the first of the three hidden S-curves comes into play. In chapter 5, we talked about how a company's financial S-curve matures much later than a company's basis of competition, its capabilities, and its talent demands. In this chapter, we'll specifically look at the competition S-curve (see figure 6-1). When the competition S-curve begins to mature, the market is ripe for an entrant like Netflix. The problem is that at that point, incumbent companies might be clueless about the imminent danger because they're still ascending their financial S-curve. As a result, they will often be far too busy concentrating on refining their basic operations when, instead, they should be thinking about how the very basis of competition could be changing in their markets.

Consider that in 1997, when Netflix was just getting off the ground, Blockbuster was busy honing its fundamental business model. Recognizing that customers were frequently disappointed to arrive at a store only to find that a popular, new release was out of stock, Blockbuster flooded the shelves with these popular titles and guaranteed that they'd be available; otherwise, the customer could rent them the next time for free. And to provide such abundant supply, Blockbuster struck revenue-sharing contracts with movie studios. Through these contracts, Blockbuster received videos at low cost (about $6 apiece, down from $65) and split the rental revenues with the studios.[2] Such moves were certainly shrewd, but they only helped Blockbuster compete by the old rules of the game. Meanwhile, Netflix had decided to play a completely different game.

To be fair, Blockbuster wasn't completely oblivious to game-changing scenarios. It was, for example, looking at how the industry might one day be transformed by the downloading of movies over the Internet. But that was a long-term technological threat. The more immediate danger was the transition from bulky VHS cassettes to light DVDs, which enabled movies to be shipped cheaply through the postal system, thus altering the cost structure of the industry. Netflix took full advantage of that transition and fundamentally took the industry from one competition S-curve to another.

So, then, how can incumbent competitors like Blockbuster avoid being blindsided by upstarts like Netflix? That question was one of the primary areas of focus of our research. From analyzing high-performance businesses over long stretches of time, we found that they are generally able to avoid being "Netflixed," because they think of strategy not as a singular function but as two distinct processes, one for exploiting a core business to ride the current financial S-curve, and another for discovering and moving the organization onto a new competition S-curve. Both strategies must be executed in parallel. That might seem like an extremely difficult balancing act, but that's why so few companies achieve high performance over any extended period.

Best Buy, the giant electronics retailer, is one of those high-performance businesses that pays attention to both its financial and its competition S-curves. In its early days in the 1980s, the company was a discounter that targeted men, but it later expanded its reach to women and eliminated commissions to motivate sales-people to be less aggressive (and not so intimidating) to custom-ers who weren't technologically savvy. Then, in the mid 1990s, Best Buy continued targeting discount shoppers, but also began going after high-end consumers and families.[3] More recently, the company has concentrated on a new and profitable market seg-ment: small-business owners who need technology solutions for running their firms. But all this doesn't mean that Best Buy has abandoned its past customers. Quite the contrary. The company has instead continued to devise increasingly better ways to serve them. To appeal to busy suburban mothers, for example, its stores have improved their signage and added play areas for children.[4] In other words, Best Buy has continued to exploit its core market segments even as it has added new ones.

Generally speaking, we found that companies are more adept at exploiting a core business (riding up a financial S-curve) than they are at anticipating how a market might change (finding the next competition S-curve). The reason is because the former requires building on existing capabilities, whereas the latter necessitates dealing with greater uncertainties and often conflicting signals. Who could have imagined that in the late 1990s, the greatest dan-ger to Blockbuster was not the future technology of online video on demand but the more immediate threat of DVDs delivered through the mail?

High-performance companies make sense of such complex and ambiguous environments by deploying what we call *edge-centric strategies*. Here, we are referring to strategies with three crucial characteristics. First, they focus on the edge of customer needs and desires, always searching for the BEMI (big-enough market insight) that will lead to a substantial new line of business. Sec-ond, the strategies occur at the organization's edge, which is often led by peripheral groups and employees outside corporate head-quarters and the core business. Third, they operate at the edge of control in that they are neither centrally planned nor centrally managed. By *edge-centric,* we're not referring to strategies that are merely strung together and executed on multiple time horizons—short, medium, and long term. Instead, we are talking about strategies that fully account for how customer needs and markets evolve, such that a company can exploit both today's and tomorrow's paradigms of competition.

Deploying these strategies does not, however, displace traditional strategic planning, which still serves to allocate resources in an organized manner; rather, the edge-based strategies are complementary to traditional planning. Keeping both running simultaneously, however, requires a corporate center that recognizes the need for formal planning, yet is capable of backing intrapreneurs, protecting fledgling businesses, providing seed funding for important new ideas, and otherwise helping the organization to live more on the edge.

STRATEGY AT THE EDGE OF THE MARKET

Determining what customers want—sometimes even before they, themselves, are aware of those needs—has always been a difficult task. Market research, customer surveys, and focus groups can provide some clues, but high-performance companies go above and beyond those traditional sources of information. Moreover, they exploit new technologies, like social networking tools and cloud computing, to tap into and analyze new data from novel sources. The goal is to gain crucial insights into markets by collecting important data as early as possible.

Form a Coalition of the Wanting

As we discussed in chapter 2, customers are an invaluable source of information that can help companies identify BEMIs.

But managers have to be wary of how they tap into customer input. For instance, many companies focus their market research on a core group of customers. But if those individuals are generally content with a current product, they could have great difficulty articulating how that item might be improved. The result: market information that is stale and devoid of any insights. To prevent this, forward-thinking companies have been using an effective approach for more than a decade. They concentrate on *lead users,* customers who are using a product in the most demanding conditions. When 3M was investigating how to decrease the infection rate for surgical patients, for instance, the company didn't go to a typical hospital to interview the doctors and nurses. Instead, it focused on mobile army surgical hospital (MASH) units, among other lead users.[5]

A more recent approach is to cast an even wider net by establishing *knowledge innovation zones.*[6] Modeled after free trade zones, these innovation zones encourage the close collaboration and transfer of knowledge among various groups, including customers, academia, governmental agencies, and other stakeholders. An example is Diabetes, Attitude, Wishes, and Needs (DAWN). This global program started by Novo Nordisk involves thousands of people, including primary care physicians, nurses, endocrinologists, diabetologists, and policy makers, in addition to diabetes patients from more than thirty countries and delegates from major health associations like the World Health Organization (WHO). Founded in the early 2000s, DAWN has conducted research, hosted international summits and workshops, and developed training courses to help health-care professionals better treat patients with diabetes.

The initiative has led to important insights for Novo Nordisk. For instance, the company now realizes that physical health is but one dimension; the psychological and sociological needs of patients and their health-care providers are also important. Specifically, through DAWN research, Novo Nordisk learned that more than 40 percent of people with diabetes also have psychological issues, with an estimated 15 percent suffering from depression.[7] Because of such insights, the company now focuses less on drug development and manufacturing and more on disease prevention and treatment, and it is betting that the future of pharmaceutical companies is to provide total health care. To explore that possibility, Novo Nordisk has funded clinics in Tanzania for treating children with type 1 diabetes. That initial effort then led to a formal five-year program that commenced in 2009 and included Cameroon, the Democratic Republic of Congo, Guinea-Conakry, Uganda, and Bangladesh. Novo Nordisk is setting up clinics in those countries to offer children basic diabetes care (including free insulin) and to provide training for health-care professionals.

It's far too early to tell how Novo Nordisk's basic business will evolve, but the company didn't wait for its financial S-curve to peak before figuring out new ways in which drug companies might be competing in the future. Although health care is a unique industry with countless public implications and a wide variety of interested parties, companies in other markets could also benefit from a similar approach. A toy manufacturer could, for example, establish a knowledge innovation zone that consists of children, parents, teachers, pediatricians, and child-development experts. The key is to include not just the end user of a product but also other associated parties because they, too, can provide valuable insights.

Bring the Spies In from the Cold

The basic premise of DAWN and other similar approaches is that companies can no longer go it alone. Gone are the days when R&D was an insular process, conducted virtually all within the company walls until a new product was ready to be launched into the marketplace. Indeed, most organizations nowadays are aware of open innovation, but may still struggle with exactly how to bring outsiders into the innovation process. One effective mechanism to do so is to host open competitions.

Consider Cisco Systems. For years, the company ran an internal competition to find the best ideas for future innovations. Then in 2007, management decided to invite outsiders to participate in its I-Prize competition. "We believed that by opening ourselves to the wider world we could harvest ideas that had so far escaped our notice and in the process break free from company-centric ways of looking at technologies, market, and ourselves," explains Guido Jouret, chief technology officer of Cisco's Emerging Technologies Group. By offering a lucrative prize of $250,000, Cisco made it clear that it wasn't interested in incremental innovations; it was on the hunt for possible BEMIs. "Our goal was to find an idea that would spawn a new billion-dollar Cisco business," says Jouret.[8] Altogether, Cisco received about twelve hundred distinct ideas from innovators in 104 countries. The winner: a "smart" electricity grid that deploys sensor technology. Whether that idea will become a BEMI remains to be seen, but Cisco has already reaped ancillary benefits from I-Prize. "The competition gave us a global view of potential new business opportunities," says Jouret. "By mapping the ideas to the one hundred and four countries that produced them, we gained perspective on what solutions would be more relevant for, say, China or India than for Spain or the U.K."[9]

Cisco isn't the only company to sponsor an innovation contest. Netflix hosted one recently to improve its movie recommendation system. From more than forty thousand submissions, the company awarded a $1 million prize to BellKor's Pragmatic Chaos, a global team of researchers, statisticians, and engineers from Austria, Canada, Israel, and the United States. In fact, such competitions have become so popular that companies don't even need to set up an infrastructure to host one; they can just use the platform provided by a company like InnoCentive, which acts as a broker to connect companies that have problems to those who can solve them for a specified cash prize. Hundreds of problems have been successfully tackled in that way, to the benefit of various companies, including Procter & Gamble. Interestingly, many of the solutions have come from the most unlikely sources. Take, for example, the problem of how to keep oil from freezing when it's stored in a tank in Alaska. A chemist cleverly realized that the construction industry keeps concrete fluid enough to be poured by vibrating it and that the same machinery could be adapted to solve the petroleum industry's challenge of storing oil in cold weather.[10]

Of course, the risk of bringing outsiders into a company's innovation process is the possibility that proprietary information could be leaked. At InnoCentive, the company names are kept confidential, but the posted problems must necessarily include enough technical details to be solved. Consequently, many businesses have feared that valuable intellectual property might make its way to competitors. Because of that concern, some firms have limited the participation to just a group of trusted parties. Whirlpool, for instance, has involved its suppliers in competitions to improve its products, and it also relies on business partners like the retailers Best Buy and Lowe's for ideas.[11] Other companies work with outsiders, but in a controlled environment. 3M, for instance, has established customer innovation centers near its research labs to collaborate with key corporate customers such as the automotive supplier Visteon Corporation. Together, 3M and Visteon worked at one of those innovation centers to develop a concept vehicle that uses 3M technologies in novel applications like 3-D navigation systems and next-generation dashboards that use optical films to hide whatever information the driver doesn't want displayed.[12]

Use Experiments to Tell Signal from Noise

Often, the challenge isn't obtaining enough information about customers; the problem is having too much of it. As we discussed in chapter 2, companies can rely on new approaches like crowdsourcing techniques and other state-of-the-art analytical methods to sort through the copious data. Netflix, for instance, relies on sophisticated information technology (IT) tools to predict a customer's tastes. Even before its competition for improving its system, the company was able to make movie recommendations with remarkable accuracy. In fact, customers found that they liked Netflix's suggestions about 10 percent better (a half-star in a five-star rating system) than the choices they made on their own.[13]

Such analytical approaches can be very effective in separating signals from noise, and to investigate which of those signals to pursue, a company can run various experiments to test potential business models and fine-tune the models until they're ready for prime time. Indeed, the initial operations of many successful businesses were very different from what they eventually became. PayPal, Inc., for example, was conceived to develop security software for handheld devices before it became the popular online payment service.

To understand the power of experimentation, look no further than Amazon, which continually runs myriad experiments—delivering different versions of certain Web pages to learn which types are the most effective, for example—to determine how best to meet the market's needs. "We can show half of our customers one thing and half of customers another, and very quickly get some results back on how people actually behave," says CEO Jeff Bezos.[14] Through such test, for instance, Amazon was able to determine that free shipping would provide optimal "lift" (the increase in sales needed to justify the added expense) for orders over $25. (The company had earlier explored price points of $49 and $99, which were not as effective.) Such experimentation has also enabled Amazon to overhaul and fine-tune its fundamental business model. To wit: after years of trial and error, the company eventually succeeded in bringing third-party vendors into its platform, and that business is now a substantial portion of revenues—about 29 percent of total sales in 2008.[15]

Of course, the Web and other IT tools make it inherently easier (and cheaper) for dot-com companies like Amazon.com to run experiments than it is for other types of firms. But brick-and-mortar businesses have also been getting into the act. Harrah's Entertainment is a case in point. Under CEO Gary Loveman, the casino chain has become a powerful laboratory for testing assumptions about customers. The company routinely runs experiments to determine, for example, the types of discounts and coupons that would be most effective for enticing people to extend their stay from two days to three, or the work practices that the service staff could implement that would best enhance a customer's experience.[16] Those types of experiments are more than just episodic occurrences; they are a way of life at Harrah's, deeply ingrained into the company's culture. "There are two ways to get fired from Harrah's," says Loveman, "stealing from the company, or failing to include a proper control group in your business experiment."[17]

P&G, too, has established a corporate culture that emphasizes experimentation. Employees there are encouraged to fail early and to fail often, to eliminate dead ends quickly so that more-promising avenues can be discovered and pursued. In fact, sometimes the company celebrates failures, especially those that impart the company with valuable knowledge. But that doesn't mean that stupid mistakes will be tolerated, either. "We are not a one-strike-and-you're-out company," explains A. G. Lafley, former CEO. "Now, if you swing at the same pitch and fail in a big way a second time, we start to wonder."[18]

Whirlpool has also adopted a similar approach for failing early and often. According to Nancy Snyder, Whirlpool's corporate vice president of strategic competency creation, employees are trained to work on low-budget, fast experiments that can be completed in one hundred days. A team with a promising idea, for example, might develop a business case for it and apply for $25,000 to conduct proof-of-concept research. That emphasis on greater experimentation and the nurturing of many small potential opportunities is a sea change from the company's previous focus on large, million-dollar initiatives. In the past, recalls Snyder, "If you said, 'I'm working on a $10,000 project,' nobody would even look at you."[19]

STRATEGY AT THE EDGE OF THE ORGANIZATION

At low- and average-performance businesses, strategy is typically devised and dictated from the center of the organization. Top executives meet on a regular basis and determine which markets to enter (and which to exit), and they try to predict how the organization's basis of competition will evolve in the future. At high-performance companies, strategy is more of an organic process that frequently emerges from the periphery of the organization. Frontline employees might, for example, have key customer information that leads to a BEMI, or a regional office might have noticed some important demographic trend. Accordingly, high-performance companies have processes in place to ensure that those peripheral sources are incorporated when the company is devising and developing strategy.

Make Peripheral Businesses the Center of Attention

Savvy executives have long realized that important innovations often come from regional operations. Case in point: Vick's Cough Syrup with Honey, a new over-the-counter remedy. The homeopathic product was developed in P&G's labs in Caracas, Venezuela, for sale in Mexico and other Latin American countries. But after its success there, P&G began marketing it in the United States and Europe. Such *reverse*, or *trickle-up*, innovations not only have become a significant source of revenue for companies like P&G, they have also altered the product strategies at those organizations. The traditional approach was to develop products for consumers in the United States, Europe, and Japan and then sell stripped-down, cheaper versions of those items in emerging countries. Now companies are realizing that the "bottom of the pyramid" contains not only opportunities to sell goods but also sources of innovations.

"Many of the business solutions America needs for the next 50 years could be found in emerging markets," asserts Vijay Govindarajan, a professor at Dartmouth's Tuck School of Business.[20]

To take advantage of any opportunities that might come from peripheral businesses, many high-performance businesses have shunned top-down organizational structures. They have decentralized the decision-making process, empowering managers at local business units with enough flexibility to quickly capitalize on market opportunities. When the manager of a Best Buy store in New York City discovered a large Brazilian community nearby, he went about catering to that market segment, first by hiring employees who could speak Portuguese. Then, after learning that large cruise ships of Brazilians often stopped in New York City, he contacted the travel company, and before long, busloads of the tour groups were visiting the store for shopping sprees. "If we waited for someone in Minnesota to come up with that idea, we'd still be waiting," said former CEO Brad Anderson at the time, referring to the company's Midwest headquarters. "I believe that some of our best ideas have come from the people who are furthest removed from the CEO's office—those line-level employees who interact with our customers each and every day."[21]

A similar philosophy permeates Illinois Tool Works (ITW). In fact, decentralized decision-making is so much a part of the company that it is organized basically as a holding corporation with literally hundreds of independent business units. CEO Jim Farrell doesn't require monthly reports from those self-supporting businesses, and the corporate headquarters is a bare-bones operation, providing just accounting and other financial functions, investor relations, minimal HR support, and an R&D group that develops applications for the individual units. Moreover, whenever a particular business unit becomes too large (the cap is $50 million), ITW splits it to maintain an overall organizational structure that is flat and decentralized such that the executives making important decisions are never that far removed from the markets they serve.

Cisco takes a different approach to achieve the same objective of decentralized decision-making. The company has established dozens of internal committees of executives who are on the constant lookout for BEMIs. A council is formed for every $10 billion opportunity, a board is assembled for every $1 billion opportunity, and a working group is formed for other, more tactical initiatives. Altogether, as many as 750 executives are involved, and the goal is faster decision-making so that promising opportunities aren't missed. "Each person on a board, council, or working group has the authority to speak on behalf of their entire organization, allowing decisions to be made in real time," says CEO John Chambers.[22] According to him, the result is that the company now needs only about a week to develop a business plan for a new venture, compared with six months in the past.

Nurture Passionate Voices from the Edge

By decentralizing their decision-making, companies like ITW and Cisco are trying to ensure that they cultivate innovative voices who might not necessarily work within corporate headquarters or a core business. The classic example here is that of Arthur Fry, who conceived of Post-it notes after his bookmark kept falling out of his hymnal at church. Even though the initial market research was discouraging, Fry persevered with his idea, distributing samples to secretaries to get their buy-in. At many low- and average-performance companies, Fry's idea would never have seen the light of day, and he might have left to found a start-up to sell sticky notes. But at 3M, the product eventually became a major new line of business.

To nurture such successes, companies might sometimes need to avoid consensus decision-making; otherwise, an important minority opinion might get silenced in the process. That's the philosophy at Reckitt Benckiser, one of the high performers in our study. "If we have ten people in a room, eight of them agreeing on one thing and two passionately believing something else, we don't try to resolve it to everyone's satisfaction," explains CEO Bart Becht. Instead, Reckitt Benckiser allows those two employees to conduct small-scale experiments that would confirm (or disprove) their belief. "Sometimes our biggest ideas come that way," says Becht.[23]

A prime example is Air Wick Freshmatic, a new product that automatically sprays freshener into the air on a set schedule. About six years ago, the idea for that product originated with a brand manager in Korea, but the proposal was initially met with considerable internal skepticism. For one thing, Reckitt Benckiser had little expertise with the required technology. "This would be our first foray into something electronic, with wires, batteries, interval switches," recalls Becht. But the CEO was eventually persuaded. "If somebody wants to stand up under stress and say, 'No, I passionately believe in this. You guys are all wrong, ...' then I'm willing to take a chance," says Becht.[24] So a small project was launched, and initial testing of the concept in early 2004 with U.K. consumers was so encouraging that the company proceeded with a full-scale launch in more than thirty countries later that year. Today, Air Wick Freshmatic is sold in eighty-five countries, generating annual revenues of more than $250 million, which makes it the most successful product launch in the company's history. The success is all the more remarkable, given how easy it would have been for senior executives to table the initial concept in favor of other, less risky proposals. But that's one of the reasons why Reckitt Benckiser has been able to develop new products at such a fast clip. Typically on the order of 35 percent of the company's net revenue in the year comes from products that have been introduced within the past three years.[25]

STRATEGY AT THE EDGE OF CONTROL

Stories about the origins of blockbuster products like Air Wick Freshmatic and Post-it notes can easily mislead executives into thinking that such successes are primarily the result of serendipitous good fortune. After all, if Arthur Fry hadn't had so much trouble with his bookmark in church, would yellow sticky notes ever have been invented? On the other hand, what if Fry had gotten his idea for Post-it at a company other than 3M? Would his serendipitous eureka insight ever have made it to the market? In our study of high-performance companies, we initially looked for commonalities in the strategy processes that businesses deployed to identify and pursue BEMIs like Post-it. But we found that the commonalities weren't in the specific processes themselves but in the *nature* of those processes. Indeed, the processes at first seemed random, even chaotic and out of control. But further investigation revealed they had a definite pattern and logic. First, strategy was made episodically but continuously. Second, it required a permanent commitment but not a permanent process. Each of those seemingly paradoxical attributes requires a more detailed discussion.

Plan Episodically (but Continually)

At low and average performers, strategy tends to be made according to the calendar. Executives might convene annually, for example, to discuss, revise, or even overhaul the company's strategy. In essence, the process is regular, orderly, and predictable. Not so at high-performance businesses. Instead, strategy making at such organizations is more episodic, dictated by the hidden competition S-curve and by specific events such as the emergence of a new technology. Moreover, it is not a onetime event but a continuous series of activities; the series ebbs and flows over time, just as a company's competition S-curve does.

Consider Samsung. In the early 1990s, when the company was aspiring to become a leading player in consumer electronics, CEO Lee Kun-hee issued this stern directive to employees: "Change everything except your wife and children." Samsung then underwent a dramatic transformation to emerge as a global corporation known not just for products with reliable quality at affordable prices but also for innovative design. More recently, in early 2010,

Lee Kun-hee announced his plans to steer Samsung through another major strategic shift. "It's a real crisis now," he told employees. "Most of Samsung's flagship businesses and products will become obsolete within 10 years. We must begin anew. We must only look forward."[26]

Critics might question whether Lee is the right person to lead Samsung through that transition. After all, the CEO recently returned to the helm of the company after resigning in 2008 amid allegations that Samsung had established a slush fund to bribe governmental figures. But to his credit, Lee is not the type of person who closes the barn door after the horses have fled. Indeed, when he recently warned his employees that Samsung was in a crisis, the company was arguably at the top of its game. On the basis of revenues, it had become the largest technology company in the world, with innovative flat-panel TVs, mobile phones, and memory chips. But as we discussed earlier, that's typical of high-performance companies—they don't wait for their sales to stagnate and profits to dwindle before they adopt a new strategy that alters the basis of competition. And neither do they adhere strictly to a long-range plan that calls for transformations at regular intervals. Instead, they make key strategic changes episodically but continually in order to move smoothly from one competition S-curve to the next.

UPS is another case in point. Founded in 1907, the company has reinvented itself not just once or twice, but several times over its hundred-year history. First it was a bicycle messenger service in Seattle. Then in the 1920s, it became a delivery service for retailers, which was quite a major transformation because, at that time, large retailers all had their own fleets of delivery trucks. Next, in the 1950s, UPS became a common carrier, competing against the U.S. Post Office by eventually expanding its operations into the forty-eight contiguous states. It later became a global company in the mid-1980s and made the bold move of launching an airline. Moreover, it began offering next-day air service in the United

States. The next major move was in 1992, when UPS reinvented itself to enter the information business by launching TotalTrack, the largest package-tracking system in the world. Just a year later, it became a third-party provider of logistics services. Another major business—UPS Capital—was launched in 1998, when UPS entered the financial services market. More recently, it has begun offering a service-parts logistics service, keeping inventories of spare parts and performing warranty repairs for companies like Dell, and has also entered the heavy-freight business.

All of UPS's major strategy shifts enabled the company to move from one competition S-curve to another. None of those transformations occurred according to any regular timetable, nor were they the acts of desperation in response to any financial crisis. Instead, they were implemented episodically but continually depending on the basis of competition in UPS's current core businesses. And that's the hallmark of a high-performance company: it reinvents itself when it wants to and not when a declining financial S-curve has forced it to take action.

Make the Commitment (but Not the Process) Permanent

But exactly what process did UPS use to continually identify its next BEMI and move to that new competition S-curve? That question was a primary area of our research, but we weren't expecting to find any magic formula. And we indeed found that some high-performance companies take a deliberate approach to crafting strategy—using careful planning and top-down decision-making—while others are equally effective using a more organic, emergent approach. What surprised us, though, was the extent to which the high performers use bits and pieces of just about every known form of strategy making. That is, high-performance companies aren't bound to any one approach; they typically take the best of various approaches, using whatever works best for them at the moment in light of a given complex set of circumstances. Some high performers, for example, have set up an office of strategy management—a central body responsible for strategy across various business units and market cycles. Others have created the position of chief strategy officer, or CSO.[27] Still others have established innovation councils, temporary task forces, and business incubators.

The portfolio of strategies that must be devised for different business units, geographies, and so on, all but demand that large corporations deploy a range of strategy-making approaches. Multiple strategies also make the crafting of strategy a much less predictable process; consequently, executives, middle managers, and employees will have greater difficulty gaming the system to their advantage. If, for instance, the CEO always devises strategy, everyone will hone his or her skills to influence that individual. Or if a strategy is always determined by a biannual conference of top executives, subordinates will expend undue time and effort to steer that agenda. To avoid these sorts of restrictions on strategy, high performers vary their approach to strategy making and incorporate multiple sources to keep the process from becoming too predictable. Or they will specifically implement countermeasures. They might, for instance, temporarily have a shadow CSO replicate a strategic plan as a check against the information sources, assumptions, and logic of the original plan.

But even though high performers might not use any permanent process, their commitment to strategy making and execution is permanent. And that commitment starts from the top. At Cisco, for example, CEO John Chambers has made it clear that he wants executives to participate actively on the various councils, boards, and working groups of the company's decentralized structure that helps chart future strategy by spotting new business opportunities. Although Chambers says he doesn't want his executives to be members on more four or five such committees, he still expects them to spend at least 30 percent of their time on such work.[28]

That type of commitment can be surprisingly difficult to maintain, even for top innovating companies. When James McNerney left General Electric to become CEO of 3M in 2001, for instance, he imported GE's Six Sigma program and tighter fiscal controls. Of course, he also wanted 3M to maintain its emphasis on innovation, but the problem was that the new focus on efficiency often ran counter to that, and the results of the disconnect eventually became apparent. Previously, 3M could boast that at least one-third of its sales came from new products (released within the past five years). Under McNerney, that percentage fell to one-quarter. "Innovation is by its very nature a disorderly process," explains George Buckley, 3M's current CEO who replaced McNerney in 2005. "You can't put a Six Sigma process into that area and say, 'Well, I'm getting behind on invention, so I'm going to schedule myself for three good ideas on Wednesday and two on Friday.' That's not how creativity works."[29]

As 3M discovered, even the best-intentioned initiatives and programs like Six Sigma can have a detrimental effect on an organization's strategic goals. In our research, we found that many companies make another type of common mistake that can be just as damaging, if not more so, by equating strategy making with long-range planning. To be sure, long-range planning is a necessary task, but it does not equip companies with the ability to identify and make transitions to new competition S-curves. It is, almost by definition, heavily numbers oriented and rarely the forum for the open-ended exploration of potential opportunities. In other words, long-range planning rarely (if ever) leads to creative new thinking.

And that's exactly why we advocate the use of edge-centric strategies. Strategy itself is about renewal, and renewal is about innovation—not just technical or product innovation but also managerial, organizational, and process innovation. Think of the sweeping ways in which UPS has continually reinvented itself over the course of more than a century. Edge-centric strategies enable the types of dramatic transformations that keep high performers consistently at the top. But who are the people with the wherewithal to lead such strategic transitions? How are they selected, and how do they work together to devise and implement new strategies? In the following chapter, we will learn how high-performance companies regularly renew their top management teams to ensure that their companies never falter as they continually move from one S-curve to another.

Before You Jump to Conclusions, Ask Yourself These Questions:

1. Where is your core business on the competition S-curve? And have you identified your next competition S-curve?

2. What processes do you use to acquire new information from the fringes of your organization?

3. Does your company routinely run experiments to test its assumptions about the market?

4. If someone at the periphery of your business were to have an idea for a blockbuster product like Post-it notes, how likely would it be for your organization to bring that innovation to market?

5. Think about your last major corporate change initiative. Was it initiated as the result of declining financial performance? Or did it occur while sales were still growing at a fast clip and profit margins were healthy?

6. What process does your organization use to craft strategy? Who's involved? Is it relatively easy for people to game the system to bias it toward their own individual needs?

TOP TEAMS THAT CHANGE
AHEAD OF THE CURVE

T HE COMPUTER INDUSTRY has certainly seen its fair share of spectacular downfalls, but perhaps none approaches the tragic proportions of Wang Laboratories. Founded in 1951 by the late An Wang, a Chinese American computer engineer and coinventor of a key technology of magnetic-core memory, Wang Laboratories was at the cutting edge of the industry. For more than three decades, it gracefully made the transition from one major product line to another, from calculators to word processors to minicomputers. In its heyday, during the 1980s, the company reached revenues of $3 billion and employed more than forty thousand workers. But then everything quickly unraveled. The PC revolution had begun, and Wang Laboratories was caught off guard. The company's revenues and profits plunged, thousands of employees were laid off, and in 1992, it filed for bankruptcy protection and was eventually acquired by Getronics of the Netherlands.

Many articles have been written about the demise of Wang Laboratories. Some have blamed the company's too-fast growth, which resulted in a lack of internal controls and a deterioration of customer service. Others say that the root cause was an organizational arrogance that, among other things, prevented executives from recognizing that future products had to be compatible with the offerings of competitors like IBM. Still others point their fingers at Fred Wang, who succeeded his father and became president in 1986. All of those factors undoubtedly contributed to the company's downfall, but another level of the story often goes untold.

Fred Wang might indeed have been the wrong person to take the reins from his father. The younger Wang was just thirty-six at the time, and according to some critics, he lacked decisiveness and the ability to challenge other executives on their views. Moreover, his approach to making decisions by consensus frequently resulted in a state of analysis-paralysis that frustrated staffers. "We went to a system of design by committee," recalls a former employee. "The problem was nothing ever got out of committee."[1] But perhaps his biggest weakness was his inability to fully appreciate the importance of the capabilities S-curve.

THE DANGERS OF THE HIDDEN CAPABILITIES S-CURVE

Companies have long been aware of how products tend to mature in the marketplace. Sales typically start off slow, ramp up, and then taper off. That financial S-curve is well known to most executives, but many are unaware of another S-curve that is equally important (if not more so). To take advantage of a market opportunity, a company's capabilities will also follow a typical S-shape, first building slowly, then quickly, and then leveling off (see figure 7-1). The problem is that many executives tend to dwell on the financial S-curve when they should instead be focusing on the capabilities S-curve. The reason is simple: by the time a company's financial performance begins to taper off, it's already too late to begin building the capabilities for the next market opportunity. The time to do that is much earlier, when the financial S-curve is still ramping up but the capabilities S-curve is beginning to level off.

FIGURE 7-1

Hidden S-curve of capabilities distinctiveness

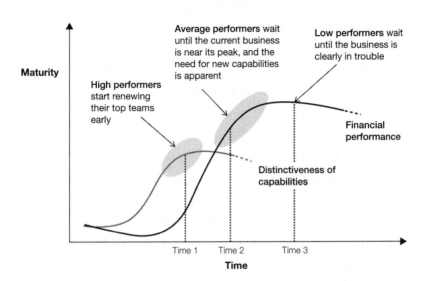

And that, in a nutshell, is where the senior managers at Wang Laboratories failed. When the sales of their word processors were still ramping up, they should have started building the organizational capabilities for the product that would eventually replace dedicated word processors, namely, PCs. But Wang Laboratories was slow out of the gate, and when it finally did introduce an IBM-compatible PC, sales never took off. What the company desperately needed in the 1980s was not necessarily a top management team that could run and expand an existing business but one that could launch a new line of products. With that in mind, Fred Wang seemed all but destined to fail, because he lacked the wherewithal to develop different technologies ahead of the capabilities S-curve. "You've got to have two or three generations in the pipeline," said a former engineer. "Wang had none."[2]

In our research, we have found that many low and average performers tend to make the same mistake that Wang Laboratories did. They manage their businesses according to their financial S-curves, leaving their businesses vulnerable when a core product line matures. In contrast, high performers make smooth transitions from one major business to another because, whether consciously or not, they are always aware of where they are with respect to their capabilities S-curve.

Now here's the tricky part. Some executives are better at running an existing business—ramping up manufacturing, expanding into different geographic markets, extending a product line with incremental innovations, and so on. Others are more entrepreneurial; their strength is in *creating* new markets. Neither type of executive is inherently better than the other, but the type of senior leadership that a company has should match its current organizational needs, as defined by the capabilities S-curve. Of course, that's much easier said than done, especially when a business is doing well. Indeed, it's the rare CEO who would be willing to step down when revenues are surging and profits are healthy. Who wouldn't want to continue riding the financial S-curve? But that's exactly when a change in top management might most be needed. Otherwise, the company could continue riding that financial S-curve for a while but then hit a wall, as Wang Laboratories did. Sadly, An Wang was in the unenviable position of having to fire his son. And although the new CEO, Richard W. Miller, implemented a massive restructuring and major shift in strategy, by then it was too late to stop the company's inexorable slide.

Without a doubt, changing a top management team ahead of the financial S-curve is an inherently difficult task. The obvious temptation is to maintain the status quo while a business is humming along. And in fact, that is exactly what many low- and average-performance companies do. But then, when that core business begins to stall, they are left scrambling to change their top management to right the ship. High performers, in contrast, are generally able to avoid such stressful transitions because the evolution of their top teams is one step ahead of the financial S-curve. In other words, they mix things up early on, well before there's any apparent reason to do so, because they recognize when it's time to jump to a new capabilities S-curve.

But how, exactly, do high performers repeatedly make such difficult transitions seemingly ahead of schedule? We discovered the crucial importance of three organizational practices. First, high performers establish a *pattern* of early top team renewal that coincides with changes in the capabilities S-curve needed to drive organization renewal. Second, they maintain in their top teams a *balance*—of cognitive styles, tenures, and viewpoints, to name just some of the elements—that keeps one foot in today and the other in tomorrow, managing simultaneously the two S-curves of financial performance and distinctive capabilities. And finally, they *organize and manage* the top team in ways that greatly increase the effectiveness and productivity of the time that the group spends working together. Those specific measures help avoid the overload that top teams typically experience in attempting to manage for both today and tomorrow.

ESTABLISHING A PATTERN OF EARLY RENEWAL

CEO transitions occur for a variety of reasons. Some happen because of planned retirements. Others occur more suddenly as the result of illness, accident, and, on occasion, improprieties. Many companies believe that this is what succession planning is all about—being able to respond quickly to the loss of a key individual. That's why many management gurus like Noel Tichy and Warren Bennis have long emphasized the importance of maintaining a leadership pipeline that never stops flowing with talent.

But simply having a string of viable replacements for top executives is not enough. Of course, the capability to replace important employees is crucial, but it is just one of the many responsibilities of succession planning. Indeed, our research showed that high-performance businesses tend to use succession planning in a fundamentally different way than other firms do. Specifically, they use it to continually renew their top management as a precursor to renewing the company. In this way, they tend to change their CEOs and other senior executives according to a timetable that implicitly or explicitly recognizes the need for company transitions along the capabilities S-curve. In other words, they don't wait for a crisis or another event that forces action. Instead, they follow a pattern that proactively seeks to bring about changes in their top teams to drive organizational transformations ahead of the curve.

Seek to Evolve Continually, Not Just to Replace

Consider Adobe Systems. When Bruce Chizen became CEO in 2000, the company was in the midst of a major transformation from being a niche player of digital artist tools to becoming a major force in the world of digital media content creation. The transformation was capped by the acquisition of Macromedia, maker of the all-important Flash technology, which enables online animation and video. That move, which Chizen spearheaded, helped position the company to compete against the established software titans in the Web-based application business. Yet, just seven years into his successful tenure at the top (at the relatively young age of fifty-two), Chizen decided to hand over the reins to Shantanu Narayen, his longtime deputy. Initially, the timing might have seemed odd, but it made good sense for Adobe, as the company anticipated a new set of challenges going head-to-head against larger competitors like Microsoft. Actually, Narayen's ascension wasn't entirely unexpected, given that the board had reportedly had him in mind for years.[3] But the move nevertheless shocked Wall Street analysts, investors, and others, which only highlighted how uncharacteristic it is for a CEO to relinquish the reins early in the business cycle, in time for a successor and a new top team to get a jump start on the company's next set of challenges.

But that's just standard operating procedure at many high performers. Take, for instance, Intel. Throughout its history, the semiconductor manufacturer has seen its CEO mantle pass through five executives—Robert Noyce (1968 to 1975), Gordon Moore (1975 to 1987), Andy Grove (1987 to 1998), Craig Barrett (1998 to 2004), and Paul Otellini (2004 to present). Not once has the company had to turn to the outside to find this talent, and the transitions have typically been orderly and well orchestrated. "We discuss executive changes 10 years out to identify gaps," explains David Yoffie, who has served on the Intel board since 1989.[4] Indeed, just months after Otellini, the current CEO, was installed in November 2004, the board had already begun planning for his successor.[5] Moreover, a past mandatory retirement age of sixty-five has helped ensure that CEOs did not overstay their welcome, and so far, Barrett has been the only one to hit that limit. Noyce and Moore both retired when they were just fifty-eight, and Grove stepped down as CEO when he was sixty-two.

One of the many lessons from Intel and other high performers is that they are not just looking for continuity when they replace their top management. Instead, their primary goal is to *evolve* the organization by evolving the top team first. In this way, succession planning is done for very different reasons than at other organizations.

When Grove stepped down from the top spot at Intel in 1998, he did so while he was arguably at the top of his game. If continuity had been Intel's overwhelming concern, Grove might have stayed for another three years, until he reached the mandatory retirement age of sixty-five. But instead, he handed the baton to Barrett, who then implemented a strategy for growing Intel's business through product extensions. That strategy ultimately had mixed results, but the point is that Barrett was trying to evolve Intel's business in ways that Grove hadn't. Indeed, each of Intel's CEOs has left his mark in different ways. Grove, for example, made the bold decision to move Intel away from memory chips in order to focus on microprocessors, a transition that established the company as a global high-tech leader. The current CEO, Otellini, has been focusing on the Atom mobile chip, which could be used in just about any device that might need to connect to the

Web, including cell phones, navigation systems, and even sewing machines (for downloading patterns).[6] In summary, Intel does not look at CEO succession as a means to maintain the status quo but as a mechanism to evolve the company by regularly renewing and refreshing its leadership.

One benefit of such a pattern of continual renewal is that it opens opportunities for talented executives to climb the corporate ladder, thus discouraging them from jumping ship. In contrast, when the CEO and other senior executives of an organization remain for extended tenures, their high-potential, ambitious subordinates will be tempted to look for opportunities elsewhere. During Scott McNealy's lengthy twenty-two-year reign at Sun Microsystems, for example, the company reportedly suffered a high rate of defections of its senior executives, which was partly attributed to the long lock that McNealy had on the top spot.[7]

Create the Right Candidate for the Right Moment

Having continual top-team evolution that anticipates the moments when new leadership is needed requires more than just a pipeline of talent; it requires development of CEO successors that are groomed and selected according to the unique circumstances of the company at the time. This means that not every potential successor will be right when the time comes, no matter how good he or she looks today. High performers name and frame the challenges they face, and they make their succession choices on that basis. So succession and leadership development must be designed with an eye to creating a variety of candidates and then selecting the candidate who is not simply the best but the best for the circumstances of the company at the time and where the business is heading.

One big mistake in leadership development or succession is to allow CEOs too much opportunity to mold their successors after themselves. Our research uncovered a number of companies that still get this wrong, allowing the CEO too much control over the succession process, and where the selection mechanism used lacks sufficient transparency. Consider AIG. Just as Intel is known for its smooth transfers of power, the American International Group has become associated with some of the rockiest transitions in recent history. When Maurice R. "Hank" Greenberg was CEO of AIG, he reportedly groomed his two sons to succeed him. But both ended up leaving AIG. Greenberg then focused on his two chief operating officers: Martin J. Sullivan and Donald P. Kanak. According to one account, Greenberg placed the name of his handpicked successor in a sealed letter that the board could open *after* he departed.[8] In 2005, Greenberg was forced to resign amid charges of securities and business fraud, and Sullivan became the new CEO. Under Sullivan's watch, AIG suffered tremendous financial losses due to its exposure to subprime mortgages, and only a massive government bailout was able to save the company from total collapse.

For a completely different succession process, look no further than Colgate-Palmolive. Everything there begins at the business-unit level, where managers first identify talented employees. That list is then reviewed by local general managers, division heads, and other top executives, including the senior vice president of HR, the chief operating officer, the president, and the CEO. During that process, some names might be added while others are dropped, and the employees who make the cut receive challenging assignments throughout their careers, with their progress regularly tracked. For about a thousand of the best of these high-potential employees, Colgate-Palmolive brings in executive coaches from the outside to help smooth any rough edges. Those employees are also brought to the company's headquarters in New York City for a week so that they can meet with every senior executive. In addition, all functional leaders are expected to introduce to the board the top two or three individuals who might one day succeed them, and the leaders supply detailed information on the strengths and weaknesses of each of those candidates. Altogether, the board regularly tracks the top two hundred or so Colgate-Palmolive employees so that it is familiar with all internal candidates for senior positions.

Consequently, when someone receives a high-level promotion, such as when Ian Cook replaced CEO Reuben Mark in 2007, the succession is not the result of a solitary decision by any single individual. In fact, it's the culmination of thousands of decisions made by an untold number of people over the course of years.[9]

BALANCING THE TOP TEAM FOR A FOOT IN TODAY AND TOMORROW

Keeping the right people (and getting rid of the wrong ones) might seem like the simple first step of any management transition. Because the composition of a top team is usually determined largely by the corporation's strategy and structure, it is typically composed of division heads and those with profit-and-loss responsibilities, as well as key function heads. As a result, appointments to the top team can seem no more complicated than simply picking the most competent contender for the particular post that needs to be filled.

Yet, the real path to high performance is not that straightforward. Remember that the senior leadership has to do two crucial tasks: it must ride out the current financial S-curve while also making the transition to the next capabilities S-curve. This requires that the top team find a balance that can ensure continuity but is also ready to renew and evolve the business. In essence, the company has to keep one foot in today and the other in tomorrow—something that can more easily be accomplished by a top management team that is well balanced with strengths in both areas.

Get Creative to Balance Vision and Execution

Whenever there's a large transfer of power, those who haven't been selected often begin to consider their options for employment outside the organization. That can be a good thing, helping to renew and refresh the top management team. But it can also lead to the loss of valuable talent that the company might prefer to retain, especially if the defections could result in a debilitating imbalance in the top team.

When Indra Nooyi first learned that she was going to be the next CEO of PepsiCo, one of her first actions was to fly to Cape Cod to meet with Mike White, who was vacationing there. White had been her main competitor for the top position—both had been chief financial officers (CFOs) of PepsiCo—and Nooyi didn't want to lose the talents of her rival, who was considered the company's best operations man. "Tell me whatever I need to do to keep you," she told him. After thinking it over, White decided to stay at the company and Nooyi has backed up her words with actions. She reportedly lobbied the board to have White's compensation increased to just about what she was making, and she is said to have always saved a spot immediately to her right for him to sit during important meetings.[10] By retaining White, Nooyi was able to maintain a balance of strengths—his operational expertise together with her strategic acumen.

In other situations, the basic makeup of the top team members has to be overhauled if the company is to move forward. After Mark Hurd became CEO of Hewlett-Packard in April 2005, he kept the two executives who were heading the two most successful divisions: Ann Livermore (enterprise computing) and Vyomesh Joshi (printer products). But he also brought in a number of other senior managers from Siemens, PalmOne, and Dell. That change in the makeup of the company's senior leadership team helped restore some order after the tumultuous reign of the past CEO Carly Fiorina. But that doesn't mean that Hurd and his executive team were interested in returning things to the past status quo. Indeed, Hurd knew that HP needed to shake things up to keep from stagnating. Accordingly, during his tenure he challenged some of the cherished tenets of the "HP Way" by, for instance, cutting thousands of jobs and freezing pension benefits. "When things weren't right in the past, they were fixed," Hurd explained. "If things aren't right now, we've got to fix them."[11]

Other high performers have wisely used the acquisition of a major business as the perfect opportunity to bring in fresh viewpoints and to address deficiencies in their top team. When Adobe bought Macromedia, then CEO Bruce Chizen took a hard look at his senior managers to determine who had what it took to grow the company to annual revenues of $10 billion. "There were a number of executives who either didn't want to gear up for what was required, or didn't necessarily have the skills sets for what was required," recalls Chizen. "And we took that opportunity to make changes, which is why we ended up with a lot of new executives, some from Adobe, some from Macromedia, and some from the outside."[12] As it turned out, Chizen tapped more execs from Macromedia than from Adobe for key roles in the new organization. Although it's not uncommon in other mergers for executives from the acquired company to assume a predominance of the key senior positions, what was different here was that the selection was clearly based on where Adobe needed to go in the future, not simply on who were the best, most capable executives today.

In other cases, the executive team might need fresh viewpoints, though not necessarily from outside the organization, but instead from outside just the usual management ranks. After Ratan Tata took the reins of India's Tata Group in 1991, he made the bold move of replacing the old guard of executives with younger blood. Previously, Tata executives comfortably ruled their fiefdoms for ages and rarely retired. But then the new chairman began easing out those longtime execs (not surprisingly, some of those departures were acrimonious), and he instituted compulsory retirement ages to help prevent the future stagnation of his senior leadership. At Tata Tea, for instance, executives must now retire at sixty.[13] The dramatic change has opened dozens of opportunities for younger in-house talent. Brotin Banerjee, for instance, was given the responsibility of running Tata Housing Development when he was just in his mid-thirties, after he had worked his way up from Tata

Administrative Service (TAS). "If you had told me, when I joined the TAS in 1998, that I would be heading a Tata Group company in a decade, I would have laughed it off," says Banerjee.[14] Thanks to younger executives like Banerjee, Tata has grown to become India's largest private corporate group and one of the most highly respected multinationals in the world.

Guarantee Diversity of Viewpoints, Not Just People

When assembling a top leadership team, the CEO usually looks for individuals who are able to see eye-to-eye on key issues so that they all can work together in steering the organization in the right direction. That approach basically makes sense, but then a common pitfall can occur if the CEO chooses members primarily to facilitate consensus decision-making. The danger is that the team could then have a dangerous blind spot, and this is why a diversity of viewpoints is also crucial. As just one example, some members need to have a perspective that favors innovation and the enhancing of organizational assets, while others need to be more biased toward the reduction of risks and liabilities. That type of systemic tension—for instance, the chief strategy officer (who has responsibility for investing funds with uncertain returns) might butt heads with the CFO (who has the job of containing costs)—is not only natural, but also necessary to ensure that the senior management team considers all important pros and cons before making major decisions.

That's one reason why, when Mark Hurd became the CEO of HP, he brought in a mixture of senior executive talent that upped the diversity level at the company. He recruited Midwesterners to counter a Silicon Valley insularity. And he added those who had a no-nonsense profit-and-loss view of business to balance the pervading innovative engineering mentality.[15] Moreover, he enlisted people like Randy Mott as chief information officer. Mott had been the CIO of giant retailer Walmart in the 1990s, and in that capacity, he was a major customer of corporate IT products like those that HP sells. Having Mott on the senior leadership team thus provided the all-important customer perspective—a viewpoint that was especially crucial now, given how Hurd, who resigned in 2010, wanted to focus on strengthening the sales culture at HP (whereas in the past the engineering and marketing groups ruled, especially under prior CEO Fiorina).

Diverse, broad viewpoints are so important to George Buckley, the CEO of 3M, that he encourages his top executives to participate on other boards. "I want them to see what it's like to interact with a board of directors and to deal with other market conditions and other approaches to manufacturing and strategic development," he explains. Of course, the downside is that any time spent on other boards means less time clocked at 3M, and the executives will develop more outside contacts that could eventually lead to their being poached. "There's a danger that you may lose some people," acknowledges Buckley, "but in the end there are far more positives than negatives."[16]

Because one barrier to having a diversity of viewpoints in the top team is rigid organizational structures, high performers tend to blend the formal with the informal. Intel is well known for encouraging such interactions, and it encourages employees to always speak the truth to those in power. That's one of the reasons that the company has long maintained an egalitarian culture, in which executives have cubicles and not offices. When Andy Grove was heading the company, his cubicle was adjacent to that of Pam Pollace, then the vice president in charge of worldwide press relations. Only a cubicle wall separated the two executives, and sometimes, Pollace would interrupt a conversion she was overhearing to correct something that Grove or someone else had said. Grove always encouraged employees to voice their opinions, because he felt that better decisions came from a vigorous discussion of the pros and cons of any initiative. "People here aren't afraid to speak up and debate with Andy," said Ron Whittier, then a senior vice president.[17]

Never Underestimate the Power of Small Changes

Savvy executives respect the fact that it can take time for a top team to coalesce. On the other hand, a top team that's been together for too long can easily become dysfunctional. Sometimes, a new CEO just has to tweak the senior leadership that's been in place, perhaps replacing only a member or two. Interestingly, our research has found that swapping out even one or two individuals can completely change the dynamic of a top team, for good and bad. So getting the alchemy of the group right is critical and requires seeing each member as having more than a functional expertise but also a philosophy of business (for instance, whether an individual is comfortable taking well-calculated risks). In many cases, what should work on paper (based on résumés and past experiences) becomes a disaster in practice because of intangible factors.

And that's why the best leaders are careful in their selection of every member of their teams. They are always imagining the effects of replacing even a single person. Often, the problem is that CEOs are too slow to take action rather than too fast. That's what happened to Bruce Chizen when he first became CEO of Adobe. "There was a sales executive who worked really hard, who was really smart, a really nice guy, but I knew he wasn't going to take the company to the next level," recalls Chizen. "But I didn't want to deal with it. And every day that I didn't make the decision was another day lost in terms of bringing the sales to a new level." And that single decision—or nondecision—had a huge impact on the company's bottom line. "It took us at least a year longer to get to where we did," admits Chizen.[18]

ORGANIZING TO AVOID OVERLOAD

Many organizations assemble a top management team that is brimming with talent, and then they expect the group to automatically produce stellar results. After all, the individuals selected are all seasoned, highly capable, and very intelligent executives, so of course they'll provide exemplary leadership for themselves as well as the company, right? But as many companies have discovered, the overall performance of such a top team can easily be far less than the sum total of its individual parts *unless* it itself is managed properly.

One business that discovered this, but went on to recover from it, is Applebee's International, one of the world's largest full-service restaurant companies. When Lloyd Hill became the CEO, he put together a senior leadership team composed of top-notch executives, each with deep strengths and expertise in their respective areas. But the group was hardly a model of good teamwork, as turf battles prevented the collaboration of those involved. "We were definitely dysfunctional," recalls Applebee's CFO at the time.[19] Two obstacles were impeding the progress of the team members. First, they didn't have a clear idea of what issues they should be focusing on. And second, even when they did, they lacked the appropriate rules of engagement for how they would work together. Although Hill would eventually fix his executive team so that it became an effective body of leadership—he was named one of America's best CEOs by *Institutional Investor* before retiring in 2006—other companies have not been so fortunate, as their top teams have continued to be plagued by those two fundamental problems.

Getting the right issues on the table and knowing how to work together don't just happen. At high performers, we found that the secret is to deploy specific solutions to avoid some common dysfunctions. The key is to structure the top team (or teams, as we found the case to be) in certain ways and to manage that group's time together such that the most important agenda items are never given short shrift.

Create Top Teams Within Top Teams

When companies create a top management team, the temptation is to be overly inclusive. A new CEO might, for instance, automatically include all of his or her direct reports as well as any previous members of the team. In theory, such an inclusive approach makes sense. After all, a greater number of people will lead to a diversity of viewpoints, which can be helpful for problem solving. Not surprisingly, many companies have top teams that include two dozen or more people. But large memberships have a number of disadvantages. People will tend to vote in favor of alliances (either oriented toward their business function or product line) and can be tempted to engage in backroom horse-trading.

To avoid that, high performers have a much more sophisticated setup: they create a nested series of teams inside of teams. They shrink the top team to a small number—maybe between three to seven people—who are the main decision makers. This small group then receives advice from other teams so that hundreds of people might be providing important input. The key, according to a Harvard University study of top management teams, is to recognize the three different functions of senior leadership: information sharing, consulting on important decisions, and making those key decisions.[20] Having the same group perform all three functions can easily become unwieldy. And that's why some companies specifically split those tasks and clearly delineate and assign each of them to a different team. According to the Harvard research, when Brian Beamish became CEO of the base metals division of Anglo American, his top team had fourteen members from various operations and business units around the world. Beamish completely overhauled that structure for a sharper focus: a large group of the top forty managers would be responsible for sharing information across the division, a management committee would concentrate on coordinating various operations to implement large initiatives, and a small team of just four executives would make major decisions that affected the entire enterprise.[21] The change has helped Beamish avoid the syndrome of trying to do too much with the same team such that little actually gets accomplished. The creation of a hierarchy of top teams was a pattern we saw over and over again in high performers.

The concept of having just a handful of executives as the key decision-making body might seem like heresy to many companies. But the Harvard study found that the best senior leadership teams typically include no more than just eight people. Otherwise, the bigger the group gets, the more it will struggle with establishing and enforcing rules of how everyone's input will be used to make important decisions. The danger is that the team will devolve into a body that merely shares information and accomplishes little else.[22] Not only must the top executive team be small, but it must also include people who are chosen not by their title or status, but by the value they can provide in the decision-making process.

Whatever decision-making structure is used, companies should remember that it must always reflect the goals of the organization. Consider Cisco, the manufacturer of communications and networking equipment. Concerned about a growth slowdown, CEO John Chambers completely overhauled how decisions were made in the company. He created about sixty internal committees of executives to provide strategic advice about potential new projects. The goal has been to develop enough new businesses to help Cisco jump the S-curve and move beyond its core strength in Internet switches. Chambers himself knows full well the dangers of complacency. Years ago, he worked at Wang Laboratories before the company collapsed from its inability to move from one core business to another.

To avoid that same fate at Cisco, those dozens of internal committees are responsible for alerting the senior leadership team of promising new opportunities. Chambers has said that the goal is to expand the number of Cisco's new businesses to fifty (from just two in 2007). "Thirty is more than almost any senior executive thinks is manageable," says Chambers. "The real point of going to fifty is to keep people open minded."[23] To accomplish that, he expects his executives to spend more than 30 percent of their time on those internal committees, with some individuals being members of four or five.[24] The new structure has certainly helped to decentralize decision-making at the company. By one account, 70 percent of decisions are now being made collaboratively at a lower level—a huge jump from 10 percent just a couple years ago. And this, Chambers says, has enabled the company to pursue more opportunities than would have been possible in the past, when just a handful of executives were overseeing new business initiatives.[25]

Manage Down the Time Spent Managing

Not surprisingly, running a business to both the financial and the distinctive capabilities S-curves creates myriad agenda items for the top team, many more than if executives were to focus on just one curve. The problem is that the agenda items that tend to get the most attention in many companies are not the right ones. In a survey of senior executives conducted by Marakon Associates in collaboration with the Economics Intelligence Unit, the researchers found that up to 80 percent of top executives' time is spent on issues that will affect less than 20 percent of the organization's long-term value.[26] The basic issue is that senior leadership teams are often *managing* an existing business when they should instead be *developing* distinctive capabilities for the future (that is, their focus is stuck on the financial S-curve when it should be on the capabilities S-curve). To produce the most effective use of a top team's time, the time spent managing must be actively managed (usually reduced) to bring it into balance with time spent planning.

In the Marakon Associates survey of top executives, more than 95 percent of the respondents said that their company lacked a disciplined process for focusing their time on important issues.[27] That's a mind-boggling statistic, given how valuable a senior executive's time is. A part of the problem is that many top management teams don't have an effective process for running their meetings. Often, agenda items that seem to be the most pressing get discussed first, such that the team is constantly fighting fires and neglects to do a sufficient amount of strategic planning. The urgent crowds out the important.

Thus, the first necessity is to control the amount of time spent managing and to create time for planning. One way to do that is to split the discussion of tactical versus strategic issues into two types of meetings. An executive team might, for example, have weekly meetings to discuss operations and have monthly meetings (perhaps for a full day) to concentrate on strategic issues. Such procedures help ensure that senior leadership is disciplining itself to explicitly and demonstrably keep one foot in today and the other in tomorrow. At Nokia, for example, strategy development staffs are responsible for creating and maintaining a list of the most important strategic issues that the company is facing. That information is then discussed by senior executives at monthly strategy panel meetings. "Having a corporate-wide agenda makes top team members focus on common challenges instead of specific subunit agendas," notes Jarkko Sairanen, vice president and the head of corporate strategy at Nokia.[28]

One important strategic agenda item that high performers make time for is talent planning. Again, the distinction is worth nothing: Low- and average-performance companies tend to *manage* talent; high performers *plan* for it. At UPS's management committee, for example, all twelve members are responsible for compiling a list of the employees whom they've identified as potential candidates for executive positions in their division or operating unit. At the committee's monthly meeting, time is always reserved for one of the members (chosen on a rotating basis) to give an update on the people on his or her list. The process is so thorough that by the time employees make it near the top of the corporate ladder, they are already well known by the committee. In addition, UPS holds an annual leadership conference in which the senior executives and board of directors review the top two hundred managers in the company's leadership development program.[29]

But setting aside the time for important strategic agenda items is one thing; creatively and actively managing the total amount of time spent planning so that it's manageable is another. Some planning tasks the top team must handle are by their nature extraordinarily time-intensive. For example, one of the most important strategic-planning tasks for senior leadership is to identify the next big-enough market insight, or BEMI. While this is one of the most important tasks of the top team, the process also requires the executive team to separate important signals from the surrounding noise and then decide which of those signals to pursue: a massively time-intensive task. It requires a structured approach to make the most of senior executive time.

Consider, for example, 3M. When James McNerney was CEO of 3M in the early 2000s, he realized that the company's problem wasn't that it had a shortage of good ideas; it had far too many. Thanks to 3M's policy of allowing employees to spend 15 percent of their time at work pursuing their own projects, the company's innovation machine was humming along—only too well. It had more than a thousand projects in the works, and executives weren't sure which of those to pursue. So McNerney created a centralized database that included details of all those initiatives, using information collected from the company's more than seventy labs. A team of technical directors then ranked each of those projects according to various criteria like costs, expected revenues, and time to market. Then McNerney's team of senior leaders pruned that list down to about seventy-five. To make the next cut, projects had to be in promising areas of technology (like nanotechnology and fuel cells), and to help ensure the selection of possible BEMIs, the potential annual sales had to be at least $100 million.[30]

Amazingly, at many companies the top executives do not even know who is (and who isn't) on the senior leadership team. That statement might sound ludicrous, but it's more than supported by that Harvard study of top management teams. The researchers investigated more than a hundred senior leadership teams from various companies (small businesses to large multinationals) across a range of industries and countries. The results were mind-boggling. "Few CEOs know just how porous the boundaries of their top teams are—or how detrimental that is to shared decision-making," the authors concluded. "In fact, only 11 of the 120 teams we studied were in perfect agreement about who was on the team!"[31] Is it any wonder, then, why so many companies like Wang Laboratories fail to change the makeup of their top management teams ahead of the financial S-curve, given that most don't even know who is on that team to begin with?

Moreover, having the right senior executives in place is merely a necessary yet hardly sufficient condition for sustained high performance. What about the people who are supposed to be following those leaders? Specifically, how can a company ensure that it will have the talent it needs to jump to a new capabilities S-curve? Can those employees be hired from the outside, or must they be developed from within? And how can managers keep any high-potential employee from defecting to a competitor? In the next chapter, we'll learn how high performers go about ensuring that they not only have the talent they need; they have a surplus of it.

Before You Jump to Conclusions, Ask Yourself These Questions:

1. What was the reason for the last CEO transition at your company? Specifically, was it spurred by an organizational crisis or another specific event? Or was it a transfer of power that was planned for years?

2. Is your company's succession process inclusive and transparent? Who has input, and how are decisions ultimately made?

3. How small (or large) is your organization's senior leadership team that is responsible for making enterprise-wide decisions? How diverse are the thinking and learning styles of the members of that team?

4. Do the members of that top team generally spend too little time planning because they're too busy managing?

5. Is constructive conflict encouraged or avoided at your company? Do employees speak the truth to power, or are they afraid to do so?

8 HOTHOUSES OF TALENT

THE OIL AND GAS industry has been suffering a critical shortage of talent. The average age of petroleum engineers is past fifty years, and the most experienced baby boomer employees are beginning to retire in droves. Exacerbating the problem is the industry's image, which has taken repeated hits as sustainability becomes an increasingly important societal issue. Indeed, over the past thirty years, the enrollment of college students studying the geosciences has plunged, which several years ago prompted the American Petroleum Institute to investigate the shifting demographics of the industry. The results of that research were sobering. "The consequences of these trends are both severe and imminent," the study concluded.[1]

One company in that industry, though, keeps humming along: Schlumberger Ltd. The multibillion-dollar global oilfield services provider appears almost immune to the daunting statistics that plague others in the oil-field services business. It's not that the company hasn't suffered any key losses. As we noted in chapter 4, competitors regularly poach some of Schlumberger's most talented people, often luring them with huge salary raises. But the company has been able to withstand those losses and carry on with a seemingly endless supply of high-potential individuals continually rising to the top. Most of those are longtime company loyalists. Remarkably, about 80 percent of Schlumberger's senior managers and executives took a job with the organization right after graduating from school.[2]

As that figure reveals, Schlumberger makes a concerted effort and the necessary investments to grow top-notch talent from within. It maintains close relationships with universities, offering scholarships and internships, to ensure a steady supply of the best young minds. It then expends considerable resources to develop that talent: rookie employees undergo a multiyear training program in which they gain field experience and participate in intensive classroom instruction. In addition, Schlumberger encourages newer employees to post detailed curricula vitae on a company intranet so that they can be recruited for projects in business units around the world. Further, to develop a sufficient supply of managerial ranks, managers are expected to cultivate their successors. And Schlumberger doesn't suffer losses in talent lightly. The company holds a rigorous postmortem after any high-potential employee leaves; this analysis helps Schlumberger learn how to minimize further losses of valuable human capital.

Thanks to such practices, high-performance companies like Schlumberger have turned their organizations into veritable hothouses of talent: they actively create an ideal environment in which talent can grow, from seedling to maturity. In chapter 4, we described how high-performance companies attract and retain serious talent. In this chapter, we'll discuss how those organizations *grow* such top-notch employees.

UNDERSTANDING TALENT SHORTAGES

Becoming a hothouse of talent is not just an admirable, lofty goal; it is a necessary condition for all companies today, regardless of industry. In our research, we learned that talent shortages afflict virtually every industry, not just long-term, cyclical industries. In short, there are not enough exceptional individuals to go around. Despite the recent downturn, long-term economic trends have created painful shortages of talent in almost every industry. Intensified competition from increasingly connected global markets, rapid market growth from accelerated economic growth in many parts of the world, and unfavorable demographic trends like aging workforces are just some of the reasons. Notwithstanding enormous advances in the creation of electronically intermediated labor markets (including Web sites like Monster.com), companies still find it difficult to source the real talent they need easily from the market.

Yet, external labor factors are not the only causes of talent shortages in companies. Even when an industry is flush with top-tier employees, a company's business success alone can't help but create shortages of serious talent. There are at least four important ways that rapid scaling stretches a company's ability to have sufficient and appropriate talent. First is the need to find lots of talent fast. A company might be able to hire dozens (or even a hundred) top-notch employees in short order. But what happens, for example, when it needs to scale quickly and therefore hire, in many cases, several thousand first-rate employees per year? Then it will typically have to lower its standards or get creative about where to look. Second, homegrown talent is not easy to develop. It takes substantial investments and considerable time to teach employees not only the skills they need, but also the knowledge of the history and values of an organization. In companies with double-digit attrition and double-digit growth, the average tenure in the organization soon becomes so compressed that employees who are relatively new themselves are expected to train those who have more recently come on board.

Third, as companies expand into different markets and geographic regions, they naturally suffer a dilution of the corporate culture from the influx of workers of different backgrounds. This means that employees might lack a fundamental understanding of how to perform their jobs in the ways that are most aligned with the values and overall mission of the organization. Fourth, companies can experience a decrease in overall employee productivity as they grow and add layers of complexity and bureaucracy to their businesses.

Interestingly, talent shortages are not just a problem in boom times; even during economic recessions, companies can be severely talent-constrained. And it is very often this shortage of talent that prevents companies from jumping the S-curve. But another cause of talent shortage is perhaps the most surprising and counterintuitive of all: a company's own decision to cut back on growing its talent.

REAPING WHAT YOU SOW

To understand why companies do this, we need to look at the third hidden S-curve, the one that depicts the growth and inevitable leveling off of serious talent in a company (see figure 8-1). Long before the financial performance of a company matures, the amount of serious talent a company has developed or acquired shrinks as a percentage of total employees and revenues. Several factors help explain that decrease.

While going up its financial S-curve, the company has also come down the learning curve, so it no longer needs such a high ratio of serious talent to handle challenges and uncertainty. Following traditional organization design theory, companies at this stage become more hierarchical in order to reduce costs. They use more rules and formal processes to conduct the business rather than the guidance of on-the-spot experts and managers.

Another reason companies slow their production of serious talent is the growth in the intensity of competition. As a business

FIGURE 8-1

Hidden S-curve of talent development

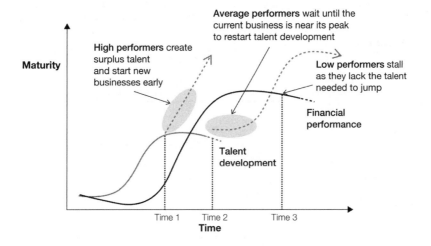

matures, more and better competitors apply downward pressure on margins. Reducing the non-revenue-generating costs of management layers and R&D experts—both these groups seemingly no longer needed—is a fast and surefire way to improve earnings, at least in the short run. And better earnings can artificially stretch the financial S-curve and disguise the underlying trend of increasing competition and declining differentiation in the marketplace. Let a business cycle downturn occur at the same time, and investor pressure will almost certainly lead to deep cuts in the levels of those costly but hard-to-replace employees.

Particularly in knowledge-work industries, where high-value employees essentially go through an apprenticeship process, large-scale layoffs and economic cycles are systemically creating skills gaps. This trend can be observed for entire age cohorts (see figure 8-2). The result is that companies are left with two painful choices. They can promote the employees they have left in those cohorts, regardless of whether the candidates for promotion have successfully demonstrated their abilities to take on greater

FIGURE 8-2

The emergence of talent cohort gaps

In challenging economic times, companies often reduce their ranks. This leads to thin spots of talent with several negative consequences, including shallower bench strength, fewer mentors, and a weakened culture as new hires are brought in from the outside to fill the gaps.

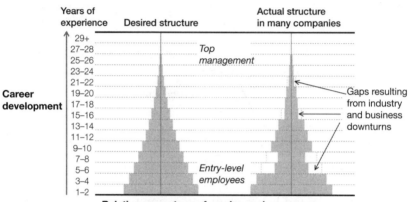

Relative percentage of employees in company

responsibilities. Or they can begin to hire large numbers of employees from outside the company, at levels for which home-grown talent would have been preferable because of the cultural glue it provides.

And there's an even more insidious danger. The talent shortages that result from these efforts to get by on a smaller proportion of serious talent eventually create problems for companies that want to embark on the next great business idea. Despite their best intentions, most maturing companies not only trim the ranks of talent, but also slow the development of serious talent somewhere in the middle of the financial S-curve. They do this in myriad ways—by curtailing investments in training and development, by encouraging in-place careers without expectations of promotion, by limiting merit promotions to when positions become open, and in countless other ways large and small. Unfortunately, when companies come under pressure, recruiting, training, and development are all viewed as semidiscretionary, and the costs of trying to rebuild lost talent that knows the ropes and is living the culture are systematically underestimated. (By contrast, GE has never reduced its training budget, even in the dark recessionary periods, like 2002 and 2008, even though "[CEO Jeff Immelt] understands that GE can call a halt to most of the company's training spending at any time, thereby improving short term numbers.")[3]

Yet, the middle of the financial S-curve is no time to give up on talent creation. In fact, that's precisely the time companies most need an injection of experienced talent to define and launch the new businesses that will begin the company's process of jumping the S-curve. Unfortunately, though, many companies wait until their financial performance has tapered and their reputation in the market has begun to wane to restart their efforts to develop serious talent, which is, of course, nearly the worst time to attempt such an endeavor.

Complicating matters is the reaction of the talent still in the pipeline as the flow of talent gets constricted. With business growth along the existing S-curve supplying the only real opportunity for advancement, up-and-comers recognize that their future rests on replacing existing people—a potential recipe for stagnation. In this environment, those who are passionate about growing new businesses will move on, and those who prefer to work with an existing business will self-select into the company and not out. This only worsens the problem, as companies are left with even fewer of the entrepreneurial (or intrapreneurial) types of employees and managers who thrive on the new-business challenges that are inherent in any attempt to jump an S-curve. The result is that the vast majority of employees and management talent that remain are all the more vested in the continuing success of the current business.

ESTABLISHING HOTBED CONDITIONS

To avoid the problems a foreshortened talent S-curve creates—and to maintain high performance over any extended period—our research shows that companies need more than just a sufficient amount of talent; they need a *surplus* of talent. Many executives might view this statement with great skepticism. After all, isn't it difficult enough finding all the talent that's necessary—let alone a surplus of it—to keep a business running? But our research has found that high performers like Schlumberger, Procter & Gamble, UPS, and others consistently maintain deep benches of excess talent through both good times and bad. (For ways to tell if you have surplus talent, see "Signs of Surplus.")

Contrast that with low and average performers. Talent shortages in general are prevalent in large companies. Nevertheless, many firms do manage to round up enough of the right people to handle the everyday challenges of a particular business. But what they are missing is the quantity of serious talent required to achieve high performance over an extended period. They are able to function under normal conditions, but then they stumble badly when trying to ramp up their operations or when trying to jump the S-curve. The solution relies on creating abundance. For companies that jump the S-curve, serious talent can no longer be foraged for in the woods of the labor market; it must be grown in a hothouse of talent.

Talent hothouses are like agricultural greenhouses. First, a company needs to start with the right seeds to ensure early, and at least moderate, success for the vast majority; then as those seedlings grow, it needs to take action to strengthen them for the challenges ahead. That preparation must include steps to increase their hardiness, so managers must regularly give employees exposure to unfamiliar ideas and ways of thinking. And throughout, the organization needs to provide adequate room for growth.

Signs of Surplus

"Where have you been hiding this person?" can be too often heard in the upper-management corridors of low-performance companies. The hoarding and hiding of talent are sure signs of a talent shortage. Some management gurus recommend managing high-potential talent at the corporate level, to avoid line-management's hoarding them. But this rather misses the point. It does nothing to address the painful underlying shortage. So what are the signs that you are successfully creating a talent surplus? Here are just a few.

Time to Think in Their Day Jobs

High performers don't need to squeeze every last ounce of juice from the orange. Since the 1920s, 3M has famously allowed its people to spend 15 percent of their time pursuing their own ideas, and the practice has been the source of some of the company's most successful products, such as Scotch tape and Post-it notes. The company maintains this policy whether the economy is booming or in recession, so talent is less likely to flee as a result of belt-tightening in tough times. Genentech has similarly allowed its researchers to spend 20 percent of their time on discretionary projects. One major example of success: in his spare time, researcher Napoleone Ferrera—hired to work on a hormone thought to be related to the reproductive system—found a gene critical to the spread of cancer. His discovery led to the development of Avastin, Genentech's anticancer blockbuster drug.[a]

A Deep Bench

Ask any sports team the secret to a winning season, and the answer is likely to be this: the quality of the players on the bench. P&G has a powerful mechanism to keep its bench deep with talent. Through its formal program Build from Within, P&G always has three qualified candidates waiting in the wings for every one of its top fifty important positions. When A. G. Lafley was head of P&G, he once remarked, "If I get on a plane next week and it goes down, there will be somebody in this seat the next morning."[b] And if Lafley had suffered such an unfortunate fate, the person replacing him would have been a fellow P&G person. "We're not going to call up a head hunter when we have a job opening because I think that would violate our culture and our values," said Lafley, who recently retired after spending his entire career at the consumer goods giant.[c]

Indeed, thanks to the company's extensive and up-to-date database that tracks more than 100,000 employees, it can react quickly to any unexpected departure of talent. "We can fill a spot in a hour ... That's the beauty of the system," boasted Lafley, who during his long tenure as CEO would meet every Sunday with HR to discuss high-potential individuals. Adds Moheet Nagrath, the head of HR at P&G, "If you train people to work in different countries and businesses, you develop a deep bench."[d] And by "deep bench," P&G is talking about several layers. "Today I could show you the next generation of successors to current leaders, the generation after that, and the generation after that," says Nagrath.[e]

Time to Grow Through Developmental Assignments

A third sign of surplus talent—enabled by a deep bench—is the ability to assign up-and-coming talent to developmental postings, rather than always pushing people up to the next big job. At high performers, there is enough good talent to fill routine openings such that decisions about next career steps can include a range of assignment opportunities that have a training and education component to them. Low performers with talent shortages simply don't have the luxury of considering longer-term benefits to the employee's career when filling open jobs.

a. Ed Frauenheim, "On the Clock but Off on Their Own: Pet-Project Programs Set to Gain Wider Acceptance," *Workforce Management,* April 2006.

b. A. G. Lafley, quoted in Mina Kimes, "P&G's Leadership Machine: The Consumer Goods Giant Has a Proven Formula to Nurture Top Talent," *Fortune,* May 20, 2009.

c. A. G. Lafley, quoted in Cliff Peale, "CEO Likes Fresh Wave," *Cincinnati Enquirer,* November 21, 2004.

d. Moheet Nagrath, quoted in Kimes, "P&G's Leadership Machine."

e. Moheet Nagrath, quoted in Jennifer Reingold, "CEO Swap: The $79 Billion Plan," *Fortune,* November 20, 2009.

Hire for Life (or Act Like You Do)

Most high-performance companies have had, at some point in their history, the intention to hire employees for life. While that time may have passed, many companies still desire to hire people for the long term—a perspective that fundamentally alters the nature of their hiring practices. They don't just look for the best résumé to fill particular positions. In fact, an individual's first job in the company is often relatively unimportant. Instead, these employers recognize that cultural fit is critical and that what matters most is the likelihood that someone will perform exceptionally well over time. All of this is reflected in how companies choose their employees and then follow up on those choices.

Hire for Long-Term Fit, Not Short-Term Needs

At high performers, hiring is generally more involved and costly, and training investment levels are higher, but these costs are offset by the better fit and longer tenure of the employees brought on board. The key question is this: how likely is this person to grow and learn within the framework of the business and its talent development approaches? This attitude is reflected in the comment of Bob Stoffel, a UPS senior vice president and thirty-year veteran with the company: "We hire people for careers, not jobs." In this way, a company like UPS might not necessarily select star performers with the best current skills or résumé; it might instead favor someone who seems more likely to flourish in the organization's specific hothouse environment.

Southwest Airlines is another high performer that takes the long view and is well known for its philosophy of "hire for fit and train for skills." Among the core values of that fit are the Golden Rule and the fundamental belief that everyone should be treated with dignity and respect. "We don't care if you're the best pilot," says Colleen Barrett, former president. "If you condescend to a secretary, you won't get hired."[4] Other important qualities the company looks for are a sense of humor and a commitment to customer service.

The Four Seasons Hotels and Resorts has a similar approach—it specifically looks for people who will thrive in a business that treats customers like kings because, quite literally, some could be.[5] That kind of customer service doesn't come naturally to everyone, and the Four Seasons is only interested in people who have an innate positive, helpful, can-do attitude. "I can teach anyone to be a waiter," says Isadore Sharp, CEO of the luxury hotel chain. "But you can't change an ingrained poor attitude. We look for people who say, 'I'd be proud to be a doorman.'"[6] Finding that kind of employee can feel like searching for a needle in a haystack. But so far, the Four Seasons sterling reputation as an employer of choice has enabled it to maintain its very selective hiring process. To staff its Doha, Qatar, hotel, which opened in 2006, it chose from an applicant pool of twenty-five thousand people for just six hundred positions.[7]

Of course, assessing large numbers of applicants for cultural fit can be costly and time-consuming. That's why some companies are turning to information technology (IT) for innovative solutions. Reckitt Benckiser, for example, has on its Web site an application that enables people to determine if they might be a good fit with its exceptionally driven culture. Called Virtual Career, the online simulation presents different business scenarios and asks prospective job candidates how they would respond. In one hypothetical situation, an employee is given two projects by the boss with the same deadline, and the employee is unsure whether both can get done in time. Should the person try to manage the boss's expectations and ask for an extension on one of the projects? Or should the person figure out exactly what needs to be done and ask coworkers for help to complete both on time? Or should the employee take a different tack and create a more off-the-wall approach to delivering on the objectives? After a choice is made, the simulation informs the candidate how well his or her response matches the company's core values, which include entrepreneurship and the desire to achieve. With their score in mind, applicants can decide for themselves whether they want to continue pursuing employment opportunities at Reckitt Benckiser. As the company's Web site readily admits, "It takes a certain type of person to thrive here."[8]

Don't Stop Choosing After Hiring

Although high performers are careful in their hiring, they are also quick to correct any mistakes they've made. Some high performers start as early as initial training to detect hires who aren't a good fit. At the Four Seasons, all the new employees must complete a three-month training program in which, through improvisation exercises, they are exposed to a wide variety of situations that they might encounter with real guests. Those who aren't a good fit for the Four Seasons culture typically leave the company quickly, while those who fit well tend to stay and build their careers there for years. The overall annual turnover rate for full-time employees at the Four Seasons is just 18 percent, roughly half the average in the industry.[9]

At P&G, hindsight is more than 20/20; it is a way of improving the hiring process. The company compares performance reviews with the assessments made by interviewers during recruiting; in this way, P&G evaluates both the employee and the effectiveness of the hiring process.[10] At UPS, the talent-identification program starts way down at the warehouse level—the place where many of the company's top executives began their careers. The process starts with functional managers identifying potential leaders, who are then tracked and regularly evaluated over the coming years. A management development committee helps assess the specific training that each of the high-potential individuals might require, such as broader functional experience or executive education classes. As the hundreds of those employees progress through the program, the best are eventually tapped for the top managerial positions. Note that the primary goal here is to provide high-caliber individuals with the development needed to achieve their full potential. This stands in contrast to other leadership development programs that focus on early selection as an excuse to avoid investing more broadly in employee development.

Management need not be the only ones to vote on the fit and potential of new employees, however. Some high performers use the informed opinion of their line employees as well. At Whole Foods, every new employee works with a team during a four-week trial period, after which members hold a vote: an employee must receive a two-thirds majority in order to stay with the team. This process applies even at corporate headquarters, where potential new members of the national IT or finance staff must also be voted in by their future colleagues.[11] Online clothing retailer Zappos.com, acquired by Amazon.com in 2009, goes as far as to offer $2,000 (along with their regular pay) to new hires that quit between the end of their first and fourth weeks of training. In doing so, they encourage their new employees to quickly judge for themselves whether they feel there is a good fit and to act on that decision.[12]

CREATING STRENGTH FROM STRESS

High-performance businesses aggressively develop the "talent muscle" in their organizations. They create environments—often highly challenging ones—for employees to acquire the skills and experience they need to climb up the corporate ladder quickly. The goal is partly to create what our Accenture colleague Bob Thomas, in his book on the topic, calls "crucible" experiences. These are life-changing events, whether on the job or not, that hold lifetime lessons that can be mined to help transform someone into a leader.[13] After A. G. Lafley led P&G in Asia during a time of economic collapse, the former CEO had this to say about that difficult period: "You learn ten times more in a crisis than during normal times."[14] Crucible experiences can—and should be—created intentionally. When Jeff Immelt was still in his early thirties and relatively young in his career at GE, he was tapped by then CEO Jack Welch and HR chief Bill Conaty to deal with the problem of millions of faulty refrigerator compressors—despite his having no familiarity with appliances or recalls. It was an experience without which Immelt says he would never have become CEO.[15]

The rationale is clear: passively waiting for natural leaders to emerge won't yield top talent in sufficient quantity. "I've seen more leaders who were born during their careers than I have seen born leaders. There's a way of helping to develop leadership," asserts Peter Brabeck-Letmathe, former Nestlé CEO.[16]

One effective approach for developing high-potential talent is to explicitly give people assignments rather than jobs. Take, for example, David Barnes, the current chief information officer (CIO) of UPS. Before being promoted into that position, Barnes had to complete several stretch assignments. In 2002, for instance, he was given the responsibility of overhauling UPS's Web site, which then was serving more than two hundred countries and handling up to 15 million package-tracking requests every day. Barnes had two years to redesign the applications on the site and update the infrastructure—all without any disruption to service.[17] It was the type of massive project that Ken Lacy, then the CIO, should have been in charge of, but Lacy assigned it to his lieutenant Barnes to see how he would respond. Barnes passed that test (and others) and eventually won the CIO spot when Lacy retired. This approach is typical at the company. Yet, success is never certain. Others Lacy tested were unable to make the leap.[18]

To manage the inherent risk that comes with assigning unfamiliar tasks to up-and-coming managers, some companies take a "popcorn stand" approach. They give employees who have leadership potential their own tiny business unit to manage—for example, the local operations of a small geographic market. The goal is to provide those individuals with the full profit-and-loss experience of running a business—leading a team, serving a customer base, negotiating contracts, and so on. And the organization gets an early look at how the employees respond to that challenge—an important piece of data because past results are typically the best predictor of a worker's future performance.

One company that provides ample opportunities for young, talented employees is Illinois Tool Works. ITW, a global manufacturer of industrial products and equipment, is organized into more than eight hundred individual business units. As we noted in chapter 3, whenever one of those units becomes too large (the maximum size is around $50 million in sales), the company splits it. For example, its original Deltar business, which sells plastic fasteners to the auto industry, has over the years been broken into more than two dozen separate units, opening up many managerial positions for young talent. "We develop managers so rapidly that a person can start running a business when he is in his twenties," says Frank Ptak, ITW vice chairman.[19]

Creating surplus talent is only partly a question of having the depth of bench required to maintain numerous operations without any hiccups; it's also about having the breadth of talent with the richness of experience needed to jump an S-curve. Having a broad range of experiences early in a career is essential for building strong future leaders who can manage both growing and maturing businesses. Too many leaders grow up repeating the same job, just on a larger scale. "If they worked for another company, they would be trapped in some function. Here they get a chance to do everything," asserts ITW's Ptak. "That gives a lot of people the chance to train and see what they can do."[20] Of course, ITW's approach means that, while many employees will swim, some may sink. But the company feels that the risks are well worth the benefits of finding out early which managers have the right stuff to become senior executives. "Some segments start out very small, perhaps $5 million to $8 million. That's a great place to try a young person," says Ptak. "If they fail, we just pick up the pieces and move on."[21]

High performers also understand that failure shouldn't necessarily be a firing offense. They encourage employees to take calculated risks, and they tolerate occasional poor outcomes as long as the results don't stem from stupid mistakes—and as long as lessons have clearly been learned. Sometimes, these companies even reward failure: P&G's feminine-care group has for several years given out the President's Fail Forward Award as part of its FemCare Delight Awards. The award goes to the "team or individual that enabled the organization to significantly learn from a failure and as a consequence enables a future project or team to move forward much faster and/or better."[22]

CULTIVATING HARDINESS THROUGH VARIETY

When creating surplus talent, it's not enough to simply hire, develop, and retain serious individual talent. Those talented individuals must work together, strengthening each other through constructive criticism and creating innovation through the intersection of ideas. One of the many benefits of growing in-house talent is the greater sense of familiarity and trust that develops, making closer collaboration possible. A former HR executive at P&G says: "When you've been in the trenches together over a number of years, it simplifies collaboration. There is a trust that you approach problems in a similar way, share a common language, and that your values are generally congruent."[23]

But the problem with being too long in the trenches together is that cultures that lack variety are often not as resilient to outside threats. To understand why, consider the humble banana. Most people don't realize that the bananas eaten throughout the world today are almost entirely from the Vietnamese Cavendish cultivar, grown from countless clippings tracing back to one original plant. The reason we eat Cavendish today is because the Gros Michel cultivar, though better suited for export, was wiped out by Panama disease in just a few short decades. The result was a temporary worldwide shortage until a reasonable substitute could be found, inspiring the still well-known 1923 hit tune "Yes, We Have No Bananas." The problem for these cultivars is that, lacking genetic diversity, they are extremely vulnerable: every disease or threat that can overcome one plant can defeat them all.

Inbred companies can easily suffer a similar fate, for example, when groupthink blinds the organization to important changes in the business environment. To discourage such insularity, high performers increase employee exposure to the wider world. Yet on the other hand, to avoid becoming a collection of iconoclasts, they offset that broad exposure with the regular use of cross-functional teaming. The goal is to achieve a delicate balance that provides the best of both worlds.

Get Employees Out More

P&G has certainly been aware of the dangers of too much insularity. In the past, conformity was the de facto rule at the company, influencing everything from how employees dressed to how they thought of themselves as "Proctoids."[24] One reason for that insularity was geographic: P&G is headquartered in Cincinnati, a relatively small city in which employees tend to live close to one another, shop at the same stores, and eat at the same restaurants. "There was a sense that you were in a club," recalls a former P&G brand manager. "The disadvantage was, people did think in similar ways."[25] And the closed environment was reinforced by the company's once command-and-control style of management. As one reporter once put it, "Behind Procter & Gamble's wholesome image is a control-obsessed company so paranoid that Wall Street analysts, employees, and the chairman himself refer to it as 'The Kremlin.'"[26]

But when Durk Jager became CEO in late 1998, he quickly went about trying to transform that culture. "At P&G, we tend to put people into a P&G box, a 'Proctoid' box, where certain behaviors and certain institutionalized ways of acting are accepted," said Jager at that time. "I don't believe in that at all. We need diversity in style. We need diversity in content, . . . and we have to move away from trying to institutionalize certain dogmas within the company."[27] But Jager, who was born in the Netherlands and came up through the P&G ranks mainly from outside its corporate center, underestimated what he was up against. His aggressive initiatives were met with overwhelming resistance, leading to his departure in June 2000, just seventeen months into his tenure. His successor, A. G. Lafley, was equally committed to getting P&G to think in broader terms, but he took a somewhat different approach.

Under Lafley, P&G implemented a variety of programs in a concerted effort to focus more on the outside world; some we mentioned in chapter 2. In the Living It program, employees reside with consumers in their homes for several days at a time to observe how those families go about their lives. The goal is to learn about the challenges and problems that consumers face on a daily basis. In the Working It program, employees are assigned to work behind a retail counter to observe what customers are buying. And in Connect and Develop, the company actively searches for new ideas from outside sources in order to satisfy the P&G mandate that half of its future innovations involve an outside partner. The Connect and Develop initiative has successfully combated the company's "not invented here" syndrome, which had been part and parcel of its insular culture. Now P&G will even partner with competitors like the Clorox Company to bring new technologies to market. In fact, hundreds of new products have been commercialized through Connect and Develop, including blockbusters like the Swiffer Duster and Mr. Clean Magic Eraser.[28]

Such programs and other initiatives have considerably loosened the P&G culture. It's not just that the company is less bureaucratic and that male employees don't need to wear ties anymore; the very zeitgeist of the organization is different. "Procter used to hire on skills, but when you got in the door there was a mold that you fit into," recalls a marketing director. "What Procter has done . . . is find more of a balance. There's not a mold now."[29]

Make Sure They're All in It Together

Iconoclasts are valuable for breaking up stale thinking. But having too many of them can result in dysfunctional behavior such as culture clashes between functions, units, and locations unless business leaders take steps to establish an environment that encourages collaboration across the organization. Again, P&G's example is instructive. In the past, employees would stay within their departmental silos, rarely interacting with other business units. Take, for instance, how the company used to develop new products. The R&D group would work on a product and then hand it off to the marketing group with minimal interactions before that transfer. "When I first joined the company, I almost never talked to my brand person except when we were launching," recalls one product researcher at P&G. "Now there are no more of these handoffs. You have to be able to speak everybody's language." Indeed, on a past project, the researcher talked to her assistant brand manager daily and even went on some sales calls.[30]

Such cross-department cooperation can do more than help large organizations function smoothly; it can also spur innovation. Consider Samsung's transformation from the world's largest memory-chip maker to the global manufacturer of stylish electronics products like flat-panel TVs and sleek cell phones. A huge reason for that success is the Samsung Value Innovation Program Center. This facility, located south of Seoul, has enabled the Korean corporation to establish a culture that emphasizes product design as well as quality. The center regularly brings together employees from design, technology, and marketing for periods of up to three months to brainstorm about new products. "It's not about selling a new product, but creating a new culture," says Lee Kun-hee, Samsung Group chairman.[31] The cross-functional approach has thus far reaped huge rewards. Samsung's LCD and plasma TVs, for example, are known for their world-class designs, helping the company to surpass previous industry leaders.

As companies ramp up their operations, their workforce often becomes much more diverse as they expand into new markets and geographies. The trick is to create strength through that diversity. "We don't want to transform a Chinese into a Chilean or an American into an Australian," says Peter Brabeck-Letmathe, former Nestlé CEO. "All we're asking for is that he or she embrace the common values that we have."[32] Indeed, high performers recognize that the objective is not necessarily to enforce a single culture. Instead, companies must maintain a strong "metaculture" at the top while also delicately managing the many subcultures that are defined by different functions, religions, countries, and so on. And, as many high performers have discovered, cross-border teams can be a very effective mechanism for spreading and establishing that metaculture.

PROVIDING ROOM TO GROW

Potted plants can't grow beyond the limits of their containers. As an organization grows, it paradoxically tends to constrict its business and management talent by constraining those individuals in small pots—creating formal processes and explicit rules in an effort to enforce consistency and maintain quality. But the danger is that those processes and rules could stunt employee growth. They could create leaders who are exceptional, but only when these leaders are operating in a predictable environment. They could also squelch initiative and creativity and might easily damage an organization's long-term future when compliance activities consume any spare time that might instead be devoted to innovative thinking. Serious talent resents having its world-class productivity reduced by the need to spend excessive time filling out forms and rigorously adhering to organizational edicts. Talented people want ample room to grow.

To provide this space, high performers first simplify essential processes, even as they add new rules and procedures. This creates headroom for change and experimentation. They then make it easy for talented employees to succeed, by providing an easy-to-follow ladder up the organization, with help provided every step of the way.

Give Them Room to Branch Out

High-performance companies reduce unnecessary complexity not only in their business models and offerings, but also in their internal processes. Organizational structures are made simpler and requirements less onerous for employees. Even seemingly small policy changes can have large effects. When Marvin Ellison was hired by The Home Depot to be executive vice president of U.S. stores, he was stunned to discover that store managers had to wade through hundreds of e-mails from the corporate office. His solution was to limit headquarters to just one e-mail a week, to be sent on Monday. And Ellison also set up a hotline for managers to complain whenever that quota had been exceeded.[33]

On a much larger scale, high performers set out to simplify their overall businesses. One effective approach is to establish global objectives, values, and practices and then allow local business units the freedom to work within that framework. Tesco, the global British retailer, is a staunch advocate of that approach. "We've told the local managers that they are to be the number one in their country, but we don't tell them how to do it," says CEO Terry Leahy.[34] So, for instance, Tesco has struck an effective balance between global and local management with Homeplus, the highly successful joint venture between Tesco and Korea's

Samsung. While Homeplus "has imported Tesco's business model, its balanced scorecard approach to performance management, its innovation programme and its operating systems," its marketing decisions are made locally, which is where Samsung and the management team that is composed mostly of local hires take a dominant role.[35] This innovative organizational strategy, which creates a "hybrid organizational culture," has allowed the British company to localize its retail offer and to adopt a store design and technique of dealing with customers that is in harmony with local Korean consumer culture. No wonder this global retailer was able to prosper in a geography where some other global players have not.[36]

Another effective approach is to guide employees with just a few simple rules. At Southwest Airlines, for example, everyone from the CEO to frontline workers makes decisions with just three goals in mind: make a profit, achieve job security for every worker, and make flying more affordable for consumers. Those simple rules help avoid the "analysis paralysis" that can afflict organizations with myriad regulations, objectives, financial targets, and the like. Moreover, the rules provide employees with the flexibility to solve problems and capitalize on opportunities quickly. Former president Colleen Barrett explains the Southwest rationale: "You cannot write a scenario for every happening that calls for common sense and good judgment."[37]

Of course, the danger of giving business units considerable autonomy is that a rogue group might stray too far from the organization's values and objectives. To avert that, high performers find ways to monitor and react to groups to redirect behavior and activities that are not strategically aligned. For example, Novo Nordisk has a team of facilitators that visits every business unit every third year. All of those individuals have backgrounds as senior specialists or managers, and they assess whether the different groups are complying with various corporate goals, such as the drive to become more sustainable. And the process is a two-way street. Whenever the facilitators discover a valuable best practice at a local unit, they then help spread it across the organization.[38] Light-handed approaches like Novo Nordisk's can go a long way to lowering group resistance—both to corporate oversight and managerial development.

Clear a Path to the Top, Step by Step

Sometimes, to truly enable employees to excel in their work, companies have to take a hard look at exactly what people are required to do, day by day. UPS has long known that its truck drivers are a crucial ingredient to its success. Experienced drivers know the fastest routes between two locations, taking into account the time of day, the weather, and various other factors. The problem for UPS was that the turnover rate for that valuable group of employees was high, partly because of the hard, physical labor required to load packages onto the trucks. So UPS separated that lesser value-added task and gave it to part-time workers, who were more affordable and easier to find.[39]

By freeing its truck drivers from loading packages, UPS enabled those employees to concentrate on what they did best, thus allowing them to excel in their jobs and get promoted more quickly. Indeed, UPS is well known for hiring entry-level workers (often part-time students) and then bringing them up through the ranks, sometimes to the very top. "We tell our human resource representatives, 'You're hiring a CEO today. We don't know who it is. But somewhere, we're hiring one. So make sure you treat that person properly,'" says John Saunders, vice president for human resources at UPS.[40]

To help employees understand what they need to do to rise in the organization, high-performance companies tend to have well-defined career paths. At P&G, a career in marketing has four milestone chronological positions: (1) assistant brand manager, who helps the brand manager develop and execute the strategy for a brand, (2) brand manager, who is held accountable for a brand's success, (3) marketing director, who is in charge of a category of brands, and (4) general manager, who oversees a global business unit.[41] Employees are continually evaluated so that they know exactly what's needed for them to climb to the next level, and their bosses (and mentors) are also held accountable for that progress.

Of course, well-defined career paths might be effective for individuals climbing the corporate ladder in traditional ways, but what about highly talented employees who don't seem to fit any defined mold? J.P. Morgan Chase & Co. plans for these outliers. Its effort has been spearheaded by CEO Jamie Dimon, who will sometimes work with the HR department to create a position for a high-potential individual when no appropriate job is available. "Our biggest sin would be to correctly identify future innovators, only to ignore them by letting them sit and stew in existing positions," Dimon says.[42]

And high-performance businesses aren't afraid of leapfrogging talented employees over those with longer tenures. After A. G. Lafley took over the reins of P&G, for example, he needed someone to run the North American baby-care division, which was then struggling. Instead of choosing one of the seventy-eight general managers with seniority, he reached lower in the organization and tapped Deborah Henretta to fill that position.[43] Lafley's move paid off. Henretta reversed twenty years of losses at the division and was later promoted to group president of Asia, overseeing a $4 billion-plus operation.

———

Many average- and low-performance companies resort to the same excuse for their shortage of talent. In bad times, they can't afford to invest in employee training, leadership development, and other HR programs. But in good times, they're too busy trying to keep up with customer demand to make human capital a priority. In contrast, high performers find the time and make the investments, whether their markets are on a downswing or an upswing. Moreover, those organizations implement mechanisms to ensure that they maintain a talent surplus. In effect, they have their sprinklers set on automatic, whereas low performers only bring out the hose when the garden is already scorched by the sun.

That kind of depth is what a talent hothouse can provide, and perhaps the strongest indicator of whether an organization has succeeded in creating such an environment is this: can it lose a number of valuable employees and not suffer a substantial drop in performance? P&G has proven it can. Consider the number of top-notch managers whom the company has lost over the years and who have all gone on to run major corporations. These include Jeffrey Immelt (General Electric), James McNerney Jr. (3M), Meg Whitman (eBay), and Steven Ballmer (Microsoft). Those talented executives were certainly a considerable loss for P&G. Yet, instead of sharing the unfortunate fate of Shockley Semiconductor Laboratory after its significant loss of talent as we discussed in chapter 4, P&G continues its dominance as a leading consumer goods manufacturer. Not many organizations could suffer that kind of loss of talent and still remain a leader in their industry. But, then, that's one of the reasons why there are so very few high-performance businesses.

Before You Jump to Conclusions, Ask Yourself These Questions:

1. Is your company a net producer or consumer of talent? That is, does it release more talent into the employment marketplace than it hires?

2. Does your company typically hire for long-term fit or for short-term needs? How does it check to ensure that a candidate will fit with the organizational culture?

3. What processes does your company use to identify talented employees?

4. How many years of experience do young, talented managers need before they are given profit-and-loss responsibilities?

5. What mechanisms does your company deploy to turn employee variety into an organizational strength? Or is diversity of viewpoint instead discouraged?

6. Do talented employees tend to leave your company with a greater measure of regret or relief? How actively do competitors poach your employees, and how substantial would their incentives have to be to succeed in luring away your top talent? Are defections investigated to minimize future occurrences?

SHARP CURVES AHEAD

EGINNING IN THE SUMMER of 2008, the global
economy suffered turmoil to a degree that
hadn't been seen in generations. As venerable
and seemingly rock-solid companies vanished and stock markets
crashed, we worried for a time that high performance was a thing
of the past. Every company seemed to be spiraling downward.
What would we be able to say?

Our concerns were misplaced. As events played out during the
global recession, the characteristics of high performance that we
have discussed in this book were more than validated. In fact, the
companies that embodied those characteristics before the crash
have generally performed better through these hard times than
other organizations. While the high performers may not have
anticipated a storm of such magnitude, they ultimately had the
mechanics and mind-sets to power through it.

Although global economic crises of a great magnitude come
only rarely, individual business crises—whether they are caused
by hungry new competitors, transformational technology, or simply the aging of an industry or a company—come with regularity.
Companies in other industries may be feeling great, in other words,
while your business (or industry) faces its own great depression.

The economic disruption that began a few years ago may not be seen again for decades—we certainly hope not. But what is rare for economies as a whole is all too common for individual companies. Crises are a regular fixture of business life, and a host of disruptive forces will cause executives to have sleepless nights in the coming years.

Advances in technology, shifts in access to talent, shrinking trade barriers, and changes in customer needs and demographics are currently threatening to disrupt companies in many industries. The message is clear—your S-curve today is much shorter than you might think. Not only are these disruptors accelerating the shift in the basis of competition, but in many industries, they are also significantly shortening the financial S-curve. Here we briefly describe just eight of the many disruptors that could change the competitive landscape and turn industries upside down in the coming years:

1. **Business analytics**—More and more companies are turning to their massive troves of data to derive and act on critical insights. They want to do much more than understand what has happened; they want to predict the future, with real-time, individualized recommendations. Analytics has already become a key differentiator for professional sports teams and for companies like Netflix and Amazon.com, and it is beginning to disrupt other industries, including insurance and pharmaceuticals. As analytical tools and practices continue to improve, they will increasingly become a source of competitive advantage.[1] (For more, see "Analytics at Work" at http://www.accenture.com/Global/Research_and_Insights/Institute-For-High-Performance/By_Publication_Type/Books/Analytics-at-Work-Results.htm.)

2. **Digital marketing**—Digital marketing is revolutionizing distribution channels, branding, customer relationship manage-

ment, and more. To apply digital marketing successfully, companies need a number of specific capabilities in areas such as social media, online search, and analytics. Advances in technology and analytical capabilities are starting to transform the digital landscape by enabling companies to use automated insights to deliver more timely and relevant content to individual customers and to engage with them in increasingly meaningful ways. Digital marketing is rapidly shortening the financial S-curve of businesses such as advertising agencies, traditional marketing companies, and print media companies. It is also poised to shorten the already-short lifespan of fashion-based products and increase the fragmentation of mass markets into niches. (For more, see "Accenture Interactive" at http://www.accenture.com/Global/Consulting/Accenture-Interactive/default.htm.)

3. **Cloud computing**—Cloud computing allows companies to use scalable, IT-enabled capabilities, including software, storage, and computing power, that an external vendor provides through the Internet. While many organizations are already finding savings and increased flexibility from the use of this new technology, the additional benefits it could deliver in the future are potentially boundless. But one thing is clear: the substantial promise offered by cloud capabilities means that advances in IT are most likely going to be made through clouds, and companies that can harness that power will be able to compete more effectively. Cloud computing has already allowed companies like Amazon.com—which runs its online retail hub on a cloud it created—to transform the basis of competition in its own industries. And this technology is poised to disrupt companies that have played a role in the traditional IT infrastructure, such as PC makers and software vendors, many of which (like Microsoft) are already looking to take on a role in the new

era of the cloud. (For more, see "Six Questions Every Executive Should Ask about Cloud Computing," at http://www
.accenture.com/NR/rdonlyres/7AFDC4E1-ACDD-4C0E-8759-
F9A90D784DD5/0/Accenture_6_Questions_Executives
_Should_Ask_about_Cloud_Computing.pdf.)

4. **Consumers in emerging markets**—In the past, Western companies have developed products at home and modified them for customers in emerging markets, almost as an afterthought. That model is starting to change. Thanks to slowing growth in developed countries and the rapid economic rise of populous countries like China and India, emerging markets will be driving global economic growth in the coming years. As these markets take on increasing significance, companies must develop innovative products specifically for them in order to stay relevant. Otherwise, they risk being preempted by local competitors. The automotive industry has already taken a step down this path, and we see other industries that are dependent on traditional R&D, like consumer goods and pharmaceuticals, starting to follow suit. On the horizon are more efforts at *frugal innovation*—designing offerings specifically for low-income market segments— and *reverse innovation,* in which new products developed in emerging markets are then modified for sale in the developed world. (For more, see "Why Less is the New More," at http://www.accenture.com/Global/Research_and_Insights/ Outlook/Journal/Feb2010/newmore.htm.)

5. **Mobility**—Mobility solutions are poised to bring networking capabilities to all of the devices that people use in their daily lives. Networked mobile phones, digital music players, and portable video devices have already shaken up their respective markets. In the future, a broad spectrum of industries, ranging from health care to automotive manufacturing, will increasingly need to incorporate these capa-

bilities into their major products to fend off competition, and industries like advertising will be reinvented as customers make more of their purchasing decisions on the go. As interoperability between devices eventually becomes the norm, mobility is sure to become a key enabler of growth and innovation, carrying special promise for emerging markets, and will provide mobile operators with a substantial new market. (For more, see "Here Comes Everything: Bringing Networking to Everyday Devices," at http://www .accenture.com/Global/Research_and_Insights/Outlook/ Networking-to-Devices.htm.)

6. **Global talent scarcity**—Companies in the developed, industrialized nations are facing critical talent shortages as well as educational deficiencies among many people entering the workforce. Indeed, a number of studies have pointed to growing concerns about the ability of educational institutions in the developed world to deliver young people into the workforce with the basic skills necessary to succeed. Other data have highlighted perennial global shortages in skilled trades, technicians, and engineers; these shortages threaten the ambitious infrastructure-development goals of many nations. Meanwhile, familiar talent pools are shrinking, and new ones are emerging. Today, Western companies competing abroad tend to rely heavily on leaders and general managers from their home countries. Few businesses have found a way to make the best use of their talent globally. Companies that are able to harness talent in emerging markets by developing a clear talent strategy with a truly global mind-set—finding new hidden pools of talent while developing and protecting their own pools of talent—will be at a competitive advantage as these markets continue to grow in significance. Other organizations will find their S-curves severely shortened as talent shortages become an

insurmountable barrier to growth. (For more, see "Where Will All the Talent Come From?" at http://www.accenture .com/Global/Research_and_Insights/Outlook/By_Issue/ Y2008/allthetalent.htm.)

7. Smart infrastructure solutions—Intelligent infrastructure has the potential to address large-scale, cross-sector challenges, such as reducing energy consumption, managing congestion, and connecting people more efficiently. Smart grids, for example, are already starting to revolutionize the electric power industry, and other energy industries, health care, and government organizations increasingly will adopt similar types of solutions. Eventually, an extensive smart grid in energy will help address the issue of climate change by allowing consumers the ability to conserve energy, tap renewable forms of it, and in general use it more wisely. In addition to innovations in technology and analytics, cooperation between the private, public, and social sectors will be needed to solve the various challenges involved, many of which will stem from the growth of megacities. The implications are not just for the energy industry. Industry sectors that create nearly everything that uses energy and serves an urban environment—appliances, automotive, lighting, and potentially even apparel as we rethink our conditioned environments, to name just a few—will need to get smarter and be ready connect if they are to succeed. And, of course, the organizations leading the way in such efforts are likely to be high performers, while the companies that remain committed to energy from traditional sources and that fail to appreciate the trend of growing urban densities are likely to wonder where their S-curves went. (For more, see "Accelerating Smart Grid Investments" at http://www.accenture .com/Global/Services/By_Industry/Industrial_Equipment/ R_and_I/World-Forum-Smart-Grid.htm.)

8. **Sustainability**—Increasingly, sustainability concerns are leading to innovations in many industries, not just in renewable energy. But some companies have thus far refused to
make the necessary substantial investments because they
fear they might cannibalize their current businesses or
lower their profits. Meanwhile, countries such as China,
Japan, and South Korea may dramatically out-invest the
traditional leading Western nations in this space over the
coming years, which could fundamentally alter the competitive balance in many industry landscapes and shorten
S-curves with new innovations and entrants. Nearly all
industries are expected to be affected, but a few industry
sectors for which there are clear and immediate implications include automotive, communications, consumer
goods and services, energy, financial services, metals and
mining, and utilities. (For more, see "A New Era of Sustainability: UN Global Compact-Accenture CEO Survey 2010"
at http://www.unglobalcompact.org/docs/news_events/8.1/
UNGC_Accenture_CEO_Study_2010.pdf.)

That your S-curve is almost certainly shorter even than you
think is why, based on our experience and High Performance
Business research, we believe you must apply the lessons absorbed
from studying the top performers—P&G, Best Buy, Danaher, UPS,
and any of the numerous other companies we have cited here—in
your own organization, and soon. You should inculcate these lessons in your people, from the top all the way down.

We recognize that executives are typically too busy to step back
from the day's raging fires to see the big picture—which, in business, rarely looks as well ordered and enticing as the paintings of
those Parisians enjoying an afternoon on the banks of the Seine.
For harried executives, we've tried to distill the critical elements
of that picture and to provide a simple language for describing it.
For companies climbing the S-curve, the key ideas are big-enough

market insights, threshold competence, and a worthy company. And for those trying to make the jump, the focus is on edge-centric strategy, top teams that change ahead of the curve, and hothouses of talent.

Simple language, challenging work. For companies with the passion and fortitude to take up the challenges, the potential to become a high-performance company (or organization) is the ultimate achievement.

APPENDIX:
HOW WE DETERMINED HIGH PERFORMANCE

WHEN WE BEGAN our research on high performance in 2003, we knew we were in it for the long haul. Defining the very term *high performance,* for one, was a challenge. Figuring out a methodology that could consistently and repeatedly identify high performers (and average performers and low ones, too) was another. And then determining what got high performers into that position and kept them there was still another.

In brief, over the years we undertook five broad sets of analysis, and Accenture continues this work today in an ongoing program of research. The findings in this book are the result, therefore, of the hard work and experience of many hundreds of participants in Accenture's High Performance Business research initiative, conducted over nearly a decade.

The first effort at analysis stemmed from our recognition that performance is relative: high performance can be judged only against low performance. We therefore invested considerable time constructing peer sets of relevant competitors, a critical underpinning of our entire research project. Next, we knew we needed a rigorous approach to assessing performance, and after numerous iterations, we developed one that has withstood critical scrutiny. We then had to develop a comprehensive understanding of what makes high performers tick. How, in the end, do they do it? For this task, we turned to Accenture's expertise, partnered with the wisdom of external experts and, of course, the insights of our clients, for an industry-by-industry view of business performance. This knowledge led naturally enough to an interest in business functions, as we determined what is necessary for mastery in a range of functional areas as a condition for high performance. And finally, we recognized that our peer sets of global companies had by design left out important local or regional players whose lessons were also significant. Thus we also undertook a number of geography-based analyses of peer sets in an effort to take into account those more local companies.

What follows is a somewhat more expansive review of each of the five main sets of analysis we have conducted since 2003. We recognize, however, that any attempt to provide a comprehensive examination of our methods and research would quickly balloon to overwhelm the book itself—rather than a book about jumping the S-curve, we would have ended up with a tome about research methodology. Fortunately, in an era of online information, we are not strictly bound by page limits: we are able to point you toward many of the research reports and articles that reside on Accenture's portal, many written by us over the years, and many others by Accenture experts with a great range of industry and functional expertise. We invite you to review this work if you want a more complete look at what lies behind the ideas we discuss in this book.

(For more on our research and findings, please visit www .accenture.com/Global/High_Performance_Business/default.htm. For a complete list of our publications from our research, please visit www.accenture.com/Global/High_Performance_Business/

Research_and_Insights/High+Performance+Business+Research+ and+Conclusions+Complete+List.htm. And for a complete list of our high-performance articles published in *Outlook,* please visit www.accenture.com/Global/Research_and_Insights/Outlook/By_ Subject/High_Performance_Business/default.htm.)

1. DETERMINING THE RELEVANT COMPETITORS

Purpose

In this analysis, we aimed to assemble sets of logical competitors whose relative performance could reasonably be assessed.

Approach

Between the fall of 2003 and the spring of 2005, we constructed and then analyzed thirty-one industry peer groups (see figure A-1). These peer sets comprised more than eight hundred companies representing more than 80 percent of the Russell 3000's market capitalization. Companies from thirty-four countries representing all continents (except Antarctica!) were included, with over half based outside North America. Since then, we have updated many of the peer sets and constructed new ones, for a total of nearly one hundred sets.

The creation of such peer sets for so many companies is not an obvious task. Creating peer sets with the intention of understanding relative performance taught us an important lesson: if the peer set is changed—by, for example, our rejecting some competitors because they are too small or too big—performance almost inevitably changes as well. While creating the peer set for beverage companies, for example, we observed that alcoholic and nonalcoholic beverage makers have very different average profits. Therefore, we could not reasonably compare companies across these sets for strategic insights. Otherwise, we would have risked coming to the conclusion that to succeed, all beverage makers should become alcoholic beverage makers. In the chemical industry, we

FIGURE A-1

Original industry peer sets examined and select high performers featured in this book

Original thirty-one industry peer sets

Airlines	Household products	Retail: drug stores
Aerospace and defense	Hypermarkets	Retail: fashion apparel
Aluminum	Industrial equipment	Retail: home improvement/DIY
Automobile suppliers	Oil and gas: nonsupermajors	Semiconductors
Automotive OEM	Oil and gas: supermajors	Software
Beverages	Office electronics	Steel
Chemicals	Personal products	Telecommunications equipment
Computer and peripherals	Pharmaceuticals	Telecommunications wireline
Food products	Rail	Tobacco
Forest products	Retail: consumer electronics stores	Utilities
Hotels		

Select high-performance companies highlighted in book

3M	Harrah's Entertainment	Porsche Automobile Holding SE
Adobe Systems	The Home Depot	Procter & Gamble
Apple	Illinois Tool Works	Reckitt Benckiser Group
Avon Products	Intel	Ritz-Carlton Hotel Company
Best Buy	Kellogg	Samsung Electronics
Cisco System	Marriott International	Schlumberger Limited
Clorox	Nike	Southwest Airlines
Colgate-Palmolive	Nintendo	Target
Danaher	Nokia	Tesco
Four Seasons Hotels and Resorts	Nordstrom	Toyota Motor
Genentech	Novo Nordisk A/S	Walmart
General Electric	Pepsi	Whirlpool

saw a similar phenomenon. Chemical companies compete with different core strategies—for example, as commodity and specialty providers.

Great care and a good deal of judgment are needed to create peer sets that lead to relevant and appropriate comparisons of performance. Where many observers have gone wrong is in highlighting differential performance using flawed peer sets, which makes their conclusions of little value. To get it right, we relied on the expertise of many longtime Accenture professionals, and we considered external professional and standard industry groupings, as well as a variety of research methods for this effort. Relative size, marketplace strategies, risk profiles, and geographic influences were among the factors considered, and assessments were made industry by industry.

2. DETERMINING THE HIGH PERFORMERS

Purpose

In this analysis, the aim was to identify high-performance businesses through careful assessment of their performance over time, measured against the logical set of their competitors.

Approach

Within each peer set, we evaluated every company, using thirteen easily available financial metrics that capture five dimensions of business performance (see table A-1). The dimensions

TABLE A-1

How to determine high performance

High performance requires outperforming peers over economic and industry cycles, and changes in leadership. We identified five critical dimensions that reveal the true nature of a company's performance, and we further subdivided those into thirteen key metrics to get an accurate reading of its performance.

Critical dimension	Metrics
Profitability	• 3-year average spread • 7-year average spread
Growth	• 3-year revenue growth CAGR • 7-year revenue growth CAGR
Positioning for the future	• 7-year change in future value relative to invested capital • 7-year level of future value relative to invested capital
Longevity	• 10-year total return to shareholders CAGR • 7-year total return to shareholders CAGR • 5-year total return to shareholders CAGR • 3-year total return to shareholders CAGR
Consistency	• 7-year median outperformance in revenue growth • 7-year median outperformance in spread • 7-year median outperformance in future value

Note: CAGR is compound annual growth rate.

and metrics were selected through an extensive study of existing methods of business performance evaluation, coupled with the research and insights of Accenture experts, including members of our shareholder value analysis practice. That group of Accenture experts is dedicated to the evaluation of company performance through statistical and numerical analyses that help CEOs and CFOs identify hidden sources of value at the operational level. In this process, we maintained a delicate balance between simplicity and comprehensiveness.

Here are the five dimensions, with a brief rationale for their inclusion:

- **Profitability**—Profitability is a key intended outcome of business, and some measure of it is central to every company's performance. *Spread* measures a company's ability to generate returns on invested capital that are greater than the relevant cost of that capital.[1] Companies that can generate returns on invested capital greater than the cost of the capital have positive spreads and are creating value. Companies that have negative spreads are destroying value. High-performance companies must generate a positive spread. Our analysis looked at both three- and seven-year average spread performance. Each time frame was given equal weight and an individual grade.

- **Growth**—Growth in revenues is a key expected outcome of business performance. *Organic growth* signals the market appreciation for a company's offerings. *Inorganic growth* is regularly fueled by funds secured through the previous success of the company. High-performance companies can grow both organically and inorganically through strategic investments in M&A activity. Our analysis looked at both three- and seven-year revenue growth performance on a compound annual basis. Each time frame was given equal weight and an individual grade.

- **Positioning for the future**—To sustain performance over time, high performers must acquire the tangible and intangible assets necessary for both current and future growth, in both existing and yet-to-be-established businesses. These investments are valued by investors in what we term *future value*, the portion of share price that cannot be explained by current earnings. Future value is a measure of investors' expectations of the value of a company's cash-flow growth, calculated as the difference between the enterprise value (the market value of debt plus equity) and the current value of operations (the value of current profitability in perpetuity). [2]

  The investments required to achieve a higher future value can diminish short-term profitability and growth. Thus, we must calculate and consider future value alongside other financial measures. The metrics we use to measure positioning for the future reflect two levels of future value. The first is the absolute growth in future value for the individual company. It is measured by subtracting the average amount of future value in the three-year period that began seven years ago, from the average over the most recent three-year period, then dividing the result by the average invested capital for the seven-year period (to control for differing levels of invested capital). We do so to account for companies that over-invest for too little market expected return.[3] The second metric is the level of future value that has been created and maintained, measured as the seven-year average of future value divided by the invested capital (to control for differing levels of invested capital). Our analysis showed that in mature, low-growth, and capital-intensive industries, future value sometimes provides little information about a business's future. In these relatively few circumstances, which are verified quantitatively, alternative measures of investment for the future were used.

- **Longevity**—High performance requires a company to have outperformed its peer group over a substantial amount of time, across business, industry, and management cycles. The long-term value of profitable growth, coupled with positioning for the future, can be determined through total returns to shareholders (TRS), measured as share price appreciation, including dividends. TRS may be flawed in the short term, but over longer periods, it closely reflects a company's health and business performance and has the benefit of being consistently and easily measured across companies. Assessment of the compound annual growth rate (CAGR) of companies' TRS over multiple time periods—ten, seven, five, and three years—highlights the companies that have successfully delivered value, regardless of the secular trends in their industries.[4]

- **Consistency**—High performance is valuable only if it is the norm, and not an occasional occurrence. For this reason, high performers must be predictable and dependable in the way they outperform their peers. We measured consistency as the percentage of years over a seven-year period that the company has outperformed the median performance of its peer set in each of three of our measures: year-over-year revenue growth, annual spread, and annual average future value divided by the average invested capital.[5]

It became clear from our research that the use of simple cut-offs to pick the high performers—like top quartile or top five companies—would yield inconsistent results. Such approaches would sometimes have resulted in different rankings for companies with nearly identical performance.

Instead, our method grades companies on a curve in their industry, and only the businesses that significantly outperform their peer set are identified as high performers. To make such assessments, we classify a company's results within its peer group (sector) by means of a standard distribution. The performance of each company in each measure was judged by its standard deviation from the mean, and we assigned a letter grade for each portion of the bell curve (see figure A-2). This meant the quantity of each letter grade assigned, A through F, was not predetermined, but resulted from the distribution of the companies' performances in the peer set (the shape of the curve). To determine the overall high-performance score for each company, we calculated the unweighted average letter grade in each dimension and then calculated the unweighted average of the five letter grades from the five dimensions (to calculate the averages, we assigned numerical values to the letter grades, with A = 4 through F = 0). Those that average A or A– (and the rare B+) are judged to be high performers. This last choice may itself sound somewhat arbitrary, but there was very nearly always a break near the top that allowed us to separate the truly exceptional from the B and C players.

FIGURE A-2

Grading a company's business performance on a curve

We applied a normal distribution to the values of the performance metrics of the companies in our industry peer groups to determine their true level of high performance. Thus, we prevented the use of arbitrary cutoffs that limit high performers to a certain number, such as top ten or top quartile.

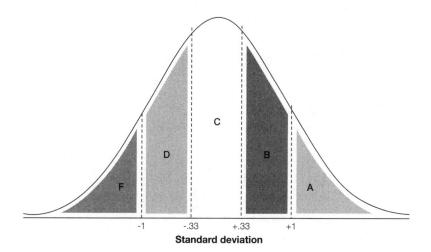

TABLE A-2

Sample high-performance scorecard

Example results

DETAILED SCORECARD FOOD PRODUCTS

PEER SET COMPANY	LONGEVITY				PROFITABILITY		GROWTH		FV		CONSISTENCY			AVERAGE SCORE
	3-yr TRS	5-yr TRS	7-yr TRS	10-yr TRS	3-yr Spread	7-yr Spread	3-yr rev. CAGR	7-yr rev. CAGR	Change	Level	Rev. growth	Spread	FV	
Company 1	B	B	B	B	A	A	B	B	B	A	A	A	A	A
Company 2	C	D	B	B	A	A	C	C	C	B	C	B	A	B
Company 3	A	A	A	A	B	C	D	D	B	C	D	D	A	B-
Company 4	B	B	B	D	C	C	C	C	B	C	C	A	A	B-
Company 5	C	C	B	C	D	C	B	B	B	C	A	D	B	B-
Company 6	B	B	A	C	C	C	C	C	B	D	A	D	C	B-
Company 7	A	A	A	B	F	F	A	A	B	A	B	F	F	B-
Company 8	F	F	F	F	A	A	C	D	F	A	D	A	A	C+
Company 9	B	A	A	A	D	D	C	B	B	D	C	F	F	C+
Company 10	C	D	F	D	B	B	C	D	F	C	F	A	A	C+
Company 11	D	D	D	D	C	C	C	D	C	C	D	B	B	C
Company 12	D	D	C	B	C	C	C	C	D	D	C	A	F	C
Company 13	C	A	D	F	F	F	A	A	C	D	B	F	F	C
Company 14	C	C	C	B	D	D	C	C	C	D	B	F	F	C
Company 15	C	D	C	B	C	D	D	D	C	D	F	D	D	C-
Company 16	D	F	D	D	D	C	D	D	B	D	F	C	D	C-
Company 17	F	D	D	C	C	D	F	F	D	D	F	B	D	D+
Company 18	D	C	D	D	D	D	F	F	B	D	D	F	D	D+
Company 19	F	F	D	F	F	D	D	F	F	F	D	F	F	D+

Note: FV is future value; TRS is total return to shareholders; rev. is revenue; CAGR is compound annual growth rate.

To test the robustness of this analysis, we also conducted analyses where we altered the weighting for each of the five categories, making each as much as 50 percent of the total (sensitivity analyses). Only on very rare occasions did such large changes of weighting have an effect on the high performers identified, and in those exceptional cases, we leaned toward inclusion.

After evaluating relative performance, we identified companies that met our strict definition of a high-performance business (see Table A-2, for example). Having identified the high performers, we then had to determine what accounted for the differences in relative performance within each peer set. This exercise has proceeded along two tracks: industry analyses and functional analyses.

3. DETERMINING THE DRIVERS AND ENABLERS OF HIGH PERFORMANCE

Purpose

In this analysis, our aim was to determine the differential strategies, actions, and organizational elements of the identified high performers that led to their differential performance.

Approach

More than three hundred people from Accenture's industry teams have been actively involved in Accenture's High Performance Business research initiative each year, with well more than a thousand individuals participating to date. In the past—and still today—these industry teams have conducted months of research using a wide range of approaches—from broad-based, in-depth executive surveys to deep statistical analyses on far more measures than named here, to determine the core drivers of differential performance within each industry peer set. The strategies and behaviors of low and average performers were evaluated as well, and where possible, failed companies remained in the evaluation sets throughout.

Of course, the effects studied and identified were not unique to high performers. In some cases, average and even low performers possess the traits we cite. But as success factors, they are overwhelmed in these companies by other negatives. This is why there is a consistency and connection among the traits we have identified. Of course, no one trait is enough to drive high performance, and merely moderate performance in an area or two will not doom a company to failure. It is in the broad and consistent application of these traits that high performance is delivered.

To better understand our industry-level analyses, it helps to read various individual reports on many of the industries studied. These reports have appeared in *Outlook,* Accenture's journal of business-thought leadership, and a few reports are listed here:

- Norbert Linn and Trevor J. Gruzin, "Banking: The Right Combination," June 2004, www.accenture.com/ Global/Research_and_Insights/Outlook/By_Alphabet/ TheRightCombination.htm

- Omar Abbosh, James C. Hendrickson, and Etienne Defarges, "Utilities: Power Plays," October 2004, www.accenture .com/Global/Research_And_Insights/Outlook/By_Alphabet/ powerplays.xml

- William N. Higbie, "Heath Care: Patient Power," October 2005, www.accenture.com/Global/Research_and_Insights/ Outlook/By_Issue/Y2005/PatientPower.htm

- John Jackson, Susan S. Mann, and John Zealley, "Consumer Packaged Goods: Cleaning Up," October 2005, www .accenture.com/Global/Research_and_Insights/Outlook/ By_Issue/Y2005/CleaningUp.htm

- John Jackson and C. Keith Barringer, "Alcoholic Beverages: Spirited Performance," May 2007, www.accenture.com/ Global/Research_and_Insights/Outlook/By_Issue/Y2007/ SpiritedPerformance.htm

- John Jackson, C. Keith Barringer, and Jan M. Mueller, "Packaged Goods and Nonalcoholic Beverages: Recipe for Success," May 2007, www.accenture.com/Global/Research_and_Insights/Outlook/By_Issue/Y2007/RecipeforSuccess.htm

- Kumu Puri, "Consumer Electronics: Competing for the Digital Consumer," May 2008, www.accenture.com/Global/Research_and_Insights/Outlook/By_Issue/Y2008/CompetingConsumer.htm

- David A. Rossi et al., "Forest Products: Out of the Woods?" May 2008, www.accenture.com/Global/Research_and_Insights/Outlook/By_Issue/Y2008/OutWoods.htm

Many other articles on industry-level analyses appear on Accenture's Web site.

After the initial industry analyses and determinations of performance drivers, these drivers were aggregated and analyzed across industries, leading to a hypothesis of the building blocks of high performance. Afterward, the building blocks and S-curve-jumping ideas and framework were brought back to the industry teams and tested in the field, through efforts that included interviews with executives at companies in our peer sets and interactions with companies through our global client work. The insights generated by these teams helped us to identify the three building blocks of scaling an S-curve, detailed in chapter 2 through chapter 4 of this book, and to flesh out the subcomponents of this foundation. The information from these teams also led us to the insights on how to jump to the next S-curve after scaling one.

4. FUNCTIONAL MASTERY ANALYSIS

Purpose

The purpose of this analysis was to determine the relative importance of business-function capabilities—in areas like supply-chain management, customer relationship management, and human capital development—in the creation of high performance.

Approach

Accenture's global service lines (our groups of professionals organized along functional areas, such as talent and organization performance, supply-chain management, customer relationship management, finance and performance management, process and innovation performance, and strategy) and cross-functional groups researched the contribution that mastery of functional capabilities in key functional areas makes to high-performance businesses. Each of these groups conducted extensive, detailed studies of a wide-ranging set of capabilities within its domain. As part of this research, Accenture's function-oriented teams conducted surveys across thousands of companies, resulting in the creation of a number of unparalleled benchmark data sets. These data sets helped us to analyze the value of capabilities at the level of the individual company.

To better understand our functional-level analyses, it helps again to read various individual reports that have appeared in *Outlook,* Accenture's journal of business-thought leadership. To name just a few:

- Marianne Seiler, Paul F. Nunes, and Jeffrey D. Somers, "Marketing Mastery Matters," May 2006, www.accenture.com/ Global/High_Performance_Business/Research_and_Insights/ MarketingMastery.htm

- James M. Benton, Susan Cantrell, and Meredith A. Vey, "Making the Right Investments in People," October 2004, www.accenture.com/Global/Research_and_Insights/ Outlook/By_Alphabet/MakingPeople.htm

- "High Performance IT," Web page pointing to IT articles, www.accenture.com/Global/Research_and_Insights/By _Role/HighPerformance_IT/default.htm

Many other reports on functional-level analyses appear on Accenture's Web site.

5. GEOGRAPHY-BASED PEER SET ANALYSES

Purpose

In these analyses, the goal was to evaluate and determine the drivers of high performance in competitor peer sets that are not dominated by global players.

Approach

In 2005, Accenture began the analysis of geography-based peer sets for countries like China as well as for regions like the Nordic countries. In some industries, these geographies have markets that are dominated by local players (though some may also participate in global markets). It is therefore important to understand the competitive strategies and the drivers of high performance within the geographic area. For example, Accenture recently conducted a sizable study of German companies in six industries, which we analyzed relative to their European peers and which totaled 350 companies. Teams have also completed repeated studies of companies in multiple industries in the Netherlands and Belgium. All these analyses were carefully constructed to ensure that (1) only industries served by a significant number of companies not in our global peer sets were assessed (that is, only where there was an important and flourishing regional marketplace) and (2) the regional industry selected was not dominated by a very high market share of international competitors. After conducting each of these analyses, we then compared the performance of the geography-based peer sets with the performance of the global peer sets to gain a regional or national perspective of high performance. These regional findings have been an essential component of our overall insights into high performance.

Individual reports on many of these geography-based studies have been published. To cite just a couple:

- Gong Li, Andrew Sleigh, and Paul F. Nunes, "China Rising," May 2008, www.accenture.com/Global/Research_and _Insights/Outlook/By_Issue/Y2008/ChinaRising.htm

- Gong Li, Andrew Sleigh, and Paul F. Nunes, "A Tale of Two Chinas," June 2009, www.accenture.com/Global/Research _and_Insights/Outlook/By_Issue/Y2009/TaleChinas.htm

Other geography-based analyses of business performance appear on Accenture's Web site.

THE RESEARCH CONTINUES

Perhaps this statement comes under the category of "needless to say," but we're not finished researching business performance. There will always be new topics that require exploring, new business successes that astound, and old conundrums that may finally yield themselves to better analysis or to clever and insightful metrics. Recently, for example, we've been concentrating on developing diagnostics to measure such traditionally "soft" management areas as employee engagement and cultural cohesion. Our goal in these cases is to obtain an even firmer grasp of what makes for "a worthy company."

Or take another subject that suddenly dominated every management thinker's radar screen a couple of years ago: risk. In light of the rather shocking downturn that began in 2008, we had to carefully evaluate how our high performers had weathered the storm, and to carefully examine the way companies need to manage risk in the future. (For more on how companies effectively manage their risk-bearing capacity, see "It's All about Balance," by Bill Spinard and his colleagues, at www.accenture.com/Global/ Research_and_Insights/Outlook/outlook-journal-2010-balance-risk.htm.)

And this brings us back to where we started, to bring home our final point. While we discovered that many of the companies we had identified as high performers did take a significant hit during the recent downturn, nearly all have made a significant recovery since. High performance, while never assured or certain, is, after all, about the long term—strategies, capabilities, and culture that hold strong, regardless of the circumstances. Thus, even as our research continues to evolve, we are confident that the principles we have laid out—for climbing, and then for jumping, the S-curve—will endure.

NOTES

CHAPTER 1

1. Leslie Helm, "TV Maker Fades to Black; Zenith to Sell Majority Stake to S. Korean Conglomerate," *Los Angeles Times*, July 18, 1995, D-1.

2. Alfred D. Chandler Jr., *Inventing the Electronic Century: The Epic Story of the Consumer Electronics and Computer Industries* (New York: Free Press, 2001), 32.

3. Maurice Bamfather, "Method in the Madness," *Forbes*, July 5, 1982, 85.

4. Eben Shapiro, "Zenith Bets the Store on New TV," *New York Times*, March 10, 1990, section 1, 31.

5. Frederick H. Lowe, "Why LG Went After Zenith: Control of HDTV Was a Key Issue," *Chicago Sun-Times*, July 21, 1995, 35.

CHAPTER 2

1. Lars Rebien Sorensen, quoted in Wayne Koberstein, "Knowing Its Niche," *Pharmaceutical Executive* 19, no. 10 (October 1999): 44–58.

2. Ibid.

3. Measured by volume, from Novo Nordisk Annual Report 2008.

4. Jonathan V. Last, "How Everybody Got Game: Videogames, Ever More Easily Learnable, Are No Longer the Special Province of Male Adolescents and Twentysomethings," *Wall Street Journal*, December 15, 2009.

5. Tesco, "Talking Tesco: Competition Commission—Listening," www.tesco .com/talkingtesco/listening/.

6. Fiona Briggs, "Tesco Drives Growth Through Innovation," *Talking Retail*, June 1, 2007.

7. "Simon Uwins: Chief Marketing Officer, Fresh & Easy Neighborhood Market, Subsidiary of Tesco PLC," *Mass Market Retailer* 25, no. 17 (October 20, 2008): 100.

8. A. G. Lafley and Ram Charan, *The Game-Changer: How You Can Drive Revenue and Profit Growth with Innovation* (New York: Crown Business, 2008): 48, 96.

9. Jeffrey R. Immelt, Vijay Govindarajan, and Chris Trimble, "How GE Is Disrupting Itself," *Harvard Business Review*, October 2009, 56–65.

10. Josh Bernoff and Charlene Li, "Harnessing the Power of the Oh-So-Social Web," *MIT Sloan Management Review* (spring 2008): 36–42.

11. Ibid.

12. Cushing Anderson and Ali Zaidi, "Leveraging Companywide Innovation with SOA: The Wells Fargo Case Study," buyer case study 214128, IDC, Framingham, MA, September 2008.

13. Teresa Watanabe, "Yukiyasu Togo: The President of Toyota USA Learns How the Locals Think by Diving into the Culture," *Los Angeles Times*, February 11, 1991; and Doron P. Levin, "Too American for Its Own Good?" *New York Times*, October 27, 1991.

14. Jeffrey K. Liker, *The Toyota Way: 14 Management Principles from the World's Greatest Manufacturer* (New York: McGraw-Hill, 2003), 43.

15. Jim Henry, "Lexus Was High-Stakes Gamble That Paid Off Big: Eiji Toyoda Decides to Let the Americans Create a New Premium Brand," *Automotive News*, October 29, 2007.

16. Ibid.

17. Liker, *The Toyota Way*, 44.

18. The Auto Channel, "Toyota Mourns Former Executive Yukiyasu Togo," July 25, 2000, www.theautochannel.com/news/press/date/20000724/press021300.html.

19. Gerard J. Tellis and Peter N. Golder, "First to Market, First to Fail? Real Causes of Enduring Market Leadership," *MIT Sloan Management Review* (winter 1996): 65–75.

20. Ibid.

21. Liker, *The Toyota Way*, 52.

22. Andrew Pollack, "Honda Insight; High-Mileage, High-Stakes Hybrid," *New York Times*, June 4, 2000; and Dan Lienert, "Honda Insight Vs. Toyota Prius," *Forbes*, February 2, 2005.

23. Liker, *The Toyota Way*, 60.

24. Micheline Maynard, "Say 'Hybrid' and Many People Will Hear 'Prius,'" *New York Times*, July 4, 2007.

25. David Magee, *How Toyota Became #1: Leadership Lessons from the World's Greatest Car Company* (New York: Portfolio, 2007), 109.

26. Ibid., 220.

27. Masami Takimoto, quoted in Peter Fairley, "Inside Toyota's R&D Strategy: A Veteran Describes Multiple Research Efforts on Clean Vehicles," *Technology Review*, March 16, 2009.

28. Henry W. Chesbrough, *Open Innovation: The New Imperative for Creating and Profiting from Technology* (Boston: Harvard Business School Press, 2003).

29. Henry W. Chesbrough, "The Era of Open Innovation," *MIT Sloan Management Review* (spring 2003): 35–41.

30. Genentech Web site, www.gene.com/gene/index.jsp.

31. Bill Trombetta, "Industry Audit 2009," *Pharmaceutical Executive*, September 1, 2009.

32. Genentech, "Horizon 2010: Corporate Overview," Web page, www.gene.com/gene/about/corporate/growthstrategy/mission.html.

33. David Stipp, "How Genentech Got It," *Fortune*, June 9, 2003.

34. Gene Marcial, "Why Genentech Is the Biotech of Choice," *BusinessWeek*, June 16, 2008.

35. Genentech, "Genentech Early Development Pipeline," online summary page, April 15, 2010, www.gene.com/gene/pipeline/pdf/early-pipeline.pdf.

36. Genentech, "Roche Group Early-Stage Development Pipeline," online summary page, April 15, 2010, www.gene.com/gene/pipeline/pdf/roche_group_pipeline.pdf.

37. Miranda Hitti, "FDA OKs Avastin for Glioblastoma: FDA Approves Avastin to Treat the Brain Cancer Glioblastoma That Progresses Despite Other Treatment," *WebMD Health News*, May 6, 2009, www.webmd.com/cancer/brain-cancer/news/20090506/fda-oks-avastin-for-glioblastoma.

38. Arlene Weintraub, "Genentech's Gamble: Behind the Biotech Pioneer's Quest to Conquer Autoimmune Disease," *BusinessWeek*, December 5, 2007.

39. Genentech, "Rituxan RA Fact Sheet," Web page, www.gene.com/gene/products/information/immunological/rituxan/factsheet.html.

40. Sydney Finkelstein and Shade H. Sanford, "Learning from Corporate Mistakes: The Rise and Fall of Iridium," *Organizational Dynamics* 29, no. 2 (2000): 138–148.

41. Max Jarman, "Iridium Satellite Phones Second Life," *Arizona Republic*, February 1, 2009.

42. Robert Swan, quoted in Linda Himelstein with Gerry Khermouch, "Webvan Left the Basics on the Shelf," *BusinessWeek*, July 23, 2001.

CHAPTER 3

1. Steven Prokesch, "People Express: A Case Study; Can Don Burr Go Back to the Future?" *New York Times*, July 6, 1986.

2. Paul Stephen Dempsey, "Prepared Testimony of Paul Stephen Dempsey Before the House Committee on Transportation and Infrastructure Aviation Subcommittee," Federal News Service, June 15, 2000.

3. For lost sales figures, see David Welch, "Oh, What a (Hideous) Feeling," *BusinessWeek*, February 15, 2010, 21–22.

4. Andrew Clark, "Toyota Boss Akio Toyoda Apologizes Ahead of U.S. Grilling," *Guardian Unlimited*, February 23, 2010.

5. Norihiko Shirouzu, Mariko Sanchanta, and Yoshio Takahashi, "Toyota Sales Halt Raises Quality Questions," *Wall Street Journal*, January 27, 2010.

6. Paul Indrassia, "Toyota: Too Big, Too Fast," *Wall Street Journal*, January 28, 2009.

7. George Kacher, quoted in Alex Taylor III, "Porsche's Risky Recipe: Wendelin Wiedeking Has Produced Higher Profits for Nine Straight Years; But Will the Spicy New Cayenne SUV Give Tradition-Minded Customers Heartburn?" *Fortune*, February 17, 2003.

8. Alex Taylor III, "Can You Believe Porsche Is Putting Its Badge on This Car? Believe It! With Sales of Its Sports Cars Zooming, Porsche Wants to Cash in on the Sport-Utility Phenomenon. Traditionalists Are Horrified," *Fortune*, February 19, 2001.

9. Chris Poole, "2010 Porsche Cayenne S Hybrid Review and Prices," Consumer Guide Auto, http://consumerguideauto.howstuffworks.com/2010-porsche-cayenne-hybrid.htm.

10. Paul Sonne, "Product Tweaks Power Reckitt," *Wall Street Journal*, February 11, 2010.

11. Jeffrey K. Liker, *The Toyota Way: 14 Management Principles from the World's Greatest Manufacturer* (New York City: McGraw-Hill, 2004), 47.

12. Chester Dawson, *Lexus: The Relentless Pursuit* (Singapore: John Wiley & Sons (Asia) Pte Ltd, 2004), 69.

13. Jack Ewing with Moon Ihlwan, "Staying Cool at Nokia: How New Design Chief Alastair Curtis Keeps the Hot Handsets Coming," *BusinessWeek*, July 17, 2006, 62.

14. Reena Jana, "Innovation Trickles in a New Direction," *BusinessWeek*, March 11, 2009.

15. Sara Corbett, "Can the Cellphone Help End Global Poverty?" *New York Times* Magazine, April 13, 2008.

16. Jim Kittridge, quoted in Charles J. Murray, "Cisco TelePresence Launches New Era of Video Conferencing," *Design News*, October 22, 2007.

17. Bart Becht, quoted in "Picking Winners at Reckitt Benckiser," *Outlook* (Accenture) 2005, no. 3 (2005): 37–41.

18. Navi Radjou, quoted in C. J. Prince, "Game-Changing R&D," *Chief Executive*, June 2007, 46.

19. Thomas B. Lawrence, Eric A. Morse, and Sally W. Fowler, "Managing Your Portfolio of Connections," *MIT Sloan Management Review* (winter 2005): 59–65.

20. John Gartner, "The Starving Actor: Why TiVo Has Never Turned a Profit," *Technology Review* 108, no. 9 (2005): 36–38.

21. Ibid.

22. Vijay Govindarajan and Julie B. Lang, "Wal-Mart Stores, Inc.," Case 2-0013 (Hanover, NH: Tuck School of Business at Dartmouth, 2002).

23. Tom Dellner, "Cover Story: A Makeover for Avon," *Electronic Retailer*, March 2009.

24. Katrina Brooker, "It Took a Lady to Save Avon: Elegant and Poised, with a Will of Iron, Andrea Jung Knows How to Win," *Fortune*, October 15, 2001.

25. Poole, "2010 Porsche Cayenne S Hybrid."

26. Andy Serwer, "The Hole Story: How Krispy Kreme Became the Hottest Brand in America," *Fortune*, July 7, 2003.

27. Melanie Shanley, "Batting for Krispy Kreme: Celebrity Franchisees," *Fortune*, July 7, 2003.

28. Melanie Warner, "Krispy Kreme Tumbles into the Red," *New York Times*, November 23, 2004.

29. "A Manager's Guide to Human Irrationalities," *MIT Sloan Management Review* (winter 2009): 53–59.

30. Chris Zook and James Allen, "Growth Outside the Core," *Harvard Business Review*, December 2003, 66–73.

31. Frank Ptak, quote in Tim Stevens, "Breaking Up Is Profitable to Do," *Industry Week*, June 21, 1999, 28–32.

32. Illinois Tool Works, 10-K Report (Glenview, IL: Illinois Tool Works, 2007), 10.

33. Thomas H. Davenport, Jeanne Harris, and Ajay Kohli, "How Do They Know Their Customers So Well?" *MIT Sloan Management Review* (winter 2001).

34. Jonathan Fahey, "The Lexus Nexus," *Forbes*, June 21, 2004.

35. Dawson, *Lexus*, 124.

36. Ibid., 140.

37. Ibid., 121.

38. Martin Peers, "iPhone Is at the Core of Apple," *Wall Street Journal*, January 27, 2010.

39. David Harding, Sam Rovit, and Catherine Lemire, "Staying Cool When Deal Pressures Mount," *Mergers & Acquisitions* 39, no. 12 (2004).

40. Nanette Byrnes et al., "Branding: Five New Lessons," *BusinessWeek*, February 14, 2005.

CHAPTER 4

1. "Interview with Gordon E. Moore," March 3, 1995; available at http://www-sul.stanford.edu/depts/hasrg/histsci/silicongenesis/moore-ntb.html.

2. S. Eric Bartz, quoted in Nanette Byrnes and Amy Barrett, "Star Search: How to Recruit, Train, and Hold on to Great People; What Works, What Doesn't," *BusinessWeek*, October 10, 2005.

3. Elizabeth Craig, Jeanne G. Harris, and Henry Egan, "How to Engage and Retain Analytical Talent" research report (January 2010). Available at http://www .accenture.com/NR/rdonlyres/E6DB36D5-D333-4318-A839-FD6A6208C19B/0/ Accenture_How_to_Engage_and_Retain_Analytical_Talent.pdf.

4. Brian Hindo, "A Dynamo Called Danaher: The Rales Brothers' Sprawling Conglomerate Makes Everything—Especially Money," *BusinessWeek*, February 19, 2007.

5. Julia Kirby, "Reinvention with Respect: An Interview with Jim Kelly of UPS," *Harvard Business Review*, November 2001, 72–79.

6. A. G. Lafley and Ram Charan, *The Game-Changer: How You Can Drive Revenue and Profit Growth with Innovation* (New York: Crown Business, 2008), 272–275.

7. Jeff Frazier and Tanya Lewis, "Office Party," *Medical Marketing & Media* 43, no. 9 (September 2008): 68.

8. Byrnes and Barrett, "Star Search."

9. Lesley Kump, "Teaching the Teachers: Best Buy Keeps Its Sales Humming by Making Sure Its Sales Force Is Well Trained," *Forbes*, December 12, 2005, 115.

10. Amy Joyce, "Circuit City's Job Cuts Backfiring, Analysts Say," *Washington Post*, May 2, 2007.

11. Phil Thomas, quoted in Amy Golding, "Cutting to the Chase," *Marketing*, August 12, 2009.

12. Dave Barnes and Thomas Wailgum, "Nothing Succeeds Like Succession: New UPS CIO Dave Barnes Is the Latest Product of a Culture That Values Succession Planning," *CIO* 18, no. 14 (May 2005): 1.

13. Elizabeth Craig, John R. Kimberly, and Peter Cheese, "How to Keep Your Best Executives," *Wall Street Journal*, October 26, 2009. See also Elizabeth Craig, Chi T. Pham, and Sarah Bobulsky, "Rethinking Retention: If You Want Your Best Executives to Stay, Equip Them to Leave," research report, Accenture Institute for High Performance, June 2008.

14. Lea Myyrylainen, quoted in Robert Levering and Milton Moskowitz, "Best Companies to Work For: 10 Great Companies in Europe," *Fortune Europe*, February 4, 2002, 30.

15. Haig R. Nalbantian and Richard A. Guzzo, "Making Mobility Matter," *Harvard Business Review*, March 2009, 76–84.

16. Mike Eskew, quoted in Barnes and Wailgum, "Nothing Succeeds Like Succession," 1.

17. Donald N. Sull, "Managing by Commitments," *Harvard Business Review*, June 2003, 82–91.

18. Ellen Galinsky, quoted in Patrick J. Kiger, "Flexibility to the Fullest: Throwing Out the Rules of Work; Best Buy Frees Corporate Employees to Work Wherever They Want, Whenever They Want—As Long As They Reel in Results," *Workforce Management*, September 25, 2006, 1.

19. Cali Ressler, quoted in ibid.

20. Peter Cheese, Robert J. Thomas, and Elizabeth Craig, *The Talent Powered Organization: Strategies for Globalization, Talent Management and High Performance* (London: Kogan Page, 2008), 168–169.

21. Frank Jossi, "Clocking Out," *HR Magazine*, June 2007, 46.

22. Jody Thompson, quoted in ibid.

23. John Moynihan, quoted in ibid.

24. Cal Darden, "Focus First on People," *Leadership Excellence*, March 1, 2005, 8.

25. Ibid.

26. Wendy Cooper. "A Philosophical Approach to High Performance," *Outlook* (Accenture) 2006, no. 1 (2006): 20–25.

27. Frazier and Lewis, "Office Party."

28. Robert J. Thomas, Jane C. Linder, and Ana Dutra, "Inside the Values-Driven Culture at UPS," *Outlook* (Accenture) 2006, no. 3 (2006): 18–29.

29. Jeff Frazier, quoted in Frazier and Lewis, "Office Party."

30. Jim Kelly, quoted in Kirby, "Reinvention with Respect."

31. Kirby, "Reinvention with Respect."

32. Byrnes and Barrett. "Star Search."

33. Robert J. Thomas, "Crucibles of Leadership Development," *MIT Sloan Management Review* (spring 2008): 15–18.

34. Charles D. Ellis, *The Partnership: The Making of Goldman Sachs* (New York: Penguin, 2008).

35. H. Lawrence Culp Jr., quoted in Cooper, "A Philosophical Approach to High Performance."

36. James Bowman, *Honor: A History* (New York: Encounter Books, 2006), 44.

37. H. Lawrence Culp Jr., quoted in Brian Hindo, "A Dynamo Called Danaher."

38. Kirby, "Reinvention with Respect."

39. Dave Barnes, quoted in Thomas, Linder, and Dutra, "Inside the Values-Driven Culture at UPS."

40. Jeffrey K. Liker, *The Toyota Way: 14 Management Principles from the World's Greatest Manufacturer* (New York: McGraw-Hill, 2004), 47–50.

41. Edward E. Lawler III, *Talent: Making People Your Competitive Advantage* (New York: John Wiley & Sons, 2008), 213.

42. Levering and Moskowitz, "Best Companies to Work For."

43. Jena McGregor, "Breeding Grounds for New CEOs," *BusinessWeek*, April 30, 2009.

44. Phil Thomas, quoted in Golding, "Cutting to the Chase."

45. Byrnes and Barrett, "Star Search."

CHAPTER 5

1. Melissa Allison, "Starbucks Aims for Growth, But Not Seven New Stores a Day," *Seattle Times*, May 17, 2010, available at http://seattletimes.nwsource.com/html/coffeecity/2011886583_starbucks_aims_for_new_growth.html.

2. Tony Dokoupil, "Is the Mall Dead?" *Newsweek*, November 12, 2008; Kris Hudson and Vanessa O'Connell, "Recession Turns Malls into Ghost Towns," *Wall Street Journal*, May 22, 2009.

3. Brad Stone, "Amid the Gloom, an E-Commerce War," *New York Times*, October 11, 2008.

4. Matthew Olson and Derek Van Bever, *Stall Points: Most Companies Stop Growing—Yours Doesn't Have To* (New Haven, CT: Yale University Press, 2008), 28.

5. Chris Zook, *Unstoppable: Finding Hidden Assets to Renew the Core and Fuel Profitable Growth* (Boston: Harvard Business School Press, 2007), 40.

6. Jim Collins, *How the Mighty Fall: And Why Some Companies Never Give In* (Boulder, CO, 2009).

7. Olson and Van Bever, *Stall Points*, 28.

8. Ibid., 36.

9. "Corporate Facts: Walmart by the Numbers" (March 2010), available at http://walmartstores.com/pressroom/FactSheets/.

10. Based on Accenture research on *Fortune* Global 500 data, conducted in 2010 for this book.

11. Jim Collins, *Good to Great: Why Some Companies Make the Leap and Others Don't* (New York: Harper Collins, 2001).

12. Relevant works include Jack Welch with John A. Byrne, *Jack: Straight from the Gut* (New York: Business Plus, 2001); Jack Welch with Suzy Welch, *Winning* (New York: HarperBusiness, 2005); Dave Ulrich and Steve Kerr, *The GE Work-Out: How to Implement GE's Revolutionary Method for Busting Bureaucracy & Attacking Organizational Problems—Fast!* (New York: McGraw-Hill, 2002); and David Magee, *Jeff Immelt and the New GE Way* (New York: McGraw-Hill, 2009).

13. Wikipedia contributors, "List of Acquisitions by Nokia," Wikipedia, May 8, 2010, http://en.wikipedia.org/wiki/List_of_acquisitions_by_Nokia.

14. "Transfer of Nokia's Line Fit Automotive Business to Novero GmbH Completed," *PR Newswire*, June 16, 2008.

15. Reuters, "Illinois Tool Says to Divest Two Businesses," Reuters Web site, August 12, 2006, http://uk.reuters.com/article/idUKN1134418820080812.

16. Adam Penenberg, "All Eyes on Apple," *Fast Company*, December 2007.

17. Steve Hamm and William C. Symonds, "Kodak: Mistakes Made on the Road to Innovation," *BusinessWeek*, September 14, 2007.

18. Michael Lewis, *Moneyball: The Art of Winning an Unfair Game* (New York: W.W. Norton and Company, 2004).

19. Christopher Rhoads, "Motorola Looks Past the Razr," Associated Press Financial Wire, April 27, 2007; Motorola, Inc., Annual Report (Schaumburg, IL: Motorola, Inc., 2005, 2006).

20. Motorola, Inc., Annual Report (Schaumburg, IL: Motorola, Inc., 2007, 2008).

21. Rhoads, "Motorola Looks Past the Razr."

CHAPTER 6

1. Timothy J. Mullaney, "Netflix: The Mail-Order Movie House That Clobbered Blockbuster," *BusinessWeek*, May 25, 2006.

2. Daniel Kadlec, Andrew Keith, and Aixa M. Pascual, "How Blockbuster Changed the Rules," *Time*, August 3, 1998.

3. Bala Chakravarthy and Peter Lorange, "Continuous Renewal, and How Best Buy Did It," *Strategy & Leadership* 35, no. 6 (2007): 4.

4. Ranjay Gulati, *Reorganize for Resilience: Putting Customers at the Center of Your Business* (Boston: Harvard Business Press, 2009).

5. Eric von Hippel, Stefan Thomke, and Mary Sonnack, "Creating Breakthroughs at 3M," *Harvard Business Review*, September–October 1999, 46–57.

6. Debra M. Amidon, "Knowledge Zones Fueling Innovation Worldwide," *Research Technology Management* 48, no. 1 (2005): 6.

7. Soren Skovlund, "Diabetes Attitudes, Wishes, and Needs," *Diabetes' Voice* 49, special issue (2004): 4–11.

8. Guido Jouret, "Inside Cisco's Search for the Next Big Idea," *Harvard Business Review*, September 2009, 43–45.

9. Ibid.

10. Cornelia Dean, "If You Have a Problem, Ask Everyone," *New York Times*, July 22, 2008.

11. Kevin C. Desouza et al., "Crafting Organizational Innovation Processes," *Innovation: Management, Policy & Practice* 11, no. 1 (2009): 6.

12. Mary Tripsas, "Seeing Customers as Partners in Invention," *New York Times*, December 27, 2009, Business Section, 3.

13. Thomas H. Davenport and Jeanne G. Harris, "What People Want (and How to Predict It)," *MIT Sloan Management Review* (winter 2009): 23–31.

14. "Jeff Bezos: 'Blind-Alley' Explorer," *BusinessWeek*, August 19, 2004.

15. Brad Stone, "Amid the Gloom, an E-Commerce War," *New York Times*, October 12, 2008.

16. Interview with Erik Brynjolfsson in Michael S. Hopkins, "The Four Ways IT Is Revolutionizing Innovation," *MIT Sloan Management Review* 51, no. 3 (spring 2010): 51–56.

17. Gary Loveman, quoted in Erik Brynjolfsson and Michael Schrage, "The New, Faster Face of Innovation," *Wall Street Journal*, August 17, 2009.

18. A. G. Lafley, quoted in J. P. Donlon, "Lafley's Law: If You Want to Win Become a Game-Changer," *Chief Executive*, July–August 2008, 48.

19. Nancy Snyder, quoted in Ann Pomeroy, "Cooking Up Innovation," *HR Magazine*, November 1, 2004, 46.

20. Vijay Govindarajan, quoted in Reena Jana, "P&G's Trickle-Up Success: Sweet as Honey," *BusinessWeek*, March 31, 2009.

21. Brad Anderson, quoted in Matthew Boyle, "Q&A with Best Buy CEO Brad Anderson," *Fortune*, April 30, 2007.

22. John Chambers, quoted in Venkat Ramaswamy, "Competing Through Co-Creation: Innovation at Two Companies," *Strategy & Leadership* 38, no. 2 (2010): 22.

23. Bart Becht, "Building a Company Without Borders," *Harvard Business Review*, April 2010, 103–106.

24. Ibid.

25. Ibid.

26. Lee Kun-hee, quoted in "Return of the Overlord: South Korea's Industrial Giants," *Economist*, April 3, 2010.

27. For more on chief strategy officers, see R. Timothy S. Breene, Paul F. Nunes, Walter E. Shill, "The Chief Strategy Officer," *Harvard Business Review*, October, 2007, 84–93.

28. Ben Worthern, "Seeking Growth, Cisco Reroutes Decisions," *Wall Street Journal*, August 6, 2009.

29. George Buckley, quoted in Brian Hindo, "At 3M, a Struggle Between Efficiency and Creativity," *BusinessWeek*, June 11, 2007.

CHAPTER 7

1. Charles Stein, "A High-Tech David Faltered as Goliath," *Boston Globe*, November 27, 1989, Business Section, 1.

2. Ibid.

3. Jon Fortt, "New Adobe CEO Faces Web Challenge," *Big Tech*, November 14, 2007, available at http://tech.fortune.cnn.com/2007/11/14/new-adobe-ceo-faces-web-challenge/.

4. David Yoffie, quoted in G. Pascal Zachary, "How Intel Grooms Its Leaders," *Business 2.0*, July 2004, 43–45.

5. Kim Gerard, "Succession in the Valley," *Chief Executive*, June 1, 2005, 44.

6. Ellen McGirt, "Intel Risks It All (Again)," *Fast Company*, November 2009, 88.

7. Zachary, "How Intel Grooms Its Leaders."

8. "Succession Screw-ups: It Matters How Companies Pick—or Don't Pick—Their Next Boss," *BusinessWeek*, January 10, 2005, 84.

9. Ram Charan, "Ending the CEO Succession Crisis," *Harvard Business Review*, February 2005, 72–81.

10. Betsy Morris, "The Pepsi Challenge," *Fortune*, March 3, 2008, 54.

11. Mark Hurd, quoted in Adam Lashinsky, "The Hurd Way," *Fortune*, April 17, 2006, 92.

12. Bruce Chizen, quoted in Fortt, "New Adobe CEO Faces Web Challenge."

13. Suman Layak, "The Bombay House Shuffle," *Business Today*, November 1, 2009.

14. Brotin Banerjee, quoted in "Tata Companies: Young CEOs Occupy Drivers' Seat," *Daily the Pak Banker*, November 13, 2009.

15. Quentin Hardy, "Hewlett-Packard's Mark Hurd: He Wants It All," *Forbes*, April 12, 2010, 74.

16. George Buckley, quoted in "When Leaders Seek Leaders," *Chief Executive*, January–February 2009.

17. Ron Whittier, quoted in John H. Sheridan, "Andy Grove: Building an Information Age Legacy," *IndustryWeek*, December 15, 1997.

18. Bruce Chizen, "Decisions: Bruce Chizen Adobe Systems," *Management Today*, May 1, 2005, 26.

19. Ruth Wageman et al., "The Structure of Success," *Associations Now*, January 2008.

20. Ruth Wageman et al., "Behind the Seniors," *People Management*, January 10, 2008.

21. Ibid.

22. Ibid.

23. John Chambers, quoted in Ben Worthern, "Cisco CEO John Chambers's Big Management Experiment," *Wall Street Journal*, August 5, 2009.

24. Ben Worthen, "Seeking Growth, Cisco Reroutes Decisions," *Wall Street Journal*, August 6, 2009.

25. Worthen, "Cisco CEO John Chambers's Big Management Experiment."

26. Michael C. Mankins, "Stop Wasting Valuable Time," *Harvard Business Review*, September 2004, 58–65.

27. Ibid.

28. Jarkko Sairanen, quoted in Yves L. Doz and Mikko Kosonen, "The New Deal at the Top," *Harvard Business Review*, June 2007, 98–104.

29. Thomas Wailgum, "Nothing Succeeds Like Succession: New UPS CIO Dave Barnes Is the Latest Product of a Culture That Values Succession Planning," *CIO*, May 1, 2005, 1.

30. Donald N. Sull and Dominic Houlder, "How Companies Can Avoid a Midlife Crisis," *MIT Sloan Management Review* (fall 2006): 26–34.

31. Wageman et al., "Behind the Seniors."

CHAPTER 8

1. Leslie Haines, "Industry Gearing Up for Coming 'Crew Change,'" *Oil & Gas Investor* 25, no. 8 (August 1, 2005): 38.

2. Nanette Byrnes and Amy Barrett, "Star Search: How to Recruit, Train, and Hold on to Great People; What Works, What Doesn't," *BusinessWeek*, October 10, 2005.

3. David Magee, *Jeff Immelt and the New GE Way* (New York: McGraw Hill, 2009), 78.

4. Colleen Barrett, quoted in J. P. Donlon, "Air Herb's Secret Weapon," *Chief Executive*, July–August 1999.

5. Though privately held, the size and historical success of the Four Seasons Hotels and Resorts led to their assessment in our Hotels and Resorts peer set.

6. Isadore Sharp, quoted in Jeffrey M. O'Brien, "A Perfect Season," *Fortune*, February 4, 2008, 62.

7. O'Brien, "A Perfect Season."

8. Reckitt Benckiser, "Virtual Career Game," Web page, www.rb.com/careers/virtual-career; and Reckitt Benckiser, "Life at Reckitt Benckiser," Web page, www.rb.com/careers/right-for-you.

9. O'Brien, "A Perfect Season."

10. Douglas A. Ready and Jay A. Conger, "Make Your Company a Talent Factory," *Harvard Business Review*, June 2007, 68–77.

11. Gary Hamel, "Break Free!" *Fortune*, September 19, 2007.

12. Tony Hsieh, "Opinion: Your Culture Is Your Brand," *Brandweek*, June 8, 2010, www.brandweek.com/bw/content_display/news-and-features/retail-restaurants/e3i81776746af85635377b6c387a8478e7f.

13. Robert Thomas, *Crucibles of Leadership: How to Learn from Experience to Become a Great Leader* (Boston: Harvard Business Press, 2008).

14. A. G. Lafley, quoted in Geoff Colvin, "How Top Companies Breed Stars," *Fortune*, September 20, 2007, available at http://money.cnn.com/magazines/fortune/fortune_archive/2007/10/01/100351829/index.htm.

15. Colvin, "How Top Companies Breed Stars."

16. Igor Reichlin, "Best 20 Companies for Leaders: Getting the Global Views," *Chief Executive*, October 2004.

17. Thomas Wailgum, "Nothing Succeeds Like Succession: New UPS CIO Dave Barnes Is the Latest Product of a Culture That Values Succession Planning," *CIO* 18, no. 14 (2005): 1.

18. Ibid.

19. Frank Ptak, quoted in Tim Stevens, "Breaking Up Is Profitable to Do," *Industry Week* 248, no. 12 (1999): 28–32.

20. Ibid.

21. Ibid.

22. A. G. Lafley and Ram Charan, *The Game-Changer: How You Can Drive Revenue and Profit Growth with Innovation* (New York: Crown Business, 2008), 210.

23. Jon Younger, Norm Smallwood, and Dave Ulrich, "Developing Your Organization's Brand as a Talent Developer," *Human Resource Planning* 30, no. 2 (2007): 21.

24. Jenn Abelson, "'Proctoids'? Shaving Company's Ranks May Clash with New Culture," *Boston Globe*, June 12, 2005.

25. Mina Kimes, "P&G's Leadership Machine: The Consumer Goods Giant Has a Proven Formula to Nurture Top Talent," *Fortune*, May 20, 2009.

26. Alecia Swasy, *Soap Opera: The Inside Story of Procter & Gamble* (New York: Simon & Schuster, 1994).

27. Randy Tucker, "P&G's Jager Will Drive for Diversity: Procter & Gamble's Incoming CEO Plans to Retool the Company's Conformist Culture," *Cincinnati Enquirer*, December 27, 1998.

28. Lafley and Charan, *The Game-Changer*.

29. Cliff Peale, "P&G Scrubs Stodgy Image," *Cincinnati Enquirer*, November 21, 2004, 1A.

30. Ibid.

31. Lee Kun-hee, quoted in Jeong Hyeon-ji, "Value Innovation Changes Samsung's Culture," *Korea Herald*, September 21, 2007.

32. Peter Brabeck-Letmathe, quoted in Igor Reichlin, "Getting the Global View," *Chief Executive*, October 1, 2004, 44.

33. Miguel Bustillo, "Home Depot Undergoes Renovation," *Wall Street Journal*, February 24, 2010, B2.

34. Terry Leah, quoted in D. E. Bell, "Tesco, Plc," Case 9-503-036 (Boston: Harvard Business School, 2002).

35. Yong-Gu Suh and Elizabeth Howard, "Restructuring Retailing in Korea: The Case of Samsung-Tesco," *Asia Pacific Business Review* 15, no. 1 (2009): 29–40.

36. Jin-Hyuk Kim, "TESCO Homeplus: Adding Creativity to the Discount Retail Store Business," *SERI [Samsung Economic Research Institute] Quarterly* 2, no. 2 (April 2009): 78.

37. Colleen Barrett, quoted in Robert Gandossy, "The Need for Speed," *Journal of Business Strategy* 24, no. 1 (2003): 29–33.

38. Mette Morsing and Dennis Oswald, "Sustainable Leadership: Management Control Systems and Organizational Culture in Novo Nordisk A/S," *Corporate Governance* 9, no. 1 (2009): 83.

39. "Everybody's Doing It: Companies of All Stripes Have Become Aware of the Need to Gather Talent," *Economist*, October 7, 2006.

40. Robert J. Thomas, Jane C. Linder, and Ana Dutra, "Inside the Values-Driven Culture at UPS," *Outlook* (Accenture) 2006, no. 3 (2006): 18–29.

41. Younger, Smallwood, and Ulrich, "Developing Your Organization's Brand."

42. Jamie Dimon, quoted in Jeffrey Cohn, Jon Katzenbach, and Gus Vlak, "Finding and Grooming Breakthrough Innovators," *Harvard Business Review*, December 2008, 62–69.

43. Robert Berner, "P&G: New and Improved; How A. G. Lafley Is Revolutionizing a Bastion of Corporate Conservatism," *BusinessWeek*, July 7, 2003.

CHAPTER 9

1. For more, see Thomas H. Davenport, Jeanne G. Harris, and Robert F. Morison, *Analytics at Work: Smarter Decisions, Better Results* (Boston: Harvard Business Press, 2010), and an overview of the book at "Analytics at Work, Summary," www.accenture.com/Global/Research_and_Insights/Institute-For-High-Performance/By_Publication_Type/Books/Analytics-at-Work-Results.htm.

APPENDIX

1. Spread = ROIC – WACC, where ROIC is the return on invested capital and WACC is the cost of capital. WACC = debt / EV × K_d × $(1 - T_r)$ + equity / EV × K_e , where EV is the enterprise value of the company (debt + equity), K_d is the cost of debt, T_r is the marginal tax rate (determined by country of operations), and K_e is the cost of equity. K_e = risk-free rate + beta (market risk rate – risk-free rate), wherein the beta we use is industry beta rather than company-specific beta.

2. This is an improvement over the use of price earnings (PE) ratios because PE ratios do not account for differences in debt levels between otherwise identical companies.

3. Average future value from the past three years and the first three years is used to adjust for any abnormal future values in one year. For example, if a company has an abnormally poor year due to unanticipated events, it is not likely that the market will penalize it, and thus future value will remain high.

4. Calculated on the basis of compound annual growth rate (CAGR) and weighted equally for all time frames. For companies with no more than seven years of public data but not ten, longevity is scored using a 33.3 percent weighting for the seven-, five-, and three-year TRS.

5. For industries where future value is not used, revenue growth and spread are each weighted at 50 percent.

INDEX

Note: Page numbers followed by *f* denote figures; those followed by a *t* denote tables.

ACKNOWLEDGMENTS

This book is truly the work of a cast of thousands, and we are glad for the chance to express our thanks to all who have contributed to the project over the years. Within Accenture, hundreds have participated directly in the ongoing program of research each year for more than seven years. Many more have made that research real and useful to clients and to the broader business community. From outside Accenture, numerous clients, scholars, and consultants have given their time, experience, and expertise to the project. We are deeply grateful to all who have participated for sharing their individual and collective wisdom with us.

We also thank the many client executives we have had the privilege of working with over the years. Their quest for understanding and their generosity of spirit have allowed us to test and forge these ideas in a crucible of real-world sensibility. Thanks for keeping us on track.

This kind of program does not begin—nor last this long—without the dedication of key individuals. For their sponsorship and strong, sustained support, we thank Accenture's top management team over the past eight years, especially Joe Forehand, Bill Green, Adrian Lajtha, Roxanne Taylor, Steve Rohleder, and Mark Foster.

Also critical to the success of the research was the long-time backing of the Accenture Institute for High Performance. We are indebted to its entire membership for their support, but particularly Bob Thomas, its executive director. From leading original research as part of the program in its earliest days to being a valuable reader of manuscripts near the end, his support and contributions have been prized and unwavering. We must also single out Elizabeth Craig for reading numerous drafts and providing insightful comments. And we thank Mark Spelman for his stewardship of the Institute and unflagging encouragement and support.

Thanks also to Accenture executives David Mann, Narendra Mulani, Walt Shill, and Mike Sutcliffe, who stepped up early to make the project a success, volunteering their time and leadership to develop key elements of the program and our thinking. Trevor Gruzin and Olly Benzecry also provided great insight and valuable support from the earliest days. Our gratitude as well to the many high-performance business program leaders in our industry groups who over the years have driven the research program down deep into our business—particularly John Jackson, who was an inspiration as well as a true craftsman. We must also thank those who worked tirelessly to make our geography-specific research so successful, including Joost A.C.N. de Haas, Sanjay Jain, Gong Li, Harsh Manglik, Raghav Narsalay, Yali Peng, Andy Sleigh, and Bo Wang.

Hundreds of researchers studying scores of industries do not just organize themselves, so we must recognize Anita Thompson and Daniel Huedig, who stepped up to lead the program management office for the High Performance Business research. They each left their mark on the outcome as tireless advocates of the research and by delivering valuable insights to clients from the work. Their intellectual contributions were also substantial, making them true founders of this book. We also thank Peter Franz, who has played a crucial role in leading the formalization and industrialization of high-performance business research, turning it into usable assets for our client teams.

We probably would not have gotten very far if we had been unable to devise a new and compelling definition of *high perfor-*

mance early on, one that could take our understanding further as we stood on the shoulders of giants. For their expert knowledge of corporate finance, and for their vision and passion in those early days and throughout, we thank Mike Ostergard, Mike Princi, John Ballow, Brian McCarthy, and Craig Savarese.

The findings would be little more than curiosities without strong marketing support to help craft the messages and to effectively communicate them, and so we thank Accenture's many industry marketing leads. In particular we thank Jean Ostvoll, one of our earliest and greatest supporters, for all her efforts.

Throughout the years we were also fortunate to have had Accenture's *Outlook* publication to help us test, form, and promote the research findings and ideas as they emerged. We own an enormous debt to David Cudaback, *Outlook*'s editor-in-chief, and to editors Tish Burton and Jackie Kessler for their efforts to make our work accessible and just plain better.

We save our deepest thanks for last, for those individuals without whom this book could simply not have been written. We thank Anna Caffrey, who pulled together the research from dozens of industries and hundreds of companies over the course of many months. Without her tireless efforts, we would have many times been unable to proceed. To David Light, who served as a sounding board throughout the development of this book and whose years of editorial efforts to sharpen the ideas were at times Herculean, we offer humble gratitude. We also express deep thanks to Alden Hayashi, who stepped into the breach to quickly turn thinking into writing (and rewriting and rewriting), allowing us to finish what we started, and to Erik Calonius, who offered both his insights and significant writing skills to help us embark on the journey.

For helping to bring the work across the finish line, we owe thanks to Shelby Prichard, Maia Pelleg, Laine Monaldo, and Charlene Hou, who never tired of sweating the details. And we thank our early readers of the complete draft, especially Wayne Borchardt and Matt Reilly, whose feedback was surgical in its precision and amazing in its completeness.

Throughout the book's development, we enjoyed the support and patience of the exceptional professionals at Harvard Business Review Press. We thank our editor, Melinda Merino, who saw the vision and trusted us implicitly from day one. We are grateful to Allison Peter, who made sure the finished product was letter-perfect, and to Courtney Schinke, who kept us managing all the assorted details of publishing. At *Harvard Business Review*, we thank Julia Kirby for listening patiently to all parts of the storyline over the years and for her dead-on feedback. Any remaining weaknesses remain our fault, and our fault alone.

At last we come to those who perhaps give the most, the ones who in many ways have less choice than the outright volunteers—our families. Paul thanks his wife Joan, who is not just the glue that keeps it all together in his life, but who is all the really good parts as well (and who is still his cheeseburger). And he thanks his children, Jonathan, Charlotte, and Michael, who fill his days with joy and who each contributed in their own particular way to making this book possible. Paul is also grateful to his brothers, Marcus and Joseph, who are perhaps his harshest critics, but are more beloved for it. And he thanks his mother for her heartfelt question of the past few years, "How's the book coming?"

Tim thanks his wife, Michele, for her love, support, and coaching over the years, and his children, Vicki, Francesca, and Venetia, for their interest and encouragement throughout the endeavor. He would also like to acknowledge the contribution of several friends—Fred Harburg, David Burnham, Brad Stackhouse, and Cannon Garber—and his wife Michele in helping develop, refine, and test his thinking in long evenings of intense debate over a bottle (or two) of red wine.

ABOUT THE AUTHORS

Paul Nunes and Tim Breene are senior executives at Accenture and the founders and coarchitects of the company's High Performance Business research program, begun in 2003. This program's contributions were recognized as one of the ten most influential in advancing management thinking on business performance in "Toward a Theory of High Performance" in *Harvard Business Review*. Nunes and Breene have coauthored over a dozen articles on the program's research findings, and the results of their research have been featured in leading publications. They have also collaborated on such groundbreaking *Harvard Business Review* articles as "The Chief Strategy Officer" and "Selling to the Moneyed Masses."

Paul Nunes is the Executive Director of Research at the Accenture Institute for High Performance. He is coauthor of the award-winning book *Mass Affluence: 7 New Rules of Marketing to Today's Consumers* (Harvard Business School Press, 2004). His writings have appeared in numerous publications, including *Harvard Business Review*, *MIT Sloan Management Review*, *Conference Board Review*, *Strategy and Leadership*, *Optimize*, *ComputerWorld*, *Wired*, and others. His research has also been featured in many news outlets, including the *New York Times*, *Wall Street Journal*, *USAToday*, BusinessWeek .com, Forbes.com, *Los Angeles Times*, and *Chicago Tribune*. He was recently awarded a U.S. patent for his method of improving companies' innovation processes. He lives near Boston.

Tim Breene is CEO of Accenture Interactive, Accenture's pioneering initiative to help companies navigate the transformation of marketing in the digital age. From 1999 through 2009, he served as a member of Accenture's Executive Leadership Team in a variety of roles, including group chief executive of Management Consulting and chief strategy and corporate development officer. In a business career spanning almost forty years, Breene also held senior leadership positions in the retail, consumer goods, and advertising industries before joining Accenture. His experience includes both senior line management roles and direct involvement in startups and acquisitions. He lives in a suburb of Boston.